A History
of the Swedish People

A History
of the Swedish People

TOLD BY

VILHELM MOBERG

Translated from the Swedish by
PAUL BRITTEN AUSTIN

PANTHEON BOOKS
A Division of Random House, New York

24689753

Library of Congress Cataloging in Publication Data

Moberg, Vilhelm, 1898-
A history of the Swedish people.

Translation of Min svenska historia.
CONTENTS: pt. 1. From Odin to Engelbrekt.
1. Sweden—History. I. Title.
DL648.M613   948.5   72-3411
ISBN 0-394-48192-5

M 687 h

Manufactured in the United States of America

Contents

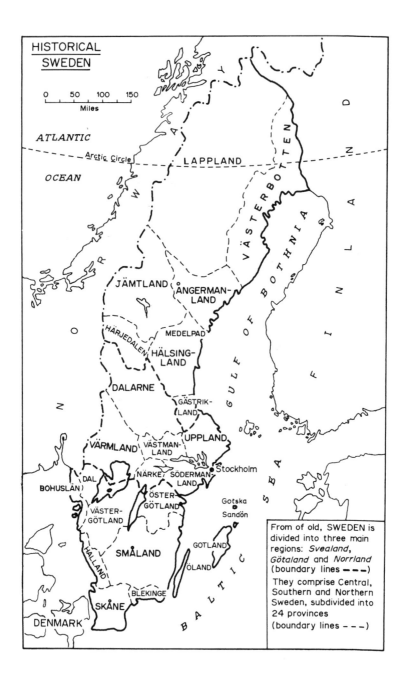

HISTORICAL
SWEDEN

0   50   100   150
Miles

ATLANTIC

- - - Arctic Circle

OCEAN

LAPPLAND

VÄSTERBOTTEN

GULF OF BOTHNIA

FINLAND

JÄMTLAND

ÅNGERMAN-
LAND

HÄRJEDALEN

MEDELPAD

HÄLSING-
LAND

DALARNE

GÄSTRIK-
LAND

VÄRMLAND

VÄSTMAN-
LAND

UPPLAND

NÄRKE

SÖDERMAN-
LAND

Stockholm

DAL

BOHUSLÄN

ÖSTER-
GÖTLAND

VÄSTER-
GÖTLAND

Gotska
Sandön

SMÅLAND

GOTLAND

HALLAND

ÖLAND

BLEKINGE

SKÅNE

DENMARK

BALTIC SEA

From of old, SWEDEN is
divided into three main
regions: *Svealand*,
Götaland and *Norrland*
(boundary lines ━ ━ ━)

They comprise Central,
Southern and Northern
Sweden, subdivided into
24 provinces
(boundary lines - - -)

Foreword

Vilhelm Moberg is the great epic author of Sweden today. His books are read and his films are seen by the entire country.

Like the great majority of the nation, he stems from peasant stock. The quality of his work comes from his effortless, and therefore natural, identification with the nameless in history: the stubborn, hard-laboring, often rebellious, poor rural people. Through the centuries and until recent decades (when Sweden became a welfare state ahead of all other countries), the peasants have been suppressed, squeezed, made to suffer and often to perish. Their destiny was harsh, even when the mighty above them shared peacefully the fruits of power, and oppression of the common people became much worse during the frequent wars when the rulers struggled for power.

About this huge majority of people the sources are scanty, and history is filled with the often crazy behavior of their overlords. When Vilhelm Moberg turns the searchlight on the lives of the anonymous common people, he uses whatever the records can tell. He uses, too, the storehouse of reminiscences and oral traditions from his youth, when peasant society was still almost static. To these sparse sources, he has added the intuitive power of his creative genius, to come to know what has never been known.

In earlier works Vilhelm Moberg has shown an extraordinary capacity to portray emigrants from his home province to the United States as the humanely warm individuals they were, imagining, laboring, and loving. In this book—which he has named, with both pride and modesty, *Vilhelm Moberg's Swedish History*—he displays the same rare gift, though painting with a broader brush on a wider canvas.

—Gunnar Myrdal

The history of Sweden is the history
of her commons

The Author on his History

I HAVE BEEN READING SWEDISH HISTORY for sixty years. My first textbook in the subject was *The History of the Fatherland* for Lower School Classes, by C. T. Odhner, twelfth revised edition. In its pages I was to learn 'how under God's guidance the human race has gradually progressed toward ever greater enlightenment and refinement.' In the introduction to his history Odhner goes on: 'History does not relate *everything* that has happened, only what was important or remarkable. The Muse occupies herself only with those races and individuals who have done something memorable and had some major influence on the destiny of the human race.'

In this history book I learnt how our Swedish armies once stood arrayed at Breitenfeld, Lützen and Narva; but they told me almost nothing about my own ancestors who had made up those armies. Nor did I learn from my other school textbooks what life for my own people had been like in past times. Which was the same as to say that peasants, soldiers, servants and backwoodsmen, not being admitted to that history, had never done anything memorable.

In 1866 the Swedish Government appointed a commission to draw up directives for the contents of history books. Such textbooks should breathe a 'patriotic spirit' and foster 'national political aware-ness.' The secretary of this commission was C. T. Odhner, who was afterwards himself given the task of writing Swedish history books for our schools. In carrying it out, according to one contemporary judge of such matters, 'he meticulously and successfully' followed the instructions in the drawing up of which he himself had played a part. Odhner became our prime exponent of the nationalistic school of history-writing. Several generations of young elementary school and grammar school Swedes have formed their notions of their country's past under the impress of 'Big Odhner' and 'Little Odhner.'

Swedish schoolchildren today, I suppose, are reading quite different history books. The idea behind teaching my own generation history was to bring us up as loyal Swedish subjects, submissive to God, the King and the authorities, for exactly the same reasons, that is, as we were taught Christianity. If we had to learn Luther's catechism by heart, it was to impress upon us that 'one and all shall be submissive to him that beareth the rule, forasmuch as all authority is of God; and that authority which is, she is even sent by God.'

In this way I, an innocent schoolboy, gained a distorted idea of my own country's history: not from the facts included in our history books, but from those they left out. E. H. Carr, an internationally famous English historian, writes (*What is History?*): 'It used to be said that facts speak for themselves. This is, of course, untrue. The facts speak only when the historian calls on them: it is he who decides to which facts to give the floor, and in what order or context.'

As the scope of my reading became wider I realised that most Swedish history was only about a single little group of individuals: the decision-makers, who on the people's behalf had decided what conditions it should live under. The great mass of the country's inhabitants had not been admitted. True, latest research has taken a sociological turn. But what I missed were the Swedes who had sown the fields and reaped them, who had hewn down forests, cleared roads, built the king's palaces, his castles and fortresses, the cities and cottages. Of all these people who had paid the taxes, salaried all the clergymen, bailiffs and officials, I had caught only occasional glimpses here and there. In all those armies that had fallen for the fatherland in other countries I missed the rank and file, their wives who had waited for them at home, the whole class of serving men and women, the labourers who had always been subject to a special law, known as *Tjänstehjonslagen* – The Statute of Servants. Nor could I find the unpropertied vagabonds, the 'defenceless' (*försvarslösa*), who owned neither land, house nor home.

So I made up my mind to write of these people in times past whom history had forgotten. I began with *Ride this Night!* (1941) and in 1949 went on with *The Emigrants*. I wrote of those who, like the 17th-century peasants who had fought for their freedom against the threat of aristocratic domination, had had to find themselves new homes in another continent and who also had largely been over-looked by our historians. My novels about them are thoroughly documented. In fact, long before the genre became fashionable in our contemporary Swedish literature, they were documentary novels.

In the present work I carry on this imaginative historical writing in another form: as a narrative history.

The past only exists by virtue of our knowledge of it, and changes with that knowledge. By knowing about it we create it, and each new access of knowledge transforms it. This process will go on until the end of time. As I see the matter, a historian's task is to recreate vanished worlds, to penetrate the lives of long dead generations. He must try to see their circumstances as they saw them, and so come to understand their age in the same light as they themselves did. Obviously, this is an unattainable goal. But to anyone like myself who – be he professional historian or not – is spellbound with curiosity as to what has happened on this earth before him, it is a task that exerts an irresistible fascination.

Besides being a scientific historian, anyone who sets out to give a complete and reliable picture of people in the past, their environments and societies, must also be a political scientist, a sociologist, an economist, a military historian, a theologian, a historian of law, of the church and of ideas, a linguist, an ethnographer, an ethnologist, and a psychologist. No one can possess such universal knowledge.

Personally I am no expert in any of these fields, so at least I have no reputation to lose. All I have arrogated to myself in embarking on this enterprise is any historical writer's freedom of movement, and have put this freedom to my own uses.

My view of history has mainly been determined by my own experience of Swedish people, derived from my own background. First and foremost let me say this: had I been born in another milieu or come from another social class, I should have written quite another history.

When writing a history no one can avoid certain incontestable events. No one can so far reinterpret facts as to assert that Christian II of Denmark defeated Gustav I of Sweden, that Gustavus Adolfus survived the Battle of Lützen, or that Anckarström, pointing his assassin's pistol at Gustav III, missed him. What we know for certain about the past, particularly the prehistoric and mediaeval past, is sadly inadequate, and when it leaves us in the lurch all we can do is try to discover what was the most probable course of events. Trevelyan describes history in 'the most important part of its business, not as a scientific deduction from a few incontestable facts, but an imaginative guess at the most likely generalizations.' For me it is precisely this that is history's great fascination. I narrate objective facts. But my interpretation of them is my own, and subjective.

Two principles underlie this work, and should be explicitly mentioned. One appears in its motto: *The history of Sweden is the history of her commons.* In the original Swedish text I use the word *allmoge* – which today means 'peasantry' – in its old Swedish sense of 'the whole people'. In fact my history's main theme is the *Swedish common man*. I have made considerable use of local history and tried to describe the Swedish people from within. I have visited the scenes of great historical events and tried to envisage them on the spot. As I see it, history cannot be based exclusively on old documents, statutes, decrees and regulations, on letters and notes. What was written in those documents which are no longer extant? No one knows. Had they survived, they might have changed history entirely. Documents do not yield us the whole picture.

All too often it is the human beings who disappear in this welter of source materials. In this book I have done my best to find them.

My intention is to make my own journey through Sweden's history, pausing primarily in areas the experts have hurried past or, after only a summary examination, abandoned. If, on the one hand, I stress facts which I consider insufficiently exploited or dwell on more or less overlooked events, on the other I have hurried past or briefly mentioned all that is well-known in Swedish history and has been described in hundreds of other works. Such are my book's limitations.

My second working principle has been this: In my historical

journey I move incessantly to and fro between past and present. Comparisons and analogies with past times, it seems to me, can illuminate and explain our own age; and contemporary instances can illumine and explain the past. I have tried to bring history close to the living. And the living close to history.

As a historical writer I am at the utmost a simple layman, an apprentice who has chiefly learnt his craft from three masters, two Englishmen and one Swede. Trevelyan recommends a close study of Macaulay's *History of England* to all who wish to write a narrative history. But the same recommendation applies to Trevelyan himself. To me he is the greatest English historian of modern times. Hardly anyone, alas, any longer reads my Swedish master: Anders Fryxell. In 56 years Fryxell wrote his *Stories from Swedish History for the Young*, in forty-six parts. Dean of Sunne, in Värmland, he wrote history on the basis of Christian values and from a Christian point of view. Obviously, he suffers from the limitations of his own time. But he wrote in a simple, clear, lively fashion, and therefore succeeded better than all the professionals in getting Swedes to read their own history. Fryxell was never recognised as a scientific historian; but his work asked questions and raised problems that forced on new investigations, with fresh results. It was from Fryxell that Strindberg and Heidenstam derived most of their source materials for their own historical writings, and he did pioneer work in weeding out four traits that had dominated all our older national Swedish histories: 1. ultra-royalism. 2. ultra-patriotism. 3. ultra-heroism. 4. historical casuistry. Anders Fryxell, born in a home where the ideas of the age of Enlightenment were still admired, remained faithful to them all his life. His mother had instilled in her son a hatred for tyrants and warrior kings. According to what he tells us himself, Mrs Fryxell used to say of Napoleon: 'I wish he could be punished for all his slaughter by having to go through a childbirth for every human being who was shot on his account'. (A. Fryxell: *Min historias historia*).

Her son's stories from Swedish history are strongly anti-heroic in tone and intent. Fryxell made short work of that view of history which stipulates a special code of behaviour for kings, statesmen and commanders of armies, which does not apply morals to politics and sees one and the same action as despicable and criminal when committed by a private person, but permissible, even admirable, when committed by a king, politician, general or some other potentate.

Following in Fryxell's footsteps, I apply the principle of the equality of all men before history's law. When passing judgment on the actions of historical personages, I use one and the same footrule, irrespective of their social standing.

Taine condemned Macaulay because 'his historical justice is like the Last Judgment, in being no respecter of differences in gifts, rank, dignity and talent, but only of the distinction between virtue and vice'. In the same way Bishop Agardh of Karlstad attacked the great historian who was a dean in his own diocese: 'Fryxell measures Swedish history against the footrule of the Ten Commandments'. Another contemporary critic compared the Dean of Sunne to the Old Testament prophets who passed judgment on long dead historical personages by measuring them against the stone tablets of the Law.

My point of view is not that of a believing Christian; nevertheless it often coincides with my master's. Obviously, men are indistinguishable from the age in which they live, and must not be considered outside its context. But I do not judge our history's men of violence – and they appear in great numbers – *only* as products of the spirit of their age and environment. I call their evil deeds by their proper name. After all, many good and peaceable individuals, living at the same time, resisted the spirit of their age and environment, and refused to let it set its stamp on them. For me, a murder committed in the 14th century is still murder. Morally, it can never be prescribed.

My Swedish history is in the first place the quintessence of my sixty years reading. So I have found the task of listing all my sources beyond me. Nor have I tried to. Footnotes only irritate the reader unnecessarily, and most people skip long lists of titles at the foot of each chapter – an unsatisfactory solution to the problem anyway, as the reader cannot know which of the listed works any given statement has been taken from. Instead, I have experimented with a third method: I have worked my source references into the body of the text. For the Middle Ages two main sources should be stressed: *The Provincial Laws of Sweden* and *Kulturhistoriskt lexikon for Nordisk Medeltid*. The latter is a large inter-Scandinavian reference work, so far in fourteen volumes and still not complete. Otherwise, the source references in the text have been restricted to little-known or more controversial cases which may arouse doubts in the reader.

As far as possible I have absorbed the results of the latest research into my narrative – without having any illusions as to their permanency.

I had not travelled far into our history before I was seized with a feeling of amazement; and the longer I read, the stronger grew my feeling. How has this people whom I have tried to follow down the ages managed to survive all the evils that have befallen them; all the wars; all the catastrophies; the almost regular recurrence of pestilence and famine; all the want; all the oppression, all the deprivations? *How have they managed to survive at all?*

My reader, I believe, will ask the same question.

The Swede as Bondsman

BEFORE TURNING TO PEOPLE in prehistoric Swedish society, a chapter must be devoted to those Swedes who found themselves wholly outside that society and had no stake in it, who were not regarded as human beings at all. The bondsmen – '*trälar*'. They, too, were our ancestors. But although they formed an important part of the population in prehistoric times and the Middle Ages, our historians have devoted little space to them. Our Swedish history books are fond of acclaiming our immemorial liberties. Our equally immemorial Swedish 'thraldom' – the Swedish word *thräldom* is almost the same – has been left in the shadow. Indeed, our earliest historians did not so much as know that this institution had ever existed. 'Thraldom', bondage, slavery, simply *could* not have occurred in a country which since time immemorial we Swedes have regarded as the home of liberty on earth.

National history was being written as early as the 16th century. In his works on the kings of the *Svear* and the *Götar*, *Historia de omnibus gothorum sveanorumque regibus*, Johannes Magnus asserts definitely that the Swedes 'have never, neither when they were Heathens or yet since they are become Christians, been oppressed under any bondage'. Johannes Magnus regards all who would assert anything else as 'scoffers' who out of ignorance or conceit would ruin their fatherland.

The author of our first vernacular history was Olaus Petri (1493–1552). He was also our first historian to treat of bondage in Sweden. In his *Swedish Chronicle* he refers to the subject several times. His brother, Laurentius Petri, came to the same conclusion in his own research. Unquestionably, bondage *had* once existed in Sweden. But Laurentius supposed that it could only have been foreigners who

8

were bought and sold and treated as slaves in primitive times. He did what he could to rescue the myth.

Johannes Messenius lived in a later age. On the basis of new sources he had discovered, he declared that Johannes Magnus, in his history, had let his imagination run away with him: it was Olaus Petri who had been right. And from that day to this no historian has denied it.

Even so, our Swedish historians have paid the subject scant attention. Bondage is mentioned by them as something self-evident, and therefore not worth looking into or describing more closely. Hans Hildebrand's study of the Swedish Middle Ages, *Sveriges Medeltid*, runs to 3,125 pages. Of these, only half a page deals with bondage, even though for three of the mediaeval centuries bondage had been a feature of Swedish life. Slavery in its Swedish form finds little place, either, in Geijer's (1783–1847) reflections on slavery in the world at large. His poem *Odal Bonden*, the action of which is supposed to take place in an age when peasants kept bondsmen, ignores the institution altogether. It would have reduced the effect of his portrait, otherwise factually correct and great poetry, of the free Swedish peasant.

An academic thesis on the rights of bondsmen in Sweden, by N. Calonius, printed in 1836, is of course out of date. I have made use of it, but not as a main source.

As far as I have been able to discover, there is only one modern summary of this subject: Emil Sommarin's *Träldomen i Norden*, a 24-page pamphlet published by Verdandi. Legal historians, following Sommarin, have written a few essays illuminating the bondsmen's juridic status. But on this subject our provincial laws are our only real source and, inasmuch as they codify the legal rules governing bondage in primitive and mediaeval society, are indispensable for any research into its history. Otherwise conditions on Iceland, as mirrored in that country's literature, would seem to have had their equivalent in Sweden.

No one knows when bondage began in Scandinavia. Probably it had existed in Sweden for millennia. Certainly, the institution was already established in ancient Greece several hundred years before the birth of Christ, and the Arabs took it over from the Greeks. A song in the Older Edda, the Rigstula or Rigsmål, tells of its origins in the North. The Asa gods, like the gods of the Greeks, were much given to making approaches to beautiful earthly women and lying with them. One day Heimdal, 'a powerful and crafty Asa god', was walking along the seashore when he came to a poor little shack, where he was received by a woman called Edda. The god spent the night in the shack. With the woman 'he stayed for three days, and thereafter went his way'. In the Rigstula we are told of the consequences, nine months later:

> A son was born to Edda;
> him sprinkled she with water,
> dark of hue,
> and naméd *Träl*.

> Wrinkled the skin was
> upon his hands,
> crooked knuckles
> malformed nails,
> stubby fingers
> and ugly face,
> bowed back
> and long heels.

> He with an effort
> bowed his strength
> bound rope of hemp
> burdens bore
> dragged home timber
> all the day long

By and by this strong and able bondsman got himself a wife:

> Came to the farm
> bow-leggéd maiden
> scarred of sole,
> sunburned arms
> and hooked nose.
> Was called *Tir*.

Träl and Tir, the swarthy-hued man and his woman, had many children. They did the peasant's heaviest and dirtiest work. They 'made fences, spread dung on the ploughed fields, tended swine, grazed goats and dug up peat.' Then the bondsman's and bonds-woman's children, in their turn, had children:

> Of them are descended
> all bondsmen born.

Continuing his journey, Heimdal, that mighty and sexually potent god, came to the farm of a prosperous peasant. There again he spent the night, lying with a woman of the house. Her name was Amma. When nine months had gone by, she too bore a son:

> In cloth swaddled
> pink and lovely
> gleaming eyes
>
> Oxen he tamed
> and plough made,
> timbered dwellings
> and lofty barns;
> fashioned carts,
> followed the plough.

The god's son with this peasant woman was handsomer and his duties were more respectable than those of his half-brother born in the wretched shack. He was called *Karl*, and became the first ancestor of all free-born men.

He got himself a wife of his own class and had children with her:

> Brought home the maiden
> with hanging keys
> and goatskin kirtle
> wed with Karl.
>
> Husband and wife
> they lived together,
> distributed favours,
> made their beds,
> set up home;
> children they bore,
> contented dwellt.
> Thus began all clans of peasants

The myth relates how Heimdal had a third son with a human woman. He became the first ancestor of the 'jarlar' – the lords.

Bondsmen and freeman, that is to say, were half-brothers, begotten of the same god; but this did not mean they were regarded as relations, still less as equals. The bondsman may have been the other's brother. He was certainly not his fellow. Träl was placed outside the human community, socially beyond the pale. Prehistoric Sweden, that is to say, recognized only one social class: the free-born. It was the only classless society we know of in our whole history.

The bondsman's sole function in life was to serve the freeman. He did the heaviest work, such as mostly required mere muscle. Society's view of the bondsman is expressed in Old Norse by the neuter word *man;* i.e., a-human-being-as-a-thing, as opposed to the masculine word *madr*, the human-being-as-individual. The word *träl* comes from the Greek word for servant; but it also seems to have had something to do with the word for a runner. In Old Swedish it is sometimes synonymous with cowardly. Dark skin, short hair, long heels – such were characteristics of the bondsman. Whores, too, were recognizable by their short-cropped hair.

For the peasant, the bondsmen provided indispensable labour. They carried out such tasks as were beneath the dignity of the free-born. They fed the swine, sheep and goats, and cleaned up after these, the smallest and least regarded animals, the beasts of the poor. Even among animals there was hierarchy. Horse and ox were creatures of higher rank; and it was not beneath the dignity of the master to look after them. The peasant ploughed the field. His bondsman tended the swine.

No bondsman was ever allowed to carry weapons. Sword and spear were the exclusive privilege of the free-born, a status symbol. In the High Song of Odin we read:

> Weapons and clothing
> give to the man:
> Weaponless man lacks courage.

According to the myth, the social order was of divine origin and so might not be called in question. Actually the simple fact of the matter was that the stronger had enslaved the weaker, and society reposed upon their exclusive possession of weapons. The unfree man could only use the tools of work, the hoe and dung-fork. Obviously neither sword nor spear could ever be trusted in his hand.

When the bondsmen were idle their peasant owners had to appoint overseers, to make sure they were not robbed of their labour. These overseers, a sort of superior bondsmen, enjoyed special privileges. It was exactly the same system as was later to be applied by slave-owners in the southern states of America.

Bondsmen fell into four categories: 1. Prisoners of war, 2. Bondsmen born, 3. Voluntary bondsmen (*gävträlar*), i.e. men who of their own free will had handed themselves over to their owner, 4. Members of a king's guard (*hird*). In the second group, according to an Uppland document dating from the year 1292, a distinction was drawn between 'home thralls' and 'bought thralls'. Bondsmen born within the household are also mentioned in a document from Småland from the year 1282, under the heading '*Fostren*'; and a paragraph in the oldest of all provincial laws, that of Västergötland, shows they were regarded as more reliable than bondsmen who had been purchased. A '*fostre*' was entitled to own possessions. Of a bondswoman born in the household it is said that she 'carries the peasant's keys', i.e., she could represent the mistress of the house. In a case of seduction a fine of three marks was paid for this unfree woman, or four times as much as the fine for a bondswoman who had been purchased. Where a '*fostre*' was concerned, that is, a special rule applied.

Otherwise all bondsmen had the same juridic status. They were chattels, someone else's property and, as such, on a par with the beasts. They had no rights whatever. Like his cattle or any other possession, living or dead, they were merely part of a peasant's property. A bondsman's owner could dispose of him in any way he pleased: sell him, exchange him for something else, or give him away. If he so wished, he even had the right to chop off an arm or a leg, though it lay in the peasant's interest, of course, that his bondsman should be fit for work. He even had the right to slay him, providing public proclamation of the manslaughter was made the same day it was committed. There is the story of a wealthy Icelandic peasant, irascible by nature and quick to violence. From time to time a furious rage would seize upon him. Against such an attack there was only one effective remedy: to go out into the fields and kill one of his bondsmen. Whereupon his spirit recovered its equanimity.

At the sacrificial feasts (*blot*) bondsmen, as further evidence of their bestial status, would be sacrificed to the gods, together with such other male creatures as stallions, bulls, billy goats and cocks. The altar of the gods also ran red with the blood of criminals, of infirm old men, prisoners of war and foreigners (M. Calonius). The bondsmen had to assist at these sacrifices. It was they who presented the victims, human or animal, who bound them to the altar and butchered them. Hakon Jarl is said to have sacrificed his seven-year old son Erling, commanding his bondsman Skapte Karker to cut the child's throat. Their work of butchery done, the bondsmen it seems, were allowed to consume what was left of the victims after the sacrificial meal. At Yuletide feasts, weddings and funerals they were copiously plied with food and drink, yes and were even permitted to get drunk.

The provincial laws expressly place bondsmen among the cattle. Paragraph 53 of the *Manhelgdsbalk* (law of life and limb) of the Uppland Law is headed: *If any find another's cattle or bondsman*. And goes on to say: 'Should any find another's home-bondsman (*hemmahjon*), he shall have one-third of the find.' The reward for finding lost property, that is, was one-third of the bondsman's value.

For a free-man to accept gifts from a bondsman, even to walk in his company, was degrading. A bondsman who offered a free-man even a drink of water so insulted him that the affronted party was entitled to give the donor a whipping.

The district status of the unfree was also emphasized by their names. Male bondsmen, we know, bore such names as Klur, Klegge, Fjosner, Kejser, Fulner, Drumb, Lut and Leggialde, and similar female names are Drumba, Kumba, Ökkenkalva, Ysjar and Tronubeina. Such names have an ugly ring to them. Often they call to mind inferior character traits and less admirable physical attributes. If anyone was dark of hue, this determined his name. Sote (*c.f.* soot) was a common name for bondsmen in Sweden; and Svartr (black) was common in Iceland.

Bondage originated in the womb. It was passed down from generation to generation. The stock of bondsmen, that is to say, was chiefly recruited by begetting them as offspring; but it was also supplemented with prisoners taken during campaigns in foreign lands. Of the plunder brought back by our forefathers from their far-flung pillaging expeditions in the Viking age some was human booty, to be exploited as labour. Most of the Swedish Viking raids, as we shall see, went eastward. They brought home slaves from the Baltic provinces, Poland and Russia, to supplement those they already had at home. Since the inhabitants of these countries were Slavs, the word Slav, as a description of genetic origin, came to be confused with the same word in the sense of bondsman – a slave.

There is no evidence that the native bondsmen were of a different race from their lords and masters. They seem to have been as purely Swedish as their owners. It is unlikely that Scandinavian peasant society was addicted to racial prejudice. The Norsemen did not spare even the purest Aryan blood, even enslaving members of their own tribe. Nor were the numbers of prisoners brought home from the wars overseas so great that there can have been much mingling of races among the unfree. There is a mention of Welsh bondsmen, originating among the peoples of Celtic countries; and foreign women generally were particularly desirable booty for the Norsemen – they could increase the stock of bondsmen.

The voluntary bondsmen (*gävträlarna*) who sold themselves and accepted unfree status of their own free will, were the most despised of all. They gave themselves up to their creditors, perhaps, in payment of debt. Usually they came from among the very poor. If they gave themselves to a lord it was because he undertook to provide them a living. But in the provincial laws of the mid-13th century, a time when the institution of bondage had already begun to undergo a change, we find this regulation: 'None shall now give himself up a bondsman; for this by Birger Jarl hath been done away.'

The '*hird*' – the king's bodyguard – was a smaller group. The word has been revived in our own time by Hitler, whose régime in so many ways modelled itself on the manners and customs of the ancient Norsemen. A king liked to see reliable men around him and needed faithful guards to protect him. To make doubly sure of their fidelity he exercised over them absolute power of life and death.

The bondsman, says the Edda, had to work all day long. In one Icelandic saga the peasant Arnkell even makes his bondsman work through the night. They had to drive home hay by moonlight, 'because in the daytime the thralls had other things to do'. No wise master, however, subjected his own property to such excessive mal-treatment as to damage its working capacity. Strong and healthy bondsmen had the greatest value. In his own interest a peasant kept his horses and oxen in good trim; and probably he also gave his bondsmen enough to eat to keep up their strength. The lot of Scandinavian bondsmen was probably somewhat milder than that of his brother in misfortune in southern lands. Those who have studied the matter agree that he was subjected to hard, but rarely to harsh, treatment. But if he was disobedient, rebellious or neglect-ful, then out came the whip. Corporal punishment of servants, indeed, was still legally permitted in principle in Sweden as long as the Statute of Servants remained in force: which is to say, up to 1920. Under this statute, masters had the right to beat their servants moderately and in a Christian manner – a form of ill-treatment known as a 'rebuke'. Such a beating was regarded as being morally in the best interests of the victim.

Ear-cropping, a shameful punishment, was also reserved for bondsmen.

In principle an unfree man could not own property or personal belongings of any sort. Nor was he legally competent. The Law of Skåne decrees: 'If any man's bondsman be slain, he who hath slain the bondsman shall recompense the owner three marks, and before a jury of twelve shall swear on oath that the bondsman was worth no more.' The bondsman could not speak in the provincial council. If he committed a crime, it was his owner who was held responsible. Nor was marriage between bondsfolk valid without their owner's per-mission. If a bondswoman give birth to a child begotten by any other man than her owner, decrees the Law of Östergötland, the father shall pay damages of six öre for having lain with her, and furthermore recompense her owner for all working days lost during the pregnancy and childbirth. Masters, on the other hand, could make free with their bondswomen.

Sexual intercourse between free men and unfree women was very common in primitive society. This did not mean that the bonds-woman's owner could sell such children as she bore him. The Law of Östergötland decrees: 'If a peasant beget a child with his bondswoman, he may not offer his child for sale, nor keep it as a bonds-man'. Between free-born women and bondsmen, on the other hand, sexual relations were rare, and were regarded as utterly degrading to the female partner. Any free woman who bore a child to a bondsman sank to the latter's despised status; but when a bondswoman had a child with her master, the child was welcomed as an addition to the farm's labour force. According to Tacitus, women who had allowed themselves to be seduced by slaves in the Roman Empire in the days of Emperor Claudius were punished by the loss of their freedom; but their 'offspring' went free. In the 5th century the Visigoths are said to have had a law by which freeborn women who had so far forgotten the laws of honour as to have voluntarily and with their own better knowledge 'united themselves with their own bondsmen, should be burnt with them' (M. Calonius).

The various provincial laws differ in their views on children of a free man and a bondswoman. Under the laws of Skåne and Väster-götland the children inherited their mother's juridic status and became unfree; while the Law of Östergötland gave them their freedom if redeemed by their fathers within six years. The Law of Uppland – the most humane of our Swedish provincial laws – granted freedom to all children begotten by free men. It even allowed a free man and a bondswoman to marry.

Since each province had its own laws, bondsmen's status varied from one province to another. The laws of the Svear were more humane, one could say, than those of the Götar; and bondsmen were better treated in Svealand than they were in Götaland. Their pros-pects of being manumitted were also greatest among the former. In the 13th century the Svear even granted their bondsmen certain legal rights against excessive maltreatment by their owners. But by that time the gradual disappearance of bondage had already begun.

Like other goods and chattels, bondsmen could be sent to market, and were much bought and sold. During periods of severe famine it could even happen that parents sold their own children. Their motives are preserved in a folk-song still current in the 19th century. Starvation is forcing a father to sell his little girl as a slave to a sea pirate:

My father and mother they suffered great want;
and me they did sell to buy themselves bread,
in lands of the heathen to languish.
May God of his mercy console all such
as in lands of the heathen do languish.

During the Viking raids bondsmen were also acquired by purchase. English history mentions with horror one princess who, at a good price, sold a number of her serfs (peasants) to the wild men of the north.

According to Olaus Petri, bondsmen continued to be bought and sold in Sweden until as late as King Birger Magnusson's day. He even gives the price: 'Where a man had a bondsman that was his own, he sold him to whom he pleased, even as he had been a horse or other beast; the which is to be remarked in our old law books. And for a strong and healthy bondsman was commonly given two marks of pure silver'.

Two marks of pure silver was the value of a medium-sized ox – perhaps some £40 or $100 in present-day values. The price of a man varied with his age and working capacity; for a woman, with her age and comeliness. From the 11th century onward we even have the exact prices: a woman then cost one silver mark, or half the value of a moderately good ox. A male bondsman was several times more expensive and cost up to three or four marks. The highest-mentioned price is the value of four immaculate draught oxen.

The Icelandic literature describes a great slave market, annually said to have been held at Brännö, a place at the mouth of the Göta River, quite close to present-day Gothenburg. The island in those days belonged to Norway, but its central situation put it within easy reach of buyers and sellers in the other Scandinavian countries. In Viking times, Hedeby, today called Schleswig, was the largest city in Denmark and Northern Europe. It was famous – so the sources say – for its slave market. All this notwithstanding, the public sale of human beings as a regular commercial commodity does not seem to have been a major feature of Scandinavian life.

The lot of the unfree was immutably fixed in this life and continued after death. Bondsfolk were buried in special grave fields, distinct from those of the freemen. Near Edsviken, a creek in Sollentuna parish in the suburbs of present-day Stockholm, the remains of a large Viking farm have been discovered. Within its boundaries lie two different grave fields. One lies on high dry soil; the other, on low swampy ground. There is no mistaking the distinction. In the former were buried the free-born; in the latter the bondsmen.

Our free forefathers did not fancy having to share paradise with their bondsmen. Odin's Valhalla, where the free were to enjoy eternal bliss, was no place for slaves. Bondsmen, it was generally believed, were taken up after death by Thor and admitted to a less blissful heaven. Nor might any woman except the Valkyrie – Odin's serving women – pass through Valhalla's gates.

How the Swedish bondsmen experienced his own degraded status we can only surmise. If the unfree accepted their lot it was no doubt because they believed it had been apportioned to them by almighty gods. Their place in society had been allocated to them once and for all. And for so divinely established an order of things to be upset would quite simply have meant the end of the world. Inherited through many generations, bondage, as far as anyone knew, had existed since the beginning of time. Like the existence of the gods it was self-evident, and accepted as such. The bondsman, I believe, bowed to his fate as inevitable, implacable. After all, what else could he do?

Roman slaves did not. In the century before the birth of Christ the world empire was shaken to its foundations by Spartacus' revolt, a revolt which at the outset, at least, by no means seems to have been hopeless. But we know of no such revolts by bondsmen in the North. Roman slaves were obviously able to come by weapons. Swedish bondsmen could not, so we have no record of them rebelling. This does not mean, of course, they may not have attempted to. Indeed it would be extraordinary if they hadn't. Although such revolts have left no trace in history, or even in myth and legend, it seems likely that in the course of millennia some small-scale local rebellions must have occurred.

In poetry we find them mentioned in several places. But this is unhistorical. There is no evidence of any freedom movements in primitive Nordic society. 'Weaponless man lacks courage!'

What fraction of Sweden's prehistoric and mediaeval population consisted of bondsmen?

Although this is a crucial question, it can only be answered with vague estimates.

One basis for such calculations is the ratio between masters and servants. On a small owner-operated farm, over and above the labour provided by the peasant's own family, one bondsman usually sufficed. A larger farm, with ten to twelve cows and a couple of horses, would require three or four servants – at least this was the number of labourers and servant-maids employed by latter-day peasants on farms of the same size. In prehistoric society the wealthiest peasants may well have kept as many as a dozen bondsmen. King's chieftains, '*jarls*' and other great men would naturally have kept even more.

Our provincial laws devote so much space to the bondsmen, they must have made up a sizeable part of the population. In his study of the last phase of bondage in Sweden, one legal historian, I. S. Landtmanson, maintains that the bondsman made up 'a considerable fraction of the Swedish people at that time'. But since the overall size of the population is unknown, no percentage can be established.

But Sweden was not a slave state in the same sense as the oriental and Mediterranean countries, where the slave system was both more thoroughly elaborated, and where it persisted until a good deal later than among ourselves.

How many bondsmen were there in Sweden, then, for instance in the 11th century, before the introduction of Christianity, when bondage was in full flower?

Hans Forsell, Eli Heckscher, Adolf Schück, S. Sundquist and other investigators have all tried to arrive at figures for Sweden's mediaeval population. In the 14th century the figure has been estimated on the basis of the St Peter's Pence paid to Rome, a tax amounting to one penny per household. But since we do not know how many people lived in the average 14th-century Swedish household, neither does this provide a sure basis for calculations. After the 11th century we do not even have the Peter's Pence. Those who have looked into the matter, however, seem to be agreed that before the Black Death decimated them there were at least 600,000 Swedes. During the three first centuries of the Middle Ages much new land was settled and from this it would seem reasonable to assume that since the 11th century the population had increased by some 100,000. From which it follows that there must have been about half a million Swedes at that time. Of these, the bondsmen must have constituted at least one fifth: 20 per cent of 500,000 persons. For 11th-century Sweden this yields us a figure of 100,000 bondsmen.

So a good many of us present-day Swedes are their descendants.

Two factors contributed to the disappearance of bondage. One was spiritual. The other economic. The first was the introduction of Christianity. The other was developments in agriculture. Gradually, over a period of two hundred years, the institution was dismantled. Great numbers of bondsmen were ceremoniously manumitted at the '*ting*'. The provincial laws mirror this change in the status of the unfree, which occurred more slowly among the conservative Götar than among the more progressive Svear. As late as the end of the 13th century, owners were still permitted to sell their bondsmen; but in 1327 the laws of Södermanland and Uppland forbade all trading in baptized persons.

Concerning the Östergötland law book, Olaus Petri writes that it permitted the sale of bondsmen. But Birger Magnusson, king at that time, 'improved the Law of Uppland and brought it more into line with circumstances than previously.' He adds: '. . . of King Birger was it forbidden that none Christian man nor woman be sold or bought, forasmuch as Christ hath bought all Christians, therefore might none Christian be sold or bought. And this interdict hath King Birger set in his law.'

By admitting the bondsman to her communion, that is, the Church recognized him as a human being and a Christian. In the provincial laws, too, it was now decreed that even bondsmen's children should be baptized and placed under the protection of Canon Law, thus depriving masters of the right to slay them. Once baptized, the bondsman received the sacrament, was married by the priest, and his marriage was blessed by the church. A bondswoman, too, was 'churched', just like any other woman.

On masters the duty was imposed of ensuring that their bondsfolk, together with all other members of their household, kept holy the day of rest. If a bondsman was found working on a holy day, the Law of Gotland decreed his master should be fined three öre. Freedmen were not supposed to become clerics; yet we do know of cases where former bondsmen were not only ordained but even rose to be bishops.

This humaner treatment of the unfree was one of Christianity's great contributions to mediaeval Sweden.

Not that the Church was consistent in its application of Christ's doctrine of the equality of all men in the sight of God. On its own estates it long continued to practise slavery, and even up to quite recent times the Holy Catholic Church has been a slave-owner.

Christianity also changed the Swede's notions of justice. Bondsmen were liberated 'for Christ's sake'. The act, however, was not usually altogether unselfish. Only when they lay on their deathbed and were drawing up their wills did folk manumit their slaves in hopes of the gate of heaven being more readily opened to them for their generosity, and to improve their own prospects of eternal bliss. From the five provinces of Svealand and Götaland we have twenty-seven such wills manumitting bondsmen. These documents date from the end of the 13th century, and bear the signatures both of Svear and Götar: which shows that by this time bondsmen were being liberated all over the country. And it was this change in people's ways of thinking that gradually influenced the content of their laws.

Latest research gives another, purely economic reason for the abolition of bondage. It was quite simply no longer profitable for the wealthy and powerful to use unfree labour on their estates. Such labour was difficult to supervise, and even in the winter months, when there was no work for the bondsmen, they still had to be fed. On the great estates the most profitable sort of labour was that which could be employed during those times of year when it was most needed, and then laid off. Only on small farms, employing a couple of bondsmen at most, was the old system still profitable.

Right up to the first decades of the 14th century there are still traces of bondage in Sweden. Even at that late date the inventories of great men's possessions were still listing bondsmen among the assets of their estates.

In 1335, the newly crowned King Magnus Eriksson, then a youth of nineteen, set out on his '*eriksgata*' – a state progress through the realm to receive the provinces' oaths of fidelity and sanction their laws. On reaching Skara, in Västergötland, he issued his famous brief, whose ninth paragraph runs as follows: 'To the honour of God and the Virgin Mary, and for the repose of our father's and uncle's souls, we do decree it as right and lawful, that no man and woman born of Christian man or woman evermore shall in Västergötland or Värend be bondsman or bondswoman, nor bear that name; for as God hath saved us from heathens and heathendom, so hath he also saved them.' All Christians, that is, had been freed from the thralldom of sin by their Saviour. The official motive for liberating the bondsmen was purely Christian. By his decree the young king wished to bring repose to the souls of his father, Duke Erik, and his uncle Birger, in the land of the dead. It was to take effect retroactively, in the life to come.

King Magnus's brief, known as the Skara Decree, is no longer extant in the original and only known from copies. These have been reinterpreted by two modern legal historians, S. Henning (*Historisk Tidskrift*, 1930) and G. Hasselberg (*Västergötlands Fornminnesförenings Tidskrift*, 1944). Henning maintains that the old Swedish words *Waerinsko Laghsaghu*, in the decree, have been erroneously interpreted. The reference, he says, is not to Värend, but to Värmland. In those days Värend was called Tihärads Lagsaga. The men who met King Magnus at Skara during his journey round the kingdom were men of Västergötland and Värmland, and his decree applied only to their provinces. In reality however, Henning maintains, King Magnus by his decree wished to give official confirmation to a state of affairs already existing *de facto* throughout the realm: namely, that, in the eyes of Swedish law, the institution of bondage was already on the way out. Hasselberg also stresses that the decree only abolished hereditary bondage. Yet even this meant that as an institution it was doomed. The entire Swedish people were now Christians; so henceforth all children, by being baptized, would automatically become free. The remaining bondsmen were to be the last. Within a lifetime they would all have disappeared.

Among the Scandinavian peoples it was the Norwegians who were the pioneers of more human institutions. In their country they had abolished bondage as early as the end of the 12th century, or about 150 years before the Swedes did.

After 1335 it was forbidden to call anyone in Sweden a bondsman. Until then peasant society had excluded the unfree, but within that society there had been no class distinctions. Now a new grouping arose within the peasantry, and gave rise to a new class: the freedmen. The bondsmen were succeeded by a social class, the '*tjänstehjon*', or servants. These were no longer their master's chattels. They stood in a new juridic relationship to him. This, of course, did not make them his equals. But the bondsman had become a human being. Formally speaking, the transformation was to have a paradoxical result. *Only when bondage was abolished did a class society come into being.*

The freedman was master of his own life and limb. He could go from one master to another. He drew a wage for his services. He had the right to own property. He had become legally competent. Henceforward he was to be responsible for his own actions. The change in apellation from '*träl*' to '*legohjon*' meant a social promotion, the word 'hjon' originally meaning a member of the household.

Yet his freedom of movement was sharply restricted even so. All unpropertied persons were obliged by law to work, and here the law drew a clear distinction between the tax-paying land-owning peasants and the serving class; between the 'haves' and the 'have-nots'. As the law put it: 'Let him be peasant that can pay tax; let him that cannot pay tax be servant' ('*legodräng*').

Most people got their living from the soil. The soil demanded labour. Therefore society required certain of its citizens to go into service. For all persons having no means of support it introduced the principle of compulsory labour. By an 'unpropertied person' the mediaeval provincial laws meant anyone owning less than three marks. Property was calculated *in natura ;* in cattle or grain. In the provincial laws three marks were regarded as equivalent in value to 36 barrels of corn, in the national laws to 18 barrels, a sum adequate to support one person for one year.

All who did not possess these three marks were obliged by law to take service for one year at a time. 'If man or woman be commanded to take service, and are loath to do so, then shall they go free seven days and nights; thereafter they shall go into service. He that thereafter giveth them lodging, let him be fined three marks.'

Thus far the original Swedish Vagrancy Act. Servants infringing it could be condemned to severe punishments. At the beginning of the 14th century the aristocracy had prevailed upon the king to enact a law guaranteeing them labour for their estates: 'In 1303, King Birger, at the request of the great nobles, issued regulations against vagrancy: he who within one month could not shew he was serving a master was to be whipped and lose his ears, a shameful form of punishment earlier reserved only for bondsmen' (C. G. Andrae: *Kyrka och frälse i Sverige*).

The statute varied from province to province. Götland law obliged anyone without land of his own to work for the landowners at harvest-time. Refusal cost him a fine of three öre. By Västergötland Law, anyone giving lodging to a '*hjon*' who had refused to go into service should be fined thrice sixteen öre. The Uppland and Södermanland Laws, too, place much the same obligation upon the unpropertied to go into service for one year, if offered such service. The Uppland Law defines the class of people subject to compulsory labour. They were the poorest members of society: unattached folk, hired labourers, household servants and 'stavemen' – i.e. beggars. In mediaeval Sweden the line of class-distinction was drawn at three marks. It put a considerable part of the population in an exceptional social position. This legal obligation on certain citizens to take service persisted right up into the 20th century. Gustav Vasa confirmed it in a decree of 1540, regulating servants' conditions and forbidding masters and servants to contract free agreements of their own. As the centuries followed one another fresh statutes of the same sort were always being passed: in 1576, 1664, 1686, 1723, 1739, 1805 and 1858 – seven statutes, and even so I am not sure I have included them all. Not until the Statute of 1805 were free agreements permitted and servants at last allowed to have a say in fixing their own wages. The last Vagrancy Act, today a thing of the past, was enacted as late as the year 1885. Under it the county council or police could condemn any person who, having passed his 21st birthday and possessing no means of subsistence and who without looking for work wandered about from place to place, to forced labour.

'He who won't work, shan't eat' – so runs the Swedish peasants'

B

Great Commandment. An Eleventh Commandment, one might say, in force even in my own lifetime.

Christianity took over one aspect of prehistoric heathen society's view of the servant class. The bondsman may have been given human status; but unequal distribution of property still distinguished him from other people. In Luther's catechism I had to learn the following: 'Rich and poor shall be together, for the Lord hath made them all.' God's ethical world-order must not be disturbed. Like bondage, earthly class distinctions are of divine origin. Only in heaven will they be done away.

What then were the real implications of the famous Skara Statute of 1335? Bondsmen had been set free; but not having possessed the right to own property in the past they could hardly be expected to become persons of means overnight. A minority went out into the forests and there tilled soil that had hitherto been regarded as defying cultivation. During the High Middle Ages this led to a number of new villages coming into being with the word '*måla*' in their names. '*Måla*' means outlying land. Gradually these pioneers and backswoodsmen were assimilated into the class of self-owning peasants. But the great majority of the manumitted stayed where they were and became the dregs of the populace. They went on performing exactly the same tasks as before. They served the 'haves'. And under the above-mentioned statutes their freedom of movement was severely limited. Nor did security necessarily follow in the wake of freedom. Servingmen and women could even find themselves less secure than they had been before, in the days when they had been objects of patriarchal concern to their masters. The negro slaves' situation after the Civil War was exactly analogous. The liberation of the slaves did not solve the negro problem. It merely gave it new implications.

The new class of servants were hired by the half-year. If they moved from one master to another they did so in spring and autumn, at Easter and Michaelmas, usually in late April and September. After a year's service servants had a right to seven days' holiday, during which time their masters had to feed them. This is the mediaeval origin of the so-called 'free week', enjoyed by farmhands and servanthands in my own childhood. The week fell in the last week of October, from October 24 to All Saint's Day, November 1. Even in the 19th century Swedish labourers were still getting part of their wages in kind. My own parents, in service to peasants at that time, have told me about conditions in the century's last decades. My mother was born in 1864. For twelve years, from her confirmation at the age of fourteen in 1878 until her marriage to my father in 1890, she had been in service as a maid in several farmhouses in her parish. During those years her average wage had amounted to one *riksdaler* a month, cash, or twelve *riksdalers* a year. In addition she received payment in kind, in the form of a field of flax, from which she could get enough flaxen thread to weave herself a dress, and a certain number of pounds of wool from the sheep to knit herself a new pair of stockings each year. While working for one peasant she also had her own potato strip. Meanwhile my father was serving as a farmhand. The highest wages he ever received were forty riksdalers for the six summer months and twenty-five riksdalers for the six winter months. A 'summer hand' was always more in demand than a 'winter hand'. This great discrepancy in men's and women's wages was due to the much greater supply of women obliged to take service.

My parents served out their time in a part of the country where farms are small, where the family usually did the same work and ate at the same table as their employees and mixed with them socially at the same feasts, weddings and funerals. To some extent such social intercourse, both at work and afterwards, counteracted the economic class distinction. Practically no peasant could be called rich. No one lived in luxury or superfluity. Everyone did physical work, and a well-to-do peasant did just as heavy tasks as his unpropertied farmhand. All this meant that they were essentially equals. In the wealthy agricultural districts, where there were large estates, conditions were quite different. There deep unbridgeable cleavages arose between those who owned the land and those who worked it.

By compelling the landless to work, the Statute of Servants subjected this class of the population to special legislation and regulated their lives for six hundred years. Yet relations between master and servant must have been characterized by a certain degree of human consideration; after all, it lay in the master's own interest. A peasant who wanted to keep a good farmhand had to treat him decently. As a rule, the Statute was not so much interpreted by magistrates at their meetings, as in practice by each individual peasant. Relationships must mostly have been patriarchal.

But the Statute also left room for maltreatment. Even the Statute of Servants in force up to 1920 still retained a regulation concerning 'moderate whipping'. A phrase open to elastic interpretation. What, in this context, was meant by 'moderate'? (I have considered the question in my novel *The Emigrants*). The 1858 Statute had restricted a master's right to chastise his servants. We read that only 'servants under age' could be whipped. Sinister though it may seem, no one has so far asked what maltreatment has been meted out to our Swedish children with the connivance of the Swedish law. Indeed the entire question of the conditions under which the servant class lived, and their legal status, has received only the most cursory treatment by our historians. It is a subject which in many crucial respects still remains to be explored. It is true that one modern writer, Clara Neveus, has devoted a doctor's thesis to this subject. Concerning the Statute of Servants she concludes: 'It was not until 1920 that this last relic of bondage was abolished in Sweden.'

The slave system, officially abrogated in Sweden in 1335, was retained by a number of countries in the Old World, even up to modern times. It was in the British colonies of America that men first declared their freedom. But it was also there that for two centuries slavery flourished as never before. In the 17th and 18th centuries between fifteen and twenty million negroes were transported as slaves from Africa to North America. The chief agents in this traffic were Europe's most civilized peoples, the British, the French, the Spaniards, the Portuguese and the Dutch. It was a most profitable form of commerce. The Scandinavian countries, too, participated in this traffic in human lives, albeit to a lesser extent. In the 1650's the Swedish-African Company, engaged in the slave trade, built a fortress called Carlsborg near the Bight of Guinea, on the west coast of Africa. From this fort the Swedes sallied out on their slave-hunts. Compared with some other peoples' my compatriots' achievements, as international slavers were modest. But the Danes were rather more successful. A Danish historian (Thorkild Hansen: *The Slave Coast*, 1967) has written this chapter in his country's history, earlier overlooked by historians. In the days when Denmark stood at the height of her colonial power, a fort, Christiansborg, was established in what is present-day Ghana. From here the Africans who had been taken prisoner in the Danish colonies were shipped for the West Indies. According to Hansen, the Danes, in 333 voyages under sail, transported something in the region of 100,000 negro slaves to America.

Compared with the cargoes of millions of human beings shipped across the Atlantic by such other peoples as the British, these Danish slave transports, too, were quite small. All that Danish history books have to say about the matter is that Denmark was the first country in the world to abolish the slave trade. That was in 1792. Not a word about the 100,000 negroes already taken from Ghana to the West Indies in Danish ships. As for our own histories, I have so far sought in vain for any information on the Swedish West African slave fort of Carlsborg, named after King Karl X Gustav.

Quite a few place names, particularly in Southern Sweden, remain to us as memorials of our own institution of bondage. In Småland, the villages of Trälebo, Trälemåla and Trälarp; also a number of farms believed to have been named after manumitted bondsmen: Kuramåla, Summamåla and Estamåla. At all events, whether or not their names have been preserved topographically, there were once bondsmen called Kure and Summe. The city of Trelleborg, in Skåne, originally appears to have been a fortress where the king's '*hird*' had their camp. As has been seen, they too lived in a special form of slavery.

In daily speech Swedes still use the verb '*att träla*', a word, as I have said, allied to the English word 'thrall'. Admittedly, it is used much less than formerly. In popular speech I have also come across the expression '*trälknölar*', meaning the thick hard callouses which manual labourers get on the palms of their hands. The word is obsolete today, but in my youth I heard old people use it – a verbal relic from an age when a sizeable fraction of the Swedish people were owned by other Swedes.

The Swedish Peasant Celebrates
his 5,000th Anniversary

H OW OLD ARE THE SWEDES, as a people? How long has anyone
been living in Sweden? In the 17th century that learned man,
Olaf Rudbeck, thought our land the oldest in the world. He
believed it to have been inhabited even in the days of Noah and the
Flood, an epoch set at a date 2,400 years before Christ. In the 18th
century, on the other hand, the writer and historian Olof von Dalin
thought that, at the time of the birth of Christ, Sweden had still been
wholly uninhabitable. As proof he adduced the fact that the sea level
around the mainland had been thirteen fathoms higher at that time
than it was in the 18th century. Our great 20th-century student of
prehistoric times, Oscar Montelius, has asserted that 'our fair-haired,
tall, dolychocephalic ancestors' have been living here since the end of
the Ice Age; or for about 15,000 years. Biblical history apart, this
archaeologist has arrived at his view by applying evolutionary doctrine to his own science. Montelius has been our first historian to
read Sweden's history in her soil, revealing her secrets with the spade.

Montelius' view is that our own forefathers were the country's
earliest inhabitants. 'Unlike the builders of so many other countries,
we have not taken ours from some other folk.' This may be balm to
our Swedish conscience; but in point of fact Swedes were so far
from satisfied with their own original share of the Scandinavian
peninsula that they went east, crossed the sea, and there, battle-axe
and sword in hand, conquered the lands of others. No historical
truth, closely scrutinized, ever contained more than a half-truth;
hardly that!

Swedes no longer rejoice with Rudbeck that their country is the
oldest in the world. But many of us, like Montelius, would dearly
like to regard themselves as descended from the country's earliest

inhabitants and so as its pioneers, entitled to it. Many archaeologists, however, have begun to revise Montelius' findings, and the latest hypothesis, briefly, is that we cannot say with any certainty what sort of people inhabited Sweden further back in time than about 4,000 years ago, nor what may have been their origins. What races may have lived here before that is lost in obscurity. Bengt Schön-bäck, an archaeologist of the latest school, writes as follows: 'From the last 4,000 years we have no evidence of any large-scale occupation of the country by foreign peoples.'

This, then, is what contemporary research has to say on the age of the Swedes. Archaeological discoveries are also swiftly modifying our view of our own prehistory.

We may not know exactly at what point in time our first ancestors arrived in Sweden. But one thing we do know. The land that fell to their lot was no land flowing with milk and honey. Ultima Thule, at the outermost limits of the known world, was certainly no Promised Land; it offered little enough bread, let alone milk and honey. For the most part it was grimly inhospitable. Its soil was littered with stones and boulders and exceedingly hard to cultivate. Its dense forests were terrifyingly large. Its distances were endless. Summer was fleetingly brief, winter insufferably long, and the cold torment-ingly severe. As long as the sun stayed away, human beings spent their lives in dark holes and huts, lit only – as far as they could keep its flames alive – by their fire. In the long midwinter darkness, seized by an irresistible longing for *the great light*, they sent up scouts to the highest hilltops to await the great luminary's return. The instant these scouts glimpsed the first beams of light they hastened down into the valley to announce the wonderful news. In their joy people invited each other to feasts to celebrate the return of light. It was the greatest festival of the year.

The country's first inhabitants, the aboriginal Swedes, sustained themselves on game from the forest, on fish from the lakes and rivers, on berries from the earth, on the fruits of trees and bushes, on acorns, beech nuts and hazel nuts. After them came a shepherd people, who tended their wandering herds. At first they probably only had smaller creatures – *smale*, as they are still called in our old country dialects. Wandering about with their flocks of sheep, goats and swine, they searched for new grazing places for their animals and dwellings for themselves. All this was during the millennia afterwards called the warmer Stone Age.

At the end of the Stone Age, about 3,000 B.C., a new epoch began. Now people, settling down in fixed dwellings, had started to extract their nourishment from the soil. And it is now that the concept of 'peasant' – *bonde* – someone who lives in one place and tills the soil* comes into existence. Swedish peasant society was founded when the first hoe was stuck into the ground. Modern archaeological finds show that this happened about 5,000 years ago. Only by archaeological means can we approximately establish the age of the Swedish peasant.

Impressions of corn have been found in the once soft wet material of fragments of clay pots. Such finds have made it possible for experts to establish what kinds of grain were cultivated by Sweden's first peasants. They were millet, two-rowed and six-rowed barley and two sorts of wheat. Seed found in the Stone Age village at Alvastra has proved to be six-rowed barley and bones found in their dwellings' refuse heaps show that Stone Age man kept sheep, goats and pigs. It was not until later that the peasant acquired his larger animals, the horse, ox and cow.

The Swedish soil is our greatest national archive – an archive that has still only to a small extent been opened or studied. Of about half a million prehistoric remains in Sweden only a small percentage have so far been investigated. But in the last few decades Swedish archaeology has made great strides, chiefly in the excavation of the island settlement of Helgö, in Lake Mälaren, an island whose soil is yielding up some remarkable secrets.

On Helgö, near the site of old Birka, later to be the Viking capital, a hitherto unknown prehistoric centre has been unearthed; a complete and elaborate community, where the Svear carried on important crafts and had a remarkable art industry. The finds have revealed metal workshops, manufacturing tools, household equipment and ornaments of a high order of craftsmanship. Crucibles and moulds of a sort formerly believed to belong only to a much later epoch have

* Sw: *bo* = to dwell, *boende* = a dweller = *bonde* = 'peasant'. *Transl.*

also been found. The soil here has yielded up golden Roman coins, glass beakers made in France and Germany, an Irish bishop's crozier and a 5th or 6th-century Indian image of Buddha. From all this it is evident that the inhabitants of Helgö stood in contact with remote lands. Their remarkable island community is believed to have been established in the 2nd century A.D., and to have reached its peak of development in the 6th.

Another great archaeological find has recently been made on the estate of Halleby, in the parish of Skärkind, in the province of Östergötland. Here well-preserved remains of a prehistoric village have been excavated. Its houses lacked longitudinal walls, the roof being supported on timbers sunk deep in the ground. Stone fences, village streets, paths worn deep by the hoofs of cattle, all have been found at Halleby.

These finds have partially revised our notions of what our earliest peasant ancestors' buildings looked like. And it is my belief that archeology is going to modify our whole idea of Swedish prehistory and greatly extend our knowledge of our ancestors' way of life. New finds soon make every account of this subject obsolete, so here I shall only touch on it briefly. Much information still lies hidden in our great state archive.

From hoe to tractor. This could be the title of a history of Swedish agriculture. Five millennia lie between these two tools. During them appear, one after the other, the man who turned the first peat sod, the man who cleared away the rocks, stones and boulders, the tiller of the soil, the man who 'swithened' or burned over the forests, the breaker of stones and clearer of tree-stumps, the man who walked behind the plough; and, finally, the tractor-driver astride his motor vehicle. The history of agriculture is the history of thousands of years of human struggle, of men's tools: the mattock, the plough-hook, the wooden harrow, the pick, the iron-tipped quarrying iron, the iron crowbar, the primitive plough and its sophisticated modern successor.

Ages were to pass before man could develop today's efficient tools. The history of tools is a remarkable saga: the saga of those sons of toil who both made and used them.

The peasant gained his knowledge through his hands. Day after day, with patiently bowed, aching backs, the palms of their hands rúbbed raw, labourers went to and fro over the soil. Their monument to themselves is their many thousands of miles of stone walls. All this stone, which had to be lifted from the ploughed fields and laid out in these walls, has cost the sweat of many a long day's work. This age-old fight against the stones, the peasant's conquest of the country, is a historical drama, a tremendous peaceful epic never yet seen in print.

Much has been written on our ancestors' warlike enterprises. The General Staff has published its account of them in enormous official histories. Compared with these tomes little has been written about their achievements in peace time. We know what they did with sword, matchlock and cannon; but all too little about what they achieved with the tools of peace. History and poetry have both been stingy in their treatment of the peasant, his labourers and their labours. So far not even a thesis has been written on these monuments to human toil, our stone walls. Nor has any poet sung of them.

The history of the Swedish peasant begins about 3,000 B.C., when his earlier, even more primitive existence was transformed by the introduction of crops. Folk settled down and began extracting a living from the soil. As a social revolution it is only to be compared with the industrial revolution of the 20th century.

The first land to be cultivated was broken with a stone hoe. In popular country speech we still have the word *hackhemman*, literally, 'a hoe-homestead'. The tool used for scorching and burning over the forest was the rake, or *fällekratta* – *fälla* means a little patch of ploughed land in the forest. The hoe used for cultivation gradually developed into the ard or plough-hook. This, the most primitive form of plough, was simply the trunk of a young spruce tree that had grown at an angle from its root, the point sticking out at the thick end being used to rip up the soil. Such an implement was called an *ärjekrok* – *ärja* means to plough, and the other part of the name comes from the hook (*krok*) at the thick end. With such an implement the very first furrows were ploughed in Swedish soil.

The invention of the bulking-plough was a great step forward. While the plough-hook had been a one-man tool, the bulking-plough called for at least two men. One walked behind, holding the handle and steering, while the other walked by the shaft in front, dragging it along. The bulking-plough consisted of three parts: pole, share, and handle. During the Iron Age the share, which ploughed the furrow, was given an iron tip.

Before horse and ox, it was human beings – in olden times chiefly bondsmen – who had to pull the bulking-plough.

Out of the bulking-plough developed the plough with a wooden mould-board, and finally the wheeled plough and the iron plough with a curved ploughshare.

Not until the 19th century did the modern plough come into general use in Sweden. The harrow went through the same development from wood to iron. An offspring of the rake used for 'devonshire-burning' or swithening in the woods was the wooden-spiked harrow. It was still in use on farms in my own childhood. I have followed it myself as it was drawn by a pair of oxen over the ploughed field. This articulated harrow consisted of mobile pieces of wood, a foot long, into which holes had been bored for pointed teeth; it crawled over the field like a great wide snake. To lift it over all the stones in which the wooden teeth so easily fastened was a troublesome business.

These were the oldest implements for ploughing and sowing – but what did men use at harvest? No one seems to know how the later Stone Age peasant reaped his crops. Our museums contain many a cartload of stone axes and other stone implements; but as far as I know not a single stone sickle survives. Could a stone knife be made sharp enough for use as a sickle?

The peasant of a later age made his sickle out of iron or flint. From time immemorial the sickle was the woman's tool. Out of the sickle developed the scythe, which became the man's. As a threshing tool the flail, too, is immensely ancient, and has remained in use up to our own time. The grain was crushed by blows of a pestle in stone mortars or else ground between two stones.

The development of implements is a crucial chapter in the history of agriculture and a most meaningful one, full of implications and saturated with the cumulative knowledge and experience of many generations. It witnesses to the perfection of that knowledge, once possessed by all peoples of the earth, which was acquired through the hand.

The first peasants settled in the plains of Skåne and Central Sweden. But for a long while only a minor portion of their food came from the fields. For thousands of years a peasant's herds were more important to him than his ploughed fields. From his cows, sheep and goats he obtained meat, milk, butter and cheese; with cattle hides and sheep's wool he clothed his own body. But his daily bread, his industry and his living were all subject to the caprices of the weather. His life was ruled by rain and sunshine, by moisture and drought, by frost and hail, heat and cold. Whether he would have enough to fill his belly and live, or would starve to death, was something which depended entirely on the weather. There were good years and there were bad years; and what sort of year it was going to be – that depended on the weather. For him the two greatest events of the year were the sun's disappearance and its return.

In the Bronze Age the climate was mild. The grape ripened and cattle could graze the year round. The great change must have occurred about 500 B.C. It was then the cold harsh climate began which still plagues us Swedes to this day. Since then we have been unable to grow vines; nor have we been able to let our cattle graze out of doors in winter. Since then the peasant has been obliged to put up buildings to protect his beasts during the cold months of the year, and in summer has had to gather enough food to last until next spring. He has cleared meadows to yield him his dry hay, and has even had to gather leaves for his cattle. The silver birch woods were felled and the leafy twigs, bound in sheaves, were dried to provide food for his sheep and goats in winter. His horses' fodder was aspen leaves.

The peasants' first dwelling was the earthen or clay hut. Later, taking his building materials from the forest, he erected a simple log cabin; and, finally, he built the typical Swedish timber farmhouse, still to be seen in the Swedish countryside today.

The earliest dwellings were solitary remote farms. Sweden was, and still is, a land of forests. From the outset, distances between human beings and their homes were immense. The Swede's character is that of a forest-dweller.

Physically and psychologically he has been toughened by solitude. This has had a positive effect. With no neighbours to help him he has been forced to rely on himself. His isolation has also had a negative effect. It has limited his view of things, made him too sufficient unto himself, prejudiced and suspicious of strangers. He has lived an enclosed life. What has been going on on the other side of the fence has been no concern of his. The truth is banal, but inescapable: solitude has nurtured the Swede's inhibitions, made it difficult for him to consort with others in an open or natural way. On one point all foreigners agree: we are a people who find it hard to associate with our fellow-beings.

It was in this immense far-flung land that the Swedish peasant began to plough up his fields. All around him swamps, marshes and bogs spread far and wide; but then, as now, it was the forests which dominated the landscape. Such regions as Tivden, Kolmården and Holaveden were of such vast extent that they utterly cut off one province from another. Forests meant firewood; and firewood meant warmth. Not until the epoch of the horse and its rider could there be much communication between the various parts of this land of forests. Of King Sverker, King of the Svear, we read that losing his way when riding through Tiveden he almost got lost altogether in that primitive forest, of which it was said that 'its breadth extended for ten days'. For a man from Östergötland to visit a man from Västergötland meant a ten days' journey. Nature herself gave the kingdoms of the Svear and Götar their names: the former were called Nordanskogs – 'the northern forests' – and the latter Sunnanskogs – 'the southern forests'.

Sweden's quality as a land of forests appears in the names of her inhabitants. Swedes have taken many of their surnames from the forest: *Björk, Gran, Ek, Kvist, Gren, Rot, Hägg, Bok, Rönn, Alm, Lind, Lönn, Stam, Ask, Ahl, Asp* – Birch, Spruce, Oak, Twig, Branch, Root, Bird-Cherry, Beech, Mountain Ash, Elm, Lime, Maple, Trunk, Ash, Alder, Aspen. In giving themselves such names people have drawn on every tree growing in the country, as well as using every thinkable combination of branch, leaf, twig and bark. All the names of which the word *sten* (stone) forms part remind us what the Swedish soil was like. How many Swedish farms and villages do not contain such words as *skog, sjö, berg, dal, lund, ö, holm, näs* and *bäck* – forest, lake, rock, valley, grove, island, islet, promontory, stream? Our Swedish place-names too, have been given us by nature.

The earliest dwellings were homesteads, consisting of single farm-houses. Gradually they grew into villages, and peasant society came into being. The family, the oldest human community, was a large natural unit, comprising several generations. By marrying into other families it grew into tribes and clans. The clan ('*ätt*') might also be described as a large family. All its many individuals were related by marriage; welded together, they helped and defended each other against other clans, violently avenging each others' deaths. An attack on any member of the clan was regarded as an attack on all. In this firmly allied group the individual was far from being his own master. Without the others' permission and that of the clan as a whole he might not marry, move away, sell his land, or indeed undertake any action of importance. Primitive peasant society was highly con-formist. The clan's powers were dictatorial. While all due stress must be laid on the immemorial freedom of the Swedish peasant – for its time it was a remarkable and praiseworthy phenomenon – his per-sonal freedom of movement was severely limited. As a group the clan had little use for such deviants as did not accept its unwritten laws. On the other hand those who could not adapt were always free to annul their contract with it, and 'go into the forest' – or else put to sea as Vikings.

As time went by, the emergent clans formed tribes and federations of tribes. Out of these developed still larger units – whole provinces, which became politically independent powers. For long ages these units waged war on each other, fighting over small areas of land; but finally they, too, formed a federation. In this federation each pro-vince retained its own distinct laws; and when the light of history begins to fall over our country and its people in the 8th or 9th century A.D., the federation of provinces belonging to the Svear, in eastern Sweden, had already conquered that of the Götar, in Western Sweden, and had incorporated their country into its own. All this had only happened after long and bloody struggles. Out of the union of the Svear and the Götar there arose in this way a single kingdom, '*Svea rike*' – the Svea Kingdom; words which, spoken quickly, merge into *Sverige* – Sweden. But several centuries were to pass before the kingdom became a national state, in the modern sense of the word. Almost throughout the Middle Ages it was still really only a loose federation of provinces.

The old peasant society consisted of several smaller units, of which the smallest was the village. The village (*'by'*) was of paramount importance both to the peasant's workaday life and to his holidays and festivals. It stood for an immemorial community of interests and feeling. Research into the names of persons in heathen days has shown that in the era of the great migrations, the mid-11th century, the village was already an extended arrangement of dwellings. But the village system, as such, appears to be considerably older. Remains of Viking dwellings show that by then peasants were already living in solitary farms and in villages. Several factors, economic and social and, not least, technical considerations of defence, led to the growth of villages. Out of sheer self-preservation people brought their dwellings together, seeking in such a cluster protection against their enemies, against robbers and predatory beasts, against criminals, and against the starving wolves that strayed about the land in winter.

The village was the peasants' castle. Its raison d'être was mutual assistance. In illness, want or danger they came to each others' assistance. Always there was someone in the village who knew how to drive out evil with fire and steel. If a cow fell sick, it was handy to have a neighbour who knew how to cure it. Birth and marriage, death and funerals, all were the common concern of the village council. Agriculture too was carried on jointly by the men of the village. The soil was distributed in such a way that a peasant's plots of land might well be scattered in thirty different places. Since the fields were tilled simultaneously, the work had to be done on a basis of mutual understanding. The cattle went out, hoof by hoof, to graze together on the common land. Each villager drew his water from the village well, and at festivals all gathered on the same hillock, the 'court' (*hov*) of some god.

Another reason why our forefathers clustered in villages was to overcome the solitudes of a country still largely uninhabited. Sometimes the houses of the old village stood so close together that they actually leaned against each other, as if for mutual support. 'Man's joy is in man', says the Icelandic *Havamal*. A timelessly valid saying.

The village organization had many branches. Community of interest led to the founding of the *byalag*, or village's communal association. For a thousand years and more it was to constitute an independent power in peasant society. Its organ was the *bystämman* – the village council – which enforced a special order of things in the village and in all essentials gave form to peoples' lives. The council decided all common questions, regulated all work and fixed the times of sowing and reaping. One of its manifestations was a village court (*'byrätt'*) to settle disputes between the men of the village, irrespective of provincial law, and pass judgment even in criminal cases. It intervened in the villagers' daily life, organized both work and rest, and arranged the annual feasts and festivals. To it was given all power in the village. The village council had the same function in the village as a board of directors has in a company.

Chairman of the village council was the alderman, or *byäldste*. His name does not imply that the position was occupied by some old and infirm man; its responsibilities were altogether too heavy. It was the alderman's business to look after the village accounts, lead its work, and generally keep order. His activities were manifold. Often he was helped by an assistant. The post, passing in turn from one villager to another was more of a duty than an honour, and in nothing was it desirable. Town guilds are regarded as having in part been organized on the pattern of the *byalag*.

By fiery-cross, horn or drum, the alderman summoned the men of the village to meetings. In the early history of the *byalag*, fire was also used as a means of communication between the villages. Great bonfires would be lit on heights, visible far and wide and from village to village. Such bonfires were also used to sound the alarm when some enemy or danger threatened. In a deserted country, where one house lay many miles from another, fire was the original means by which people kept in contact with one another. In peasant society the flames of these hill-fires passed messages to and fro. It was also by means of fire that the authorities made their announcements to the people. And still today in Sweden we use the verb *att lysa* – literally, to 'show a light' – when we mean putting up marriage banns.

Originally, too, people were summoned to the *ting* – the provincial council – by fire: a flaming torch would be carried about by a runner.

It was the oldest form of the *budkavel* – in Scotland still referred to as the 'fiery cross'. In country speech this torch was called a *tanne*, the German word for the spruce – actually a silver spruce – which it was made of.

In early days, the minutes kept of the village council meetings and its decisions were recorded on wooden staves. Like the horn, the drum and the fiery-cross, the alderman's mallet, too, was the village's property and passed down to his successor.

The village community was an association for mutual help, for joint work and human intercourse generally. It was a collective, taking care of those interests that unite all who practise the same craft or industry. In this sense, our trade unions are a modern equivalent of the old *byalag*. The importance of the *byalag* in the history of the Swedish peasant can hardly be exaggerated. As the Middle Ages reached their climax and spiritual and temporal over-lords arose who made heavy demands for taxes, horses and transport, requiring hospitality for magnates and bishops and their huge entourages, the *byalag* assumed crucial importance. These burdens were always growing heavier and it became a matter of vital importance for the peasants to stick together. It was also the Middle Ages which saw the introduction of days of compulsory labour on taxable lands. The peasants had to work both on the royal and noble estates, and also on those of the church. At first such work seems to have been – in principle – voluntary: but gradually, as had earlier been the case with taxes, they were transformed into a legal obligation. In 1403, it was formally made law that all peasants on taxable land should do eight days' work a year on the royal estates, an obligation afterwards extended to the estates of the nobility. As the years went by, the number of such work-days was multiplied several times over.

From among the *allmogen*, the commons, arose wealthy peasants who became nobles and earls. Cleavages between social groups became broader and deeper. The difference between one man's circumstances and another's was symbolized, literally, by the quality of a man's daily bread. The bondsman's bread, baked in hot ash, was full of bran; the peasant's was a loaf of corn-bread, baked on a stone or iron slab; while on their tables the earls had wheaten loaves, baked on a bread-iron with a handle to it. All three were unleavened. None was baked in an oven.

During the Middle Ages, as Christianity came to be introduced, the village joined a larger unit: the ecclesiastical parish. Gradually, part of the village council's powers and duties were taken over by the parish council, and the administration of justice passed to a court set up in each hundred. But right up to the time of the great redistribution of the land in the early 19th century, when the Swedish village community was finally disrupted, the village council filled a crucial function in the lives of the peasantry.

Industrialization and modern communications have dissolved the *byalag*. Yet this ancient Swedish peasant community has still not quite vanished. As owner of a quarter of a homestead at Söderäng, in the parish of Väddö in the county of Stockholm, the present writer is a member of a *byalag* that still exists and functions, has its own alderman, and holds meetings. Every year we meet to elect the alderman, and all our decisions are confirmed by an antique mallet belonging to the village. Naturally, the tasks of this association are limited. It administers only such lands as are owned by the whole village in common, leases out its common fishing waters and keeps up the village roads. There is a village fund, administered by the alderman, who receives an annual fee for his duties.

The most treasured possession of this *byalag* is a big collection of old minutes from its meetings. Unfortunately, no records on wooden staves have been preserved. But a number of two-hundred-year-old documents are still in its possession. I have gone through them, and they have yielded me fresh information on the history of the Swedish peasant. They tell me how he used to govern and administer his village, they speak of his never-flagging attempts to retain control of himself and his possessions. Much in these documents treats of the villagers' struggle against higher authority, in the person of that representative of the long arm of the law: the *fogde* – bailiff – later known as the *länsman*, or sheriff.

The Swedish peasant's hatred of bailiffs is of ancient date, it too has its roots in the Middle Ages. All down the centuries it has found drastic expression in the words used by the rebellious fist-shaking peasants in my novel *Ride this Night!* When any of them is obliged to heed a major call of nature he says 'I'll give the bailiff a lift'. As a child I've often heard peasants, working in their fields and meadows, say as they went behind a bush: 'I'll just go and give the bailiff a lift'.

Väddö *byalag* no longer uses the village horn or the fiery cross to summon its meetings. These antique means of peasant communication have been superseded by the telephone. Whether any other *byalag* are still functioning in Sweden today I cannot say. Presumably Väddö is one of the last to survive.

In this work the peasant will chiefly appear in his social and civic capacity. What I shall mainly investigate here will be his relations with the authorities, with kings, noblemen and other power-holders down the ages. The peasant's dwellings, his household goods and utensils, his eating and drinking vessels, his clothes, his customs and his habits have all been described already in several large and profusely illustrated volumes. Familiar though I am with this field, it would be presumptuous of me to dwell on it. But the Swedish peasant's social standing has drawn less attention from our historians. So it will be only natural if my history devotes a good deal of space to the *byalag*. For a thousand years it has been, for the peasantry, a cohesive factor, the bulwark of their liberties; in the desolate realms and solitudes of the forests it has also expressed a real community of feeling and interests, man's search for that joy of which the *Havamal* speaks.

The fundamental notion of human collaboration and common interest on which it is based seems to me so timeless that it could well be realised even in our latter-day environments. One day, perhaps, it will be revived in another society than ours – a form of society where the human being takes his rightful place: at the centre of things.

X

The exact age of the kingdom of Sweden is a matter of debate. Presumably it can never be fixed precisely, but one gathers that it must be at least a thousand years old.

The Swedish peasant is considerably older. He is five times as old. If we regard him as having been born somewhere around 3000

B.C. – as the latest research permits us to – then, within a few decades, in the year 2000, he will be no less than 5,000 years old. As things are going at present, however, it seems doubtful whether he will live to celebrate so remarkable a birthday, and even more dubious whether he will survive it.

Throughout our history, right up to the last century, peasant society was remarkably stable and unchanging. Its foundations are in the soil, which abides, and into which it has thrust deep roots. Close communion with every aspect of nature has been one of the main sources of its vitality. In the 19th century the immemorial distribution of the soil into strips was abolished and succeeded by individual farms. But these changes in the villages' structure were only superficial. The real life of their inhabitants went on as before. This ancient peasant culture persisted, in all essentials true to itself, for a thousand years.

The peasant's world survived every strain it was subjected to. It stood up to all the stresses of war, catastrophic diseases, times of famine and starvation. When the peasant was drafted for the wars and went abroad to foreign lands, sometimes never to return, it was his wife who took his place behind ploughhook and the plough. Only in this way could the land be kept under cultivation. And when times of peace returned the population increased again, which led to the cultivated lands being extended and fresh ground broken. After each catastrophe, peasant society recovered with amazing swiftness. It was this peasant society, on which the whole realm was based, that kept its basic industry going. Always it remained immensely vital. From the peasantry, too, were recruited all the other classes of society. It was the well-spring which never ran dry.

Even as late as the end of the nineteenth century Sweden was still a peasant country. Today, a century later, it has become an industrial one. Nowadays only some 7 per cent of us Swedes get our living from the land. To grow grain for bread, or keep a milch cow, no longer supports either man or woman. What used to be our main industry has become a secondary one. Agriculture is being rationalized. Ploughed fields are being allowed to go to grass. Our farms are being abandoned. Analagous changes are occurring over most of our part of the world, and most swiftly of all in Western Europe.

Today, it seems, the funeral knell has begun to toll for 'the eternal peasant' – a romantic old expression which now no longer having any basis in reality, sounds almost ironical.

Every year, deteriorating conditions in the mother of all industries are forcing some 10,000 peasants to leave their farms; homes, in most cases, passed down to them by their forefathers, and which for centuries have been our race's one safe recourse, its one fixed point in existence. All over Sweden, country roads run past empty and deserted cottages, lifeless farms. Man and beast have departed. Not even a dog or a cat is to be seen. In many places new forests are already growing up on the ploughed fields; over the meadows a vast jungle of bushes is spreading out. The forest is taking back the land of which it was once robbed at cost of so much sweat and toil by those who cleared and tilled it.

Upon those peasants who still remain the central authorities have enjoined that, within ten years, one-third of the land still under cultivation shall be allowed to go to grass, these new forests being planted in their place. If 10,000 peasants are to continue to disappear each year – how many, one wonders, will there be in the year A.D. 2000, when the Swedish peasant celebrates his five-thousandth birthday?

A quarter of my long life has been spent among peasants and others who live close to the soil; and I have devoted the remaining three-quarters to writing about such people. First and last, I have tried to present them as human beings, as individuals, each with his own characteristic traits and quirks. It is namely my belief that peasants differ more widely among themselves than do the social classes and professions indigenous to cities or small towns. For the countryman has been less exposed, hitherto, than the town-dweller to the influence of mass culture and its media which, eradicating people's characteristic traits, lead to so much standardization and mediocrity. To me the peasant is the last individualist left in our modern society. Not that I have ever romanticized or idealized him, nor the stern conditions under which he lives. But that the soil which he has tilled for five thousand years should be allowed to grow wild and revert to forest again is a course of events which I can only regard as profoundly tragic.

Concerning the disappearance of our farmlands, the man who, at this time of writing, is the Swedish peasant's chief political representative, namely our Minister of Agriculture, has declared: 'What is happening, after all, is merely that the environment is being allowed to revert to its original state.' As a statement of fact this is correct; but as a defence of this transformation – if that is what it is supposed to be – it must be utterly unacceptable to anyone who regards evolution and progress as desirable for mankind. When has our society ever made it its goal that the environment shall revert to its original state? What we have here is a reactionary regressive movement, represented as a good and desirable one! We could also return to our original dwellings: to caves, earthen huts and holes in the ground. But it would be no solution to our housing problem.

What is happening is commonly declared to be unavoidable, necessary. For my part I do not believe in any fated development which involves the ploughed field being given over to wild beasts. And development, anyway, is a word often grossly abused, by being made synonymous with change – as if all change were necessarily for the better. If our cultivated lands disappear and the Swedish countryside resumes its aspect of five thousand years ago, when Sweden was still a land of dense and desolate forests, then I certainly cannot regard this as a 'development', in the sense of progress. Cultivation is culture; improvement, progress. And to allow cultivated land to go to wrack and ruin is reactionary.

If our ploughed fields are allowed to revert to their aboriginal condition, the loss will not only be a material one. We shall also suffer – perhaps even more crucially – a social loss. If the peasant is to disappear, and with him an inhabited countryside, then that immemorial source of vitality and health which throughout our history has sprung from man's links with nature will also vanish. For what happens when land is allowed to go to seed? How many, how long and how laborious have not been the days, how much toil of aching backs have these old fields not cost to those who lived before us? By 'allowing the environment to revert to its original condition' we simply write off the achievements of a thousand years, a millennium of persistence, effort, obstinate work, endless patience and toil. What is happening today is nothing more nor less than a *regression*.

In man's history on this earth the peasants' five thousand years are but a twinkling of an eye. Today we are in the machine age, the industrial era. Having reached the atomic age, mankind has finally succeeded in producing implements which can bring about its own annihilation. Whether that annihilation is imminent or remote, or whether it will remain no more than a possibility, is not for me to prophesy. But if the catastrophe does occur, then probably, somewhere on earth, some human beings will survive it and once again begin gradually building up a new culture. When our machine civilization, our industrial and technocratic society have all long vanished and the green grass of oblivion waves over its grave, mankind will perhaps again begin turning the sod. A second time, perhaps, they will sow it with corn. That the ploughed field which is today being allowed to go to ruin may one day become necessary to man's daily bread is by no means impossible.

100 Kings

THIS CHAPTER CAN BEGIN WITH the opening words of all fairy stories: Once upon a time there was a king. Well, in Sweden, once upon a time, there were a hundred.

In his work, already referred to, on the old kings of the Svear and Götar, Johannes Magnust lists all the regents who had reigned since King Magog (he who lived about the time of the Flood and was Noah's grandson) up to King Björn, who was a contemporary of Ansgar the missionary. Johannes Magnus lists the names of exactly one hundred kings. For this sixteenth-century Swedish historian we Swedes were the oldest, not to say the most glorious, of all the peoples of the earth.

Johannes Magnus' beautiful – but wholly fallacious – picture of the prehistory of the Swedes was accepted by his successors; for several hundred years it was regarded as true and definitive. Not until our first rationalist in this field, Olaf von Dalin, cast a critical eye upon it in the 18th century, did it begin to pale. Modern research has committed mass-murder among Johannes Magnus' kings. All, with few exceptions, have been deported from the world of reality to the realm of myth. Yet as mythical figures, sprung from legendary truth, not a few are interesting. And since they appear in our earliest history book to the number of one hundred, their very multitude, surely, should entitle them here to a chapter of their own.

In the profound darkness shrouding Sweden's prehistory the concepts 'god' and 'king' can only with difficulty be distinguished. They seem to have been virtually identical. Long ages had to pass before divinity was laid aside and the human figure emerges.

Our prehistoric kings were of different kinds and qualities. There were kings of armies; of hundreds; of provinces; tributary kings,

48

and petty kings. By and by the petty kings disappear. After the ninth century we hear no more of them. By then their Lilliputian realms had become absorbed into larger units. We hear of the populace drowning five petty kings at once in a spring beside Mora Mead, in Dalarna. Great numbers of sea-kings also existed. According to Snorre Sturlason they 'had much folk, but no land'. It was on the high seas that these monarchs held sway and kept their courts. Their royal title was nothing but a euphemism for piracy, which was their true occupation.

Our oldest Swedish chronicle is the one contained in the older Västergötland Law, considered to have been penned before the year 1250. This chronicle is no more than an appendix to the laws of that province. But from prehistoric times we possess five extant lists of kings. One such list is found in the *Codex Upsaliensis C.70*. In Sture Bolin's methodological study, evaluating our sources for research into the earliest history of Scandinavia, it receives exhaustive treatment. A fourteenth-century list of Swedish kings, containing twenty-eight names and based on exceedingly ancient Icelandic and Norwegian sources, is regarded by Curt Weibull as our oldest and as having been the first to be drawn up.

We know very little about these regents except their names. Rolls, annals and chronicles have singularly little to relate about the events of their lifetimes. But their deaths are all the more vividly and tangibly described.

In one respect these prehistoric kings are all extraordinarily alike. When they departed this life it was always by violence. Sudden death was their normal lot. Only an odd king, here and there, died from sickness. Indeed, to pass away peacefully on one's couch, to 'die like a cow in the straw', was degrading. It was a shameful 'straw' death. The way which we regard as natural for a human being to end his days was, in prehistoric times, dishonourable. Happily, most kings escaped it. They departed this earthly life in a more glorious fashion.

While travelling through his kingdom, Sveigder, King of the Svear, had a spell cast upon him by a dwarf who inveigled him into a stone cairn, and was there found dead. King Fjolner, for his part, drowned himself in a tub of mead – a beer barrel, as we should call it today. The annals relate that on that occasion His Majesty was not sober; and since they add that it befell at a Yule feast, we have no reason to doubt this statement. Without risk of being arraigned for lèse-majésté we can say that King Fjolner was dead drunk. Henrik Schück, however, has placed a symbolic interpretation upon his death. Mead was a drink for the gods, and anyone who drew his last in a whole tub of it would instantly have been united with the gods and passed on to the delights of a higher life.

Concerning King Valande, on the other hand, we are told that he was strangled one night in his sleep by the Night-Mare. This was a shameful death. The Night-Mare ('*Maran*') was a female spirit; and no death more grossly degraded a man than death at the hands of a woman. King Domalde, again, fell a victim to bad weather. A long and severe drought had caused a crop failure; whereupon the Swedes, in exchange for rain, sacrificed their ruler to Ceres. That is to say, situations could arise when a king's subjects placed more value on a spell of rainy weather than on the life of their king.

Marital squabbles, too, could prove fatal to kings. When King Domar abandoned his queen, she caused the Seeress Huld to cast so severe a spell upon him that he died of it. King Agne married the daughter of a Finnish king, by name Skjalf, who hanged him in a golden chain. Another regent, by name Ingemar, was hanged in an oak by his enterprising queen. These kings' behaviour toward their spouses must have been bad indeed to precipitate such revenge. Hanging was a death for horse-thieves and a most shameful way to end one's life.

Concerning King Egil, we are told that he was about to sacrifice a bull to the gods, when he himself fell victim to it and the furious animal gored him to death. Two brothers, Kings Alsek and Erik, falling into a violent quarrel when out riding, slew each other still sitting on their horses – with their bridles. Unfortunately no details have survived to explain the exact manner of such a simultaneous double murder; as far as I know it is the only case in Swedish criminal history where the murder weapons were bridles. Of two other royal brothers, Alf and Yngve, the annals tell us cursorily that, having killed each other, they were ceremoniously buried on the ramparts of Fyris.

Brotherly love within royal families, if we are to believe our annals and chronicles, was no more in evidence in prehistoric times than in the Middle Ages. Our kings seem to have run the gravest danger when in the bosom of their closest relatives.

So much sudden death among Swedish kings greatly reduced their average life-expectancy which in our day, as in other kingdoms, is notably high. Nowadays it is dictators and dictatorial presidents who go in constant danger of their lives. Concerning two kings, Dyggve and Domar, it is recorded that they passed away as a result of illness. Another famous exception to the rule of sudden and violent death was Aun, or Audunn, as he is called in Icelandic, whose cognomen was Ane the Old. He is thought to have been a historical personage, who perhaps reigned in the fifth century. King Ane was famed for his longevity. He lived to be two hundred, a circumstance which makes him the longest-lived of all our Swedish monarchs, more than twice as old as Gustav V, his latter-day successor on the Swedish throne, who only reached an age of ninety-two. Ane the Old had ten sons. Of these he sacrificed nine to Oden – thus gaining in exchange one more year of life for each – a spirit of sacrifice for which he is famed in the annals. During his last years King Ane became so sickly that he had to live on baby-food, taking only liquids. Like an infant with its bottle, he lay in bed, tippling milk out of a horn. He, too, we are told, died a degrading death, perishing like a 'cow in the straw' of its manger.

According to Snorre Sturlason's *Ynglinga Saga*, Odin was the first ruler of the Svear. In this chapter, therefore, as our first Swedish king, he must take pride of place. Unfortunately our Swedish system of taxation is also coeval with his reign. An old narrative records that each commoner in Svitjod whom nature had provided with a nose paid a penny to King Odin. It was called the nose-tax: a sort of personal due, or sacrificial offering. In exchange for this allegedly voluntary penny tax it was Odin's duty to see to it that the peace was kept throughout the land, and that the fields yielded good grain. Under the kings who succeeded him this tax's voluntary character was annulled, and for some inexplicable reason has never been re-introduced into Sweden from Odin's day down to our own.

After his death Odin was deservedly elevated to divine rank; so we owe special reverence to his memory.

Otherwise it was the royal clan of the Svea empire, the Ynglingar, who were to be Scandinavia's most famous dynasty. They traced their descent directly from the god Fröj. The Icelandic *Ynglingatal* lists the clan's members; some are still regarded as having been monarchs who actually lived and reigned. Such was King Anund. He is described as a most amiable regent, and his reign is said to have been a happy one. In his day peace prevailed throughout the Svea empire; harvests were abundant, and every year the fields yielded a wealth of nourishment.

Anund, in fact, was a farmer king. He had the enormous forest lands – known as Svitjod – cleared; he cultivated the desolate places and laid out roads across marshes, bogs and fells. For this he was honoured with the nickname Bröt-Anund, because he broke (*'bröt'*) fresh land. When making a tour of inspection through his kingdom he was overwhelmed by a landslide, thus dying a death wholly true to style. The farmer king's tumulus, Anundshögen, can still be seen on the Badelunda Ridge, not far from the city of Västerås.

Anund's son was a man of quite different temper. Every school-child knows him from his history book under the name of Ingjald Illråde – 'Evil-Council'. As a boy he had the misfortune to eat the heart of a wolf, and as a result grew up to be a most evil-tempered and cruel man. In my schooldays I was fascinated by the tale of the funeral feast he gave for his father. Sending out messengers throughout Svitjod, Ingjald invited various petty kings, earls and other great men to the banquet. One of the guests was his father-in-law, a petty king. Ingjald had sworn a sacred oath to extend his kingdom in every direction, and to this end had drawn up a secret plan. At the banquet he put it into immaculate effect. He celebrated his father's funeral by burning the house down over the heads of his father-in-law and five other kings, seized the dead men's kingdoms, and appointed his own sons as chieftains to rule over them.

The key to Ingjald's success in this and other extensions of his empire lay in his passion for arson. One day two petty kings, Granmar and Hjorvard, were holding a great feast on the island of Selaön in Lake Mälaren, when suddenly Ingjald attacked them, set fire to the house, and burnt both of them and all their company to death. Snorre Sturlason estimates that Ingjald Illråde slew a total of twelve kings.

Although Ingjald's daughter Åsa had inherited her father's bad character and vicious temper, he managed to marry her off to Gudröd, King of Skåne. Their marriage was highly dramatic. Åsa incited her husband to slay her brother, Halvdan; whereafter she arranged for his own murder. Having thus achieved widowhood by her own efforts, she returned to her father's house. At that time Ingjald was involved in a war with King Ivar Vidfamne ('Huge-Hug') of Denmark, whom he 'much feared'; and with good reason, for in Ivar he met his fate. Ingjald and Åsa were staying as guests on their royal estate of Räning, in Uppland, when the Danish king attacked them with an overwhelming force. Father and daughter made 'all their people dead drunk', after which they set fire to their house and perished in the flames, together with everyone else. Like his father, Ingjald's departure from this life was true to style.

The annals of the Svea kingdom assert that it had been Ingjald who, by these murderous acts of arson, had first succeeded in uniting a fragmented Sweden. Later historical research, however, has stripped him of this signal honour. As the most successful fire-bug in Swedish history his reputation is less easily assailed. Between fires and feasts there seems to have been a striking connection. In those days one only accepted an invitation to a royal banquet at peril of one's life. The Icelanders call one of Ingjald's sons Olof Trätälja – Wood Carver, or Woodcutter. Allegedly he was the first king of the Svear not to hold court at Uppsala. Nor did Olof inherit his father's fiery disposition. Instead, he followed in his grandfather's footsteps and became a farmer king. To the west he cleared the great forests of Värmland, whence his cognomen. He founded a kingdom of his own, and a Norwegian royal clan claimed him as its earliest ancestor. He too died the death traditional in his family; while sacrificing to the gods beside Lake Vänern, the house caught fire.

Count Axel von Klinckowström has written a stage play about Olof Trätälja, famous in the history of the Swedish theatre. This play's dramatic doggerel is famous for being accorded the Swedish Academy's great gold medal, its greatest distinction. Sture Bolin has said that this drama smelt offensively of timber, but as a silvicultura-list he ploughs King Olof: 'the felling of forests does not usually give rise to dramatic conflicts, though it may well give rise to con-flicts with the man whom the king has put in charge of it.'

The subjects of the old Svea kingdom treated their kings less respectfully than we do ours. They gave their kings nicknames, sometimes honourable ones, but for the most part ill-natured or satirical. Here are a few more samples of such cognomens once borne by our Nordic monarchs; Erik Weather Hat, Eric the Happy-Year, Erik the Blessed-with-Victory, Erik the Lisping and Lame, Halvdan White-Leg, Halvdan the Mild, Harald Blue-Tooth, Harald Hard-of-Counsel, Håkan the Red, Ottar Vendel-Crow, Sven Twenty-Beard, Sven Sacrifice, Olof Nose-King, Olof Hunger, Magnus Barefoot, Björn Ironside, Björn the Slippery, Emund the Sly, Emund Charcoal-Burner, Sverker Club-Foot, Ragnvald Short-Head. Twenty-five names. The list could be longer.

Sture Bolin has looked into the derivation of the two cognomens, Charcoal-Burner and Club-Foot – the word 'sly' ('*slemme*') needs no exegesis. King Emund was called the Charcoal-Burner because he punished disobedient subjects among the peasantry by burning down their houses. King Sverker, for his part, had a misshapen and awkwardly large foot. How he came to suffer from this deformation, too, makes a curious story. As a tiny child Sverker was carelessly carried by his mother. She had tied up her little boy among the pleats of her skirt. How this could have caused one of the child's feet to grow abnormally large is not explained. The word *Blåfot* may have been meant a club-foot, an inherited deformation.

These, then, are some of the hundred kings in Johannes Magnus' list. No one knows how many of them had any real existence.

Kings did not always have to be descended from the gods. Chief-tains and warriors could attain to that dignity by their skill in using their weapons. World history knows many instances of this. How else did Napoleon become emperor? In that prehistoric world little was needed for a man to entitle himself king.

Petty kings and kings of hundreds were in reality tribal chieftains, who had seized power and authority over the common people by the sword. In those days wars were not waged between whole peoples or nations. Petty kings and their warriors – individual magnates and earls who had raised themselves above the peasant class – fought over provinces and smaller districts. A great peasant rose to be a chieftain; and a chieftain could become king. But for the maintenance of power some connection with the divinity was always required. Kings secured their subjects' obedience by explaining to them they were merely carrying out a divine task.

How this link between god and king developed down the ages can be traced in the successive changes of meaning of the word *hov*.

Hov is derived from a word meaning an eminence where sacrificial feasts were held and the gods were worshipped. In the language of heathen Scandinavia, *hov* was synonymous with temple. It was a house of the gods. Later, the word came to mean a farm, a large peasant holding and the lands surrounding it, a sense it still retains in Old German, *Hof*. In Sweden *hov* became the name of a royal farm, from which it gradually came to signify the king's guard – his *hird*, his entourage, his household and all those persons who surrounded him. It is in this sense – 'court' – that the word is still used in modern Swedish.

Iceland has many farms whose names begin or end with *hov*. Originally, in heathen times, they were houses of the gods or temple groves. The word is still found in the names of large farms, farms which our prehistoric and mediaeval kings acquired for themselves in various parts of Sweden. A countryside abounding in such royal farms is the western part of Östergötland, whose fertile plains still contain many large estates. Their names bespeak their origins; Kungs Starby, Hovgården and the parish of Hov. In Stockholm the memory of the court once kept by the great Sture family lives on in a restaurant, situated on Stureplan. From *hov*, too, comes our Swedish word for a head-waiter – *hovmästare* – though in the course of the ages his duties have been largely extended. Originally, he was responsible only for the king's table, serving royal personages and their guests. Now he serves us all.

The King of Sweden still keeps his court, and the first syllable of many of his officers' titles is derived from the name of some slight eminence, hillock or temble grove, where our heathen forefathers sacrificed human beings and beasts to the wooden images of their gods. To name only a few: the king has a *Hovmarskalk* (Master of the Royal Household), *Hovjägmästare* (Master of the Buck Hounds), a *Hovintendent* (Chief Comptroller), and many others.

So history lives on in the present; and the present in history.

As has been seen, our prehistoric kings had a penchant for basing their power on divine descent. They were worshipped by their subjects as possessing supernatural powers. The common people believed their rulers could regulate natural processes as they pleased, distribute rain and sunshine as might best help the crops and promote the fertility of man and beast, producing healthy, well-fashioned offspring, free of all blemish or deformity. Under a good king the grain was plentiful, women became pregnant, cows calved, man and beast multiplied, and no monsters were born into the world. Under a bad king the grain was poor, women failed to become pregnant, cows did not calve, and the world beheld many monstrosities. As long as a ruler could prove his divine power by the happy courses of nature, he sat safely on his throne. But if the weather turned bad, or the harvest failed and famine ensued, then it could happen that the common people, to appease their gods, slew so worthless a king.

According to the Icelandic annals, Frej – or Fröj – god of the Svear, was the first ancestor of the Ynglinga clan. As the source of fertility, he was of great importance to our forefathers. On him it depended whether the grain sprouted on the fields and the cattle grew strong and manifold. Frej's image in the house of the gods in the temple at Uppsala is described by Master Adam of Bremen as having an immense phallus. An eloquent symbol of fertility. A little bronze statue found in the soil of Södermanland, also with a magnificent and all-dominant phallus, is none other than the god Frej. Swedes, it is obvious, were once phallus-worshippers. There is every indication that the maypole we still dance round on Midsummer Eve was originally a symbol of the male organ.

Each summer the wooden image of Frej, set up on a wagon, made a journey through Sweden. Carried round the country to bless the grain on the fields, the god promoted the year's growth and reproduction. It is here we probably have the origin of the '*Eriksgata*', a progress through the realm still undertaken by Swedish kings after their accession. But their journey had another purpose too. In each province they gave their subjects their royal undertaking, and in exchange took their oaths of fidelity. This traditional tour of the realm by its monarch was last revived in the 1950's, by the present king of Sweden, Gustaf VI Adolf.

As heathendom came to be ousted by Christianity, the Christians quite simply took over the monarchy's intimate relations with heathen divinity. The god-magic, indispensible to a king's power over his subjects, was retained. Nothing must disturb a people's faith in the divinity of his royal task. Inherited from heathen days, his authority was preserved; but now it was the god of the Christians whom the king represented; it was at his command he ruled and by his grace that he reigned. No doubt the kings were themselves thoroughly convinced that God had appointed them his representative.

In a royal letter dating from Knut Eriksson's reign in the 12th century, it is explicitly stated that Knut was king 'by God's grace'. The regents who followed him, no matter what relationship their mode of living might, in other respects, stand in relation to Christianity, adopted and used the same formula. Gustav Vasa, who made Sweden into hereditary monarchy in the 16th century, is not known for any deep religiosity. But he was always much concerned to point out that it was at God's command he ruled, and he made frequent use of the ancient formula.

His motto was: *Omnis protestas a deo est*, all power is of God.

This magical phrase, 'by the grace of God', worked like an incantation. No one might use it without the permission of the Church; and Holy Church did not recognize the divinity of a king's task until she had herself crowned and installed him in office by anointing him with holy oil. This made it every ruler's goal to get himself crowned as the Lord's Anointed. Only thus could he secure his people's worship, respect and obedience. Even today this formula, 'by the grace of God', is still included in laws and other acts promulgated in the king's name. In Sweden, as elsewhere, the magic of kingship retains its powerful effect on the popular mind. A recent British public opinion survey reveals that one-third of the population of Britain still believe that Queen Elizabeth possesses divine powers.

c

That all authority is divine was explained to me in nursery school in connection with the Fourth Commandment: 'Let each be submissive to that authority which hath the rule. For there is no authority that is not of God; and that authority which is, is ordained of God.' First and foremost, it was upon the king that God had enjoined and commanded 'in fatherly wise to care for us and . . . promote our true welfare.'

For eight hundred years of our history, ever since Knut Eriksson's day in the 12th century, the kings of Sweden have claimed the legitimacy which springs from having been divinely summoned to the throne. It has certainly contributed no little to the Swedish monarchy's happy survival.

Peasant Seafarers of the 9th Century

~~~~~~

TWENTY YEARS AGO I WROTE a novel about some peasant seafarers, a little group of men who left the terra firma of their native Sweden and put out into the Atlantic Ocean. These 19th-century peasants went west. They emigrated, unarmed, to the New World. Since their intentions were wholly peaceable, they needed no weapons to kill their fellow men. So their only implements were the farmer's. And since they were seeking new homes for themselves in another continent they took with them their wives and children.

Ahead lay a perilous voyage. Of the land which was their goal they knew nothing. As an enterprise for peasants it was bold even to the point of foolhardiness. A grand adventure.

A thousand years earlier they had had forerunners. Building themselves ships, those 9th-century peasants, too, had put to sea, both eastward and westward. But on their voyages they had been armed with sword, spear and shield. Indeed their enterprise was anything but peaceable. So they left their wives and children at home.

They were certainly no less enterprising than their descendants of a thousand years later, and every bit as bold and foolhardy. But there all similarity ends. The 19th-century Swedish peasant set out on a peaceful adventure. The 9th-century peasant on a warlike one. To some extent it too had been an emigration. Many of these who set out on those voyages afterwards remained behind to settle in foreign lands.

During the last two centuries of the first Christian millennium a remarkable change seems to have come over the Scandinavian peasant. From being a land-lubber he became a seaman; instead of a stay-at-home farmer, a highly mobile seafarer and warrior. A Viking.

59

The Viking raids are the first great popular movement in Swedish history. They extended the lands of the Norsemen as never before or after. Scandinavia became a great power, the most feared in Europe. The Viking ships ruled every known sea. They sailed from the Caspian to the Atlantic. On all coasts, from the Orient to North America, the Vikings made their landfalls. They captured London and forced Paris to capitulate. Throwing Russia into subjection, the Viking founded empires at Smolensk, Novgorod and Kiev. He held Constantinople in such a stranglehold that to save his capital the Byzantine Emperor was obliged to pay him heavy tribute. The Viking instilled terror into every land that had anything to do with him. The peoples of Europe regarded him as the scourge of God; the Almighty's judgment on their sins.

What can have happened to the Scandinavian peasant at this time? All down our history the Swedish, Danish and Norwegian peasantry have been a quiet and peaceful race of men, never desiring war, and resorting to violence only when obliged. Whenever they have taken up arms or left their own part of the country it has been to defend it against an enemy. They have never begrudged other folk the peace they so ardently desire for themselves. The Scandinavian peasant has only taken up arms in self-defence. How then could he suddenly become a Viking – a pirate, given to arson and the extremities of violence? How did it come about that he went murdering, plundering in foreign lands? How was it that he became a curse to peoples of which he knew nothing?

What, really, is the explanation of the Viking raids? At that time the three Scandinavian countries together contained hardly a million people. Yet the Vikings were able to set out on their raids, plundering and devastating almost the whole known world. How was such a thing possible?

A modern historian, Holger Arbman, has looked into the origins of the Viking raids (*The Vikings*, 1961). Here I shall avail myself of his latest results. But my main account of the matter is based on our modern overall view of the Viking world as it emerges in a large-scale Norwegian work: *Vikingene* (Oslo, 1967). Written by historians from Norway, Sweden, Denmark, Iceland, France, Britain and Germany, it is the fruit of a truly international collaboration and describes the latest archaeological results to which we are indebted for what is to some extent an entirely new view of the Viking Age. Contributions by Frenchmen, Germans, and Englishmen, historians from the very countries most ravaged by the Vikings, complement the archaeological evidence. The book describes our Norse ancestors not only as pirates but also as explorers and colonizers. Besides injecting fresh blood into the populations of other lands, they brought home new impulses and manners to the barbarous North. This is a positive, if hitherto overlooked, aspect of the Viking raids. The book is a truly epoch-making contribution to Viking research.

Study of these archaeological finds shows that, even if it was one of the main reasons for the Viking raids, the accepted explanation – the over-population of the Norse kingdoms towards the end of the first millennium A.D. – does not suffice. True, the peasant families lacked living space. A peasant might have many sons; but only the oldest could inherit his farm. How were the others to get a living? It is also true that an immense amount of land still remained to be cultivated. But all land with deep fertile soil was already under the plough. Clay soil could not be cultivated with the primitive tools then available, and the great areas of sandy soil, morraine and peat-lands held little attraction for an outcropper. All this would tend to make a free life on the ocean wave more tempting to the lotless sons of the peasantry than a toilsome existence ashore. Sword and spear offered a better living than hoe or plough-hook. Those who joined the expeditions, of course, staked their lives, pawning them every morning and – with luck – redeeming them with profit in the evening. For those who fell, the glories of Valhalla were waiting; so to fall in war held no terrors for them. For all these reasons the landless sons of the peasantry built themselves ships and opted for a new occupation: piracy on the high seas.

The hypothesis of over-population and famine in 9th-century Scandinavia, however, is contradicted by new archaeological finds. These testify to no poverty among the people. On the contrary, they seem to indicate that peasant society in Viking times was more prosperous than it was later to become in the Middle Ages. Foreign visitors to the kingdom of the Svear speak of a good and fertile land, whose folk lacked for none of life's necessities.

What can it have been, then, that drove the 9th-century peasant to put to sea? Real starvation, generally speaking, it cannot have been. Presumably it must often have been a sheer lust for heroic deeds; a longing for adventure; a dynamic spirit and a chance of glory. Glory and honour ('*ära*') could only be won by the sword. Of all deaths, to fall in battle was the most honourable; and to win such glory no one minded sacrificing his life. But above all they were attracted by booty; by the plunder of wealthier lands.

The prime factor that made the Viking raids possible was the Norsemen's extraordinary ability as shipbuilders, an art of which they possessed an amazing knowledge. Here they were superior to all their contemporaries. In their manner of building boats was perfect art. They built the beautiful lissom dragon ships – ships which, with a happy combination of sail and oar, carried them over the high seas.

Our latter-day marine architects are full of admiration for these Viking ships which even conquered the North Atlantic rollers.

Finds in Norway have shown us how their ships looked. One magnificent dragon-ship, found at Oseberg, is to be seen in Bygdö Museum, Oslo. But the best-preserved is that found in an old tumulus at Gokstad, in 1880. It still contained even the Viking's pots and pans, and even a sort of chess game to pass the time during days at sea. From stem to stern the Gokstad dragon-ship measured 77′ 6″, it had a maximum beam of somewhat more than 16′, and a draught of 3′ 6″. The mast is 39′ tall, with a long and powerful yard and a single square sail. This dragon-ship is considered to have had a crew of at least fifty men. There was little space on board. Room had to be left for prisoners, leaving the crew only a minimum of space in which to eat, sleep and move about. The sail would be spread as a tent against wind and weather, and in severe cold the men slept two by two in leather sleeping bags. All calls of nature were met over the railing – 'to go to the rail' was the expression used.

A Viking dragon-ship could be at sea, no matter what the wind or weather, for at least a month without needing to put into harbour. Norwegians have recreated a Viking ship modelled on the Gokstad ship, and a Norwegian crew crossed the Atlantic in it in four weeks. A 19th-century Swedish emigrant ship needed ten weeks to sail from its home port to New York. These 9th-century peasants travelled faster than their descendants who followed them westwards a thousand years later.

The lines of such vessels as have been found are a feast to the eye. In everything they made with their own hands the ancient Norsemen had a sense of beauty, and in their dragon-ships they blended beauty with efficiency. Our forefathers' striking artistic sense was so much the more remarkable for their having had no chance to develop it in academies of the fine arts. Such of their monumental art as has been preserved is particularly highly regarded by experts.

The Norsemen are thought to have been the first seafarers in history who dared to put so far out to sea that they lost all touch with land. So their transoceanic voyages are especially worthy of our admiration. These 9th-century peasants voyaged the seas without any navigational instruments; they had neither chart nor compass. By day they navigated by the sun; at night by the stars. But what about cloudy days and starless nights? How could they keep a course then? More often than not they steered a course toward foreign coasts, sailing about the wastes of the ocean without even really knowing where they were. It is unlikely they had any means of fixing their position.

For their ships to run aground or be wrecked must have been an everyday occurrence, though for lack of material we cannot say just how common it was. The Vikings held no maritime courts of enquiry. As far as possible they set their course along the coasts, sailing over creeks, sounds and inlets. They are said to have got their name from the Swedish work for a creek – *vik*. They were pirates who lurked in creeks. From offshore hiding places they made their sudden landings, taking the coastal population utterly by surprise. Such successful landings were only possible thanks to the Vikings' shallow-draught ships. Usually these vessels drew no more than about 3' of water. The crews went swiftly ashore; and before the local inhabitants had had time to put up a resistance, the Vikings had gone again. The Scandinavian kingdoms were watery lands. And it was by water that people travelled and made contact with one another. A boat was the chief means of transport, not only to lands overseas but also over smaller stretches of inland water, In Sweden it was the lakes, rivers and streams which were the indispensable lines of communication;

and it was this geographical characteristic of their own maritime kingdoms that had turned the Norsemen into ship-builders and masters of the sea. It was they who first hit on and developed the idea of the keel. Thanks to this nautical invention their boats were not only stronger but also more manoeuvrable.

But what sort of people were they really, these sea-faring peasants who a thousand years ago suddenly emerged from their own obscure corner of the world and dominated the historical scene for two centuries? Ethnically they were of Germanic origin. They spoke a North Germanic tongue, best described as Scandinavian or Old Norse. Their contemporaries called it 'the Danish tongue'. That is to say, all Vikings spoke the same language, and this must have been conducive to a feeling of solidarity among the Nordic peoples. This possession of a common tongue was later to disappear as each of the three languages went its own way.

The Norsemen were also eminent organizers and administrators. They built enormous fleets of several hundred ships. Incredible though it may seem, a figure of 350 vessels is mentioned for one such fleet. This mass of sea-going ships had to be kept together throughout a long voyage. To build such fleets and fit them out took years of preparation and called for great economic resources. For this they needed money. Our Viking ancestors' raids represented enormous investments. No poverty-stricken people could ever have organized or equipped them. The raids can only have had their basis in a prosperous society.

Doubtless it all began with a few sporadic plundering raids on neighbouring lands, which brought home a rich booty. The fame of these successful enterprises would have spread through the land like rings on water and before long have caused others to emulate them. To set out as a Viking became a profitable business. Beginning as purely private undertakings, the voyages developed into great collective affairs, not unlike the sailings of modern shipping companies.

The enterprises' success must first and foremost be attributed to the Vikings' extraordinary valour in battle. And this in turn stemmed from their religion. The Asa faith taught the Viking to scorn death, and in war this is always a great asset. Like the Japanese soldier, whose religion also made him such a factor to reckon with in the field, a Viking was assured of paradise.

Another reason for the Norsemen's victories was that the kingdoms they attacked were militarily weak. After Charlemagne's death, at the beginning of the 9th century, his continental empire had begun to crack up, and the Franks could only put up a feeble resistance. Russia, still not a state at all, fell an even easier prey. But in most cases when the Vikings attacked countries capable of organized resistance they were beaten off.

The voyages of those days also comprised a good deal of peaceful trading. Commodities were exchanged by two sorts of Norse seamen: by so-called 'travellers' (*farmän*), who were fully professional merchants; and by 'travelling peasants' (*farbönder*), whose overseas trade was merely supplementary to their main occupation on land. Finds of coins in Swedish soil have shown that they traded not only with neighbouring lands, but also with Greeks, Jews, Turks and Arabs. It is even thought the Norsemen did business as far away as Persia. Finds of Arabic coinage have been numerous, and our ancestors' contacts with the Arabs have even earned them a place in Arabic writings.

At the beginning of the 10th century the Arabic author Ibn Rustad compiled an encyclopaedia. Its contents are most interesting. Among other things, he gives a vivid description of a Viking chieftain's funeral. 'When one of their chieftains dies, they dig for him a grave like unto a roomy house and lay him therein. With him they put his clothes, golden bracelets, a great quantity of food, vessels containing drinks, and minted coins. With him in the grave they also put the woman whom he most loved, and this even while she is still alive. The grave door is closed, and she dies.'

Usually a dead Viking chieftain was burnt with his ship. His corpse would be carried on board; full sail was set; and as the ship drifted out to sea fire-arrows from the shore would set it ablaze. Who could desire a more stately departure from this earthly life?

Another Arabic writer, Ibn Fadlan, writes of a prominent Viking's ship-burial on the shores of the Volga in the 920's, where one of his men said of the dead chieftain: 'We burn him up in an instant, and in that same instant he goes straight to paradise.' Here we have a foreigner corroborating our ancestors' certainty of a life in the world to come.

Various seas washed the littorals of the North; so while the Danes and Norwegians went westward, the Swedes went east. During the latter half of the Viking Age (according to latest research) the Swedish Vikings also went west to a greater extent than has earlier been supposed. This means they must have participated in the huge and devastating raids on the British and Frankish kingdoms, the two Christian countries hardest hit by the heathen invasions. One contemporary chronicler, Ermentarius of Noirmoutier, writes: 'Everywhere the Christians fall victims to massacres, plunderings, devastations, conflagrations. They [the Vikings] take all cities lying in their path. . . They take Bordeaux, Périgueux, Limoges, Angoulême, and Toulouse, Angers, Orléans have been annihilated . . . The city of Rouen is laid waste, plundered, burnt; Paris, Beauvais and Meaux are taken. Melun's strong fortress has been levelled to the ground, Chartres is occupied; Evreux, like Bayeux [has been] plundered. Hardly a town, not a monastery, has been respected . . .'

This document dates from about the year 900. By then the Viking raids had been going on for about a century. It was during the years 879–892 that the Viking curse lay most heavily on the Frankish kingdom. People fled in masses to churches, calling on God to help them. One famous prayer reads: 'Of Thy great mercy preserve and protect our lives. Free us, O God, from the wild men of the North, who lay waste our kingdom. They murder hosts of the aged, of young men and women, yea, the very children.' God is said to have helped His people by sending the land a very bad harvest, followed by famine, thus forcing the Vikings to depart.

Even if information gleaned from French sources is partial and exaggerated, we cannot doubt that our ancestors' behaviour in the Frankish kingdom – as in the English – was extraordinarily cruel and inhuman. Their vigour deserves our admiration – they were without doubt bold, capable and practical people. But their violent deeds are worthy only of our disgust. They waged no regular wars, but fell treacherously on peaceful coastal populations who had done them no harm. Churchill has described them as incomparably the most formidable and daring race of that time, but also as 'the most audacious and treacherous type of pirate that had ever yet appeared' (*A History of the English-Speaking Peoples*).

In their own time and circumstances such behaviour was natural. War was regarded as legitimizing plunder. With prisoners one might deal as one would. The Vikings' cruelty found outlet in the way they treated theirs. Either they killed them out of hand or else took them back to their own homeland as slaves. From the conquest of Paris the sources yield us a picture of the Norseman's methods as a terrorist. Before the eyes of the citizens the Vikings executed a great number of prisoners; whereupon the terror-stricken citizens surrendered their city.

But blackmail – or 'fire-tax' – provided the Norsemen with their chief revenue. Blackmail under threat of violence was certainly known in this world long before the 9th century A.D., but the Vikings raised this particular form of criminality to the level of a fine art. By threatening to set fire to a city and lay it in ashes they extorted enormous sums of money from its citizens. The country's unwelcome guests also demanded compensation for leaving it. In 845 the Frankish king, Charles the Bald, had to pay the Norsemen 7,000 pounds in silver to get them to leave Paris. Seven years later they were back again, demanding still more cash. History calls this black- mail, paid to the Norsemen, the 'Danegeld'. Later on, in England, it rose to huge sums; but it was first levied in France. In the 9th and 10th centuries it has been calculated that the Frankish kings paid out some 40,000 pound in gold and silver to rid the kingdom of these uninvited guests. And, of course, it was the common people who had to pay. The king raised the money by taxing his subjects.

Our seafaring ancestors could be called the most impudent and successful blackmailers in history. If they succeeded in their enter- prises it was because, as warriors, they were utterly superior to all other contemporary peoples, a fact which emerges strongly from the latest Viking research. In their military techniques they were so far ahead of their time that, according to contemporary research, the rest of the world did not catch up with them until the Second World War. Their combination of swift-sailing ships, a sudden surprise landing and mobility ashore can be compared with the invasion of

Normandy in 1944, a thousand years after their conquest of the Cherbourg peninsula. Recent finds at Birka, in Lake Mälaren, have proved that they also used cavalry, enabling them to move swiftly during their landings. The Norseman was at once seaman and horseman.

His main weapon was the sword. This sword which the Vikings had developed and perfected was a French type, successfully used by Charlemagne's ever-victorious soldiers. In battle the Vikings protected their heads with simple and practical iron helmets. The horned helmets seen in all the Viking films were never used by them; they are the invention of historically ignorant film-directors. Such helmets had been worn by warriors in the Early Bronze Age, two thousand years before the Vikings. But in films they are decorative enough and give the wild Norsemen the aspect of bulls.

Insofar as the acquisition of armed power is greatness, we have every right to call the Viking Age the great age of Scandinavia. In the theatre of world history the men of the North staged a grandiose spectacle, the like of which they were never to put on again.

Patriotic historians have presented the Viking Age as an epoch of heroic deeds, worthy of emulation by us latter-day Swedes. The heroes of the dragon-ships, they thought, should reawaken our drowsy patriotism. To the early 19th-century 'Gothic movement' the Viking was an ideal figure. He became the darling of our Swedish poets, who found in his boldness and manly courage a fruitful source of poetry. After Sweden had lost Finland to Russia in 1809 their verses revived the great age of a thousand years before when the Swedes had reigned as petty kings over the Russian cities. It was a latter-day poetic revenge for our defeat. Tegnér's greatest public success was his *Frithiof Saga*. I shall not try to assess it aesthetically – even as a child the book made no appeal to me, and after I had used it to learn to parse Swedish at school, the most celebrated of neo-romantic Swedish poems ended by boring me to tears. Geijer's *Vikingen*, on the other hand, was all adventure. As such it delighted a youngster in the Red Indian stage, to whom Geijer's verses seemed to have in them the eternal roar of the ocean, symbol of boyhood's inalienable dream of freedom and adventure.

As a spurious version of the realities of the Viking Age, a romantic picture of the 'bloody play of the raid' across the sea, this poem is unsurpassed. Its rhythmically exquisite verses describe murders, rapes and every other sort of violence – as if it were all nothing but a delightful frenzy, a splendid game, a pastime reserved for real he-men and heroes, those residuaries of mankind's highest moral qualities: audacity and manly courage. The following verses could be headlined *Rape at Sea*:

> In Valand I took me a maid –
> three days she wept, and then was content;
> delightful our nuptials, as playful we went
> over the ocean wave.

In Viking life, no doubt, all this was an everyday affair, and to carry off a woman and rape her was regarded as the most natural thing in the world. But Geijer swathes his hero's abduction and subsequent rape of a virgin in a dubious poetic shimmer.

The Norsemen were barbarians. But all the peoples with whom they came into contact, except in Russia, had ancient cultures. In this respect Scandinavia lagged far behind the times. The Vikings' arrival in civilized countries must have opened their eyes to new and hitherto unknown values. The great importance to the Scandinavian peoples of this confontation of barbarism and culture has hitherto been underestimated. It was not only material plunder the Vikings brought home with them.

As founders of states they achieved great things. They colonized Russia – but soon drowned in that ocean of peoples. In France they set up their own state, the Duchy of Normandy. There too they soon merged with the local population and became naturalized French-men. Their wealthy province, the Skåne of France – still has some purely Skanian place-names.

It has been said that the Swede as an emigrant is more easily assimilable than other nationals. Perhaps that was true even a thou-sand years ago. Once the Vikings had settled down in the countries and districts they had conquered they had no great difficulty in adopting the native customs and life-style generally.

They had emigrated from a poor country, with a cold harsh climate. In these southern realms they were not slow to enjoy the sunshine, the wines and the *joie de vivre*. Existence had become young again, it offered them undreamed of pleasures and comforts. They adopted luxurious habits, dressing themselves in silk and satin. In the lands of the Orient their chieftains became pashas, and kept great harems. Of one Viking chieftain we are told that he had eight hundred concubines, outvying Solomon himself. An exaggeration, no doubt, which even if it errs by a hundred women or so witnesses to an impressive sexual potency and reminds us of the stress laid upon the Norsemen's extreme sensuality by almost all foreign visitors to Scandinavia in those days. Of this the Arabic author Ibn Fozlan cites impressive instances, and even Snorre Sturlason declares that polygamy was common in Scandinavian peasant society. Adam of Bremen, usually a highly reliable source, writes that two vices were natural to the whole population of the North: drunkenness and fornication. According to Adam, the Swedes were especially insatiable and kept at least two or three wives apiece. This was true of the men at large. Chieftains and great men had innumerable concubines.

Naturally, this confrontation between the heathen Vikings and the Christian peoples ravaged by their raids had other consequences. Hans Hildebrand and some other historians explain the raids in purely religious terms. They were, he says, God's own plan for converting the Norsemen to Christianity. The Christian peoples sought to defend themselves against the heathen plague by incorporating their lands into Christendom. It was God's plan that by ravaging Christian cities and villages, churches and monasteries, by murdering, raping, burning and plundering, the Norsemen should come to realise how dire was their own need of baptism. 'The robbery of their treasures, their plundered dwellings, the innumerable corpses, the sufferings of every sort' exhorted the pious to undertake the missionary work to the barbarian homelands. If God had sent the Norsemen out on their Viking raids, it was so that their evil deeds should show the world what bandits they were.

According to this theory, the salvation of the Norse heathen was purchased at the cost of great numbers of French and English lives. God won new souls, at the price of innumerable sacrifices within Christendom itself. The salvation of our forefathers' souls was indeed a costly affair.

The great Scandinavian expansion was a unique occurrence in world history and shook Europe for two and a half centuries, between about A.D. 800 and A.D. 1050. But though the Viking raids are the first campaigns known to us in Swedish history, they are still largely unresearched. The source materials are too scanty. Fresh archaeological finds may well extend our knowledge.

But now let us return to the place where the raids started – the peasant homesteads, where the Vikings themselves were born and brought up. It was here they armed themselves for their campaigns and every spring assembled in their *ledung* – as their organization was called. Mostly it was the young men, supernumerary sons of the homestead who, having no inheritance in the farm itself, regarded the lands beyond the seas as their rightful loot and inheritance. The Viking in Geijer's poem was fifteen when lust for adventure drove him to sea. He must have had many equivalents in reality. But the head of the household too, as an experienced and capable leader toughened by many raids, also accompanied them.

The peasant and his sons left the farm in springtime and returned – if they returned at all – in autumn. During the summer months, the season of sowing and harvesting, when all the real work of the farm was done and when labour was most needed, they were away. By the time the raiders returned, the grain was already harvested.

So who looked after their farms when they were away? This toilsome burden fell on the old men, women, children and bondsfolk. The old could do little. Children could tend sheep and cattle. This left only the women and the bondsmen to plough, sow and reap and do all the farm work. Even the heaviest jobs were done by women. For the two and a half centuries of the Viking raids the women stayed at home on the farms, waiting for their men. The head of the household, too, left in the spring and returned in autumn, to spend the winter under his sooty roof, spinning yarns about last summer's feats of arms for the benefit of his faithful and admiring family. Or again perhaps both autumn and winter pass away, and still he does not come back. No one knows whether he has fallen in battle and gone to Valhalla or is lingering in some foreign land where he has set up a new home for himself. His wife knows that not a day passes but he is casting dice, his own life being the stakes. Every evening she wonders 'Is my husband still alive?' But gets no answer.

Our histories are full of campaigns, of men's bravery, of their heroic deeds on fields of battle in Finland, in the Baltic lands, in Poland, Russia, Germany, Denmark and Norway. We are informed at length about battles won; and, somewhat more briefly, of battles lost. But while the men were away, what were their women doing at home? What sort of a life did they lead on the farm and in the soldier's cottage during the absence of the head of the household? This is a question which has but faintly interested our historians.

In their men's absence the peasant women were working in the fields. They were reaping the corn with their sickles, harvesting it, threshing it and grinding the grain that was to be their own and their children's bread. In farm and cottage they were bringing up and caring for the next generation. It was they who kept the race alive. This, too, was their achievement while waiting for their husbands. Without it the Swedish people would have ceased to exist.

Among warrior peoples this has always been women's lot: to wait for absent husbands, sons, brothers. Thus woman has waited through every war, from the 9th-century Viking raids up to our last war in 1814. Through a thousand years Swedish wives have waited for their husbands; mothers have waited for their sons. Their destinies, too, are part of Swedish history – if it is to be a history of human beings.

The 300 Years' War

Christianity hath made but slow advances in this realm, before heathen idolatry was flung down.

Olaus Petri: *En Svensk krönika*

THE FIRST CHRISTIAN MISSIONARY to Sweden was a Benedictine monk, Ansgar. He arrived in 829. The last was the Norwegian king Sigurd Jorsalafar, who in 1123 broke into Småland to convert its inhabitants, the last heathens left in Sweden. Between these two visitations lay almost exactly 300 years. Attempts at conversion had begun in the 9th century; but it was not until the 12th that Christianity became established as the country's official religion.

Three centuries of warfare were fought out between the heathen gods and the Christian god before the latter was victorious. Only to a small extent was it a war waged with weapons, though at times these could certainly also be brought into play to instil conviction. Chiefly it was a struggle between souls. We hear of one heathen king of the Svear who was so democratic as to ask his subjects whether they would permit Christian missionaries to preach their doctrine in the country. But the process of converting our forefathers was a slow one. That it took three whole centuries shows how deeply rooted was the Asa faith.

To their three chief gods, Odin, Thor and Fröj (or Frey) our ancestors were faithful to the bitter end. Each had his own function. Odin's was to help the war, Thor's to aid against the plague and famine. And Fröj was responsible for the year's harvest and for reproduction generally. He was lord of rain and sunshine. A fourth god, Balder, was a god of peace; and inevitably he met his death by

73

treachery. Unlike the gods of classical antiquity, however, I do not find any of these Nordic gods a fascinating personality. In the book we used in elementary school I only recall one amusing chapter: the stealing of Thor's hammer. This tale of Loke, who dresses up Thor as a beautiful bride for his marriage to a giant, makes an admirable tale for children. Only the mischievous Loke – the Asa faith's counterpart to the Christian devil – puts any life into the saga of the gods.

Our heathen ancestors' notion of paradise, on the other hand, is of great interest for the light it sheds on conditions under which they actually lived. Their vision of Valhalla yields information, oblique but valuable, on the Norsemen's daily life; it half opens a door on to a world otherwise closed to us. People lived in crowded, dark huts. They cohabited with cold and darkness. Such was their earthly home. How different their heavenly! Odin's hall, in Valhalla, is an enormous room with 140 doors, each wide enough for 800 men to enter abreast. This heavenly hall was of course a figment of our forefathers' wish-dreams. As with their dwellings, so with their diet. On earth they had to survive long winters when the pork, their favourite food, dwindled in tubs and barrels or else went putrid and tasted foul, and many long months were to pass before the next pig could be fattened for the slaughter. But in Valhalla the fatted hog, Särimner, was slaughtered every evening and next morning came back to life, to be slaughtered again in the evening.

Here in Valhalla the Vikings could look forward to an existence which left nothing to be desired: where they would be able to gorge themselves for ever and ever on fat pork. In everyday life corn, hops and honey could also be in short supply. The salt meat parched their throats – but the mead tubs stood empty. But in Odin's hall an endless stream of mead, and Odin's serving maids, the ever young and lovely Valkyrie were never done refilling the drinking horns. In that imagined paradise pork dripping with fat and washed down with mead was the acme of delights.

But more than all else the Norsemen were addicted to feats of arms. And of these they also had their fill in Valhalla. Every evening the champions marched out 800 men abreast through the 140 doors to do battle. All the livelong day they flung themselves on each other, sword in hand, until all were slain. But as night fell they all came back to life and returned to Valhalla, where, tended by the Valkyrie, their wounds healed spontaneously.

Such was our forefathers' paradise, the fruit of their wish-dreams, a state of perfect bliss and a vision of everything they regarded as supremely good: a heavenly kingdom where they would enjoy for ever all they had lacked in reality. Like every other imaginary paradise it had its roots in the shortcomings of an earthly life, offsetting its miseries with a state of fulfilled longing.

Since we know what our forefathers desired, we can also tell what they lacked. It is their religion that gives us insight into their real circumstances.

The Asa doctine was crude, and it was materialistic. It sacrificed human beings inhumanely to the gods. But these Asa gods were not immortal. Nor were they all-puissant. Their power over the world was strictly limited. There was only one supreme power: fate, before which men and gods alike had to bow. Among the Swedish peasantry this belief in fate has survived heathendom, providing an alternative explanation of life's mystery to Christianity. I have known many peasants, both men and women, who have declared their firm belief in a blind remorseless fate. It is their unshakable conviction that a man's lot in this life is decided even before he enters it. We must all accept our destiny. Fundamentally, these people identify fate with God, who, they believe, has decided their lot in advance. If anyone told them their faith was originally the faith of the heathen they would be deeply shocked.

The Norsemen's fatalism seems to have been basically the same as that of the ancient Greeks. The power which decided over man's life and death was in either case equally blind, equally inexorable. Only the names of the goddesses of fate and the powers of destiny differed.

From the Christian church historian Adam of Bremen we know how the heathen Svear worshipped their gods. In a famous work on the history of the Hamburg-Bremen diocese, written in the 1070's, he gives us some valuable information on their religion. Master Adam's descriptions of the temple of the gods at Uppsala are well known. Regrettably, he does not quote from any of the obscene and indecent songs sung by the Svear at their sacrificial temple feasts. In his ears the – presumably four-letter – words had so shameful a ring that it was more than he could do to bring himself to repeat them. Etymologically, too, it would be interesting to have some samples of those terrifying words Adam says were uttered by our forefathers at divine service.

The Norsemen's cruellest rites were their human sacrifices. If contemporary Christian sources are to be believed, as many as two hundred corpses of slaughtered humans and beasts could be seen simultaneously hanging in the sacred grove outside the temple at Uppsala. The mere thought of a divine service in a sanguinary atmosphere of steaming freshly butchered human flesh, where tormented living beings whimper and scream out in deathly terror, nauseates us. Yet it is a true image of the barbaric North. Human sacrifice, however, has had its place in many other religions. The Jewish, for instance. It was the God of the Old Testament who required of Abraham that he should sacrifice his son Isaac as a burnt offering; and it was the God of the New Testament who sent his only-begotten Son down to earth to be sacrificed on the cross for our sins.

Experts differ as to the exact manner in which Sweden was converted. Some think Scandinavia was christened with the sword: others that the Swedes became Christians by conviction. No doubt the truth is that the Three Hundred Years War was fought with both spirit and sword, by preaching and violence.

The Christian missionaries to Sweden came from the Carolingian kingdom and from the British Isles, the two countries most severely plagued by the fury of the Norsemen. Already Charlemagne had suppressed the refractory Saxons 'by sword and sermon' – as the method was called. His successor, Louis the Pious, wished to extend the northern boundaries of the Christian world. His motives were not all religious. Such an expansion was also part of his commercial policy. Scandinavia was needed for barter and as an export market. In 829 the Benedictine monk Ansgar came to the heathen King Björn, in the trading city of Birka. He is said to have been well received, and was freely permitted to preach. Not until long after his day, however, in the 10th century, was the real work of conversion carried out by English and German missionaries.

These Christian pioneers in the land of the Asa faith had no easy task. It was a struggle between Christian asceticism and life-denial, on the one hand, and heathen materialism and affirmation of life on the other. The heathen had to be convinced that the Christian god was superior to Odin, Thor and Fröj. The Norseman, however, was nothing if not a rationalist. If he was to worship a god, he wanted to be sure that the god was going to be of some practical use to him. Why sacrifice to a divinity who gave nothing in return? Why donate his bondsmen, his stallions, his horses and his bulls to someone who did not repay such gifts? What the Norseman wanted was aid against his enemies, a cure for illnesses, protection against the plague. In time of drought he wanted rain; in rainy weather, sunshine. He wanted fat crops and healthy foals, calves and lambs in his barns. And any god who did not give him what he wanted he abandoned.

And so it happened over and over again. The Swedes give 'the White Christ' (*Vite Krist*) a try. They accept baptism. And the missionaries go home. After a while they return – only to find that their converts have once more begun sacrificing to their wooden gods. The new god has not conquered their enemies. He has not protected them against sickness. Nor has he brought them rain in time of drought. They have found themselves loath to part with the gods of their fathers. Valhalla, with all its tangible delights and splendours, is still dear to their hearts. The Christian paradise, with its abstract disembodied delights, is a state of bliss they find it hard to envisage and which holds but little attraction for them.

So the conversion work had to begin all over again. Several missionaries are said to have died martyrs' deaths, but modern research and source-criticism has left little standing of their legends. Our oldest story of a Scandinavian saint concerns Saint Sigfrid, the apostle to Värend, in the province of Småland. According to this legend, Sigfrid came to what today is Lake Helgasjön, in the heart of Värend. With him he had his sister's three sons Unaman, Sunaman and Vinaman. Instantly an angel appeared, showing the newcomers where they should build the first Christian temple – the spot where Växjö Cathedral stands today.

King Olaf, King of the Swedes at that time, was quite willing to be baptised; and sent word to that effect to Sigrid. The missionary heard the call and departed, leaving his three nephews in Värend. During his absence things went badly for them. The devil intervened, inciting the Smålanders to rise against the missionaries. Unaman, Sunaman and Vinaman were slain by the heathen. On Sigrid's return to Värend he saw his nephews' decapitated heads floating on the waters of Lake Helgasjön. *But out of their mouths the words were still coming as before*, the disembodied missionaries were still preaching their doctrine as if nothing at all had befallen them, precisely as they had in their lifetime.

The salvaged heads of Unaman, Sunaman and Vinaman were preserved as relics in Växjö Cathedral, and can still be seen in relief on the great seal of the See of Växjö, from 1292.

For this legend research finds no basis in reality. There is no evidence whatever that Saint Sigfrid, apostle to Värend, ever existed. Or his nephews. Indeed we have no sure evidence that any missionaries of that name ever worked in Småland, nor is there anything to connect them with the Värend district. Master Adam mentions an English clerk, by name Sigfrid, who attended the funeral of Bishop Thurgot, first bishop of Skara, at Skara about the year 1030. He is only once mentioned in the sources, and they say nothing of him ever having been an apostle in Växjö, the main town of Värend. So how he came to lend his name to Sigfridsmässan, the annual fair held in February and the great event of the year in that town, is a mystery.

All these legends of saints and martyrs such as Sigfrid, Botvid, Eskil, David and Henrik, were written down a couple of centuries after the triumph of Christianity to edify the pious. But though the latest research does not regard them as source-materials for any historical events, they are valuable as expressions of our ancestors' new faith. They bear witness to other-worldly states of mind; to a belief in miracles.

For long periods during those three hundred years when the work of conversion was going forward Christians and heathens lived peacefully together in the central parts of the realm. In Olof Skötkonung's day an agreement was even reached that both Christianity and heathendom should be recognized as doctrines of equal status. The citizens of Birka practised both religions. We hear of no

armed clashes. The Swedish archeologist, Prof. Birger Nerman is of
the view that it was mainly those who confessed to the old doctrine
who favoured tolerance. The heathen were prepared to put up with
the new doctrine, providing they were allowed to go on practising
the old faith in peace. The gods, they thought, could get on together.
Why should the Christian god monopolize human worship? Why
only one god?

There was less tolerance on the Christian side. 'The Christians . . .
with their fiery faith were more prone to aggression.' Instead of
'fiery faith' (*trosglöd*) we could perhaps write 'fanaticism'.

The missionaries tried both carrot and goad on the heathen. On
occasion the Christians are said to have bought up bondsmen and
promised them their freedom on condition they let themselves be
baptized. Sometimes their zeal was so great as to make light of their
'prospect's' lives – witness the Swedish crusades eastwards to Finland.

The final struggle between heathendom and Christianity took
place toward the end of the 11th century. There were some bloody
confrontations. Of King Inge the Elder we hear that he was driven
out of the Council of the Svear with a shower of stones for refusing
to preside over the heathen sacrifices. The Christians pulled down
the heathen temples and burned the wooden images. Just before the
end of the century the temples of the gods at Uppsala, the citadel
of heathendom, were overthrown. At long last the struggle had been
decided.

Christianity had won the day. In remote parts of the country the
heathen still resisted and there were a few revolts. But that was all.
Men who remained faithful to their old gods continued to worship
them in the depths of the Småland forests, well out of reach of even
the most zealous missionaries. In the end it was the Norwegians who
succeeded where the Smålanders' own countrymen had failed. In the
early 1120's King Sigurd Jordalafar of Norway launched a crusade
into Småland and rooted out the last relics of heathendom. The year
of King Sigurd's mopping-up action against the Småland heathen
can be fixed with some accuracy. It took place the year before the
great darkness: i.e., a great and memorable eclipse of the sun which
astronomers say took place on August 11, 1123.

King Sigurd was an experienced crusader. In 1107 he had taken

part in a crusade to Christ's tomb in Jerusalem, whence his cognomen. Against the refractory Smålanders his success was complete.
According to the chronicle he ravaged them with fire and sword:
'King Sigurd set his course for a trading city called Kalmar, which he
laid waste, and thereafter ravaged Småland, exacting from the
Smålanders a tribute of fifteen hundred beasts; and the Smålanders
accepted Christianity'. The King returned to Norway laden with loot,
so we are told. His crusade was called the Kalmar '*ledung*' – raid.

In Dalarna the worship of heathen gods is said to have survived
late into the 12th century, though I am unacquainted with the
details. What is certain is that heathen rites and customs lived on
among the Smålanders for several centuries. In his *Värend och
Virdarne*, which Strindberg called 'the cornerstone of ethnography',
Hyltén-Cavallius cites a wealth of evidence for this fact, taken from
old legal documents. Even in the 17th century, five hundred years
after the official introduction of Christianity, heathen cults were still
being practised in that part of the country. The court rolls give the
names of persons who openly denied the God of the Christians and
blithely admitted that they 'called on Satan' instead. They ate and
drank in the Devil's name. He was called The Other, and was nobody
else but old All-Father Odin under a new guise. They were not
afraid of the Christian devil; so they gave his name to the divinity
of their fathers, who thus became the God of the remaining heathen.

As late as the 17th century the court rolls describe a remarkable
fertility cult in Södra Hestra parish, in the county of Jönköping.
Girls of the parish who badly wanted to get married gathered on a
heath, stripped naked, and ran races to find out who among them
should become a bride. The girls' races coming to the ears of the
clergy, an enquiry was held into their heathen activities; and it is this
enquiry that has survived. This was no jolly game, but a most serious
ritual act; a cult of the fertility god. These young women running
races over the heath had retained a memory of their forefathers'
fertility worship.

Asa cults and customs, under their new Christian names, continued to be practised unchanged by the people, and relics of
heathendom have survived even up to our own time. Believing
Christians would be shocked if someone informed them of the real

origins of many of their own rites and customs, which are entirely heathen.

In the new religion, evil was personified by the devil. The mediaeval devil was quite a decent and amenable fellow. People were not afraid to make fun of him and made jokes at his expense. It was not until the Lutheran Reformation that the devil became a really terrifying figure. Then Hell, too, became more concrete and more horrible than before. Evil also appeared in the shape of trolls, water-sprites, wood-fairies, dragons and other dangerous natural spirits, populating forests and waters. In my own childhood in Värend, at the beginning of this century, I knew many older people who firmly maintained they had seen the wood-fairy and the 'Näcken' – the water-sprite who plays his fiddle in the waterfall to lure young maidens to their doom. They also embraced a whole-hearted belief in magic, even black magic and witchcraft. Women who had just given birth and who were not yet churched were regarded as peculiarly exposed. I know of women who, before being churched, never dared go out of doors without putting a pair of shears in their skirt pocket – steel to protect them against the powers of evil. Their beasts, too, were threatened. Some peasants would never loose a cow after she had calved without first laying an iron spoke across the threshold of the cowshed for her to step over.

The Smålanders were the last Swedes to become Christians and perhaps this is why heathendom has so long retained its grip on them. At their three great annual festivals, Christmas, Easter and Midsummer, the whole Swedish people still celebrate many old Asa customs. Magical in origin, they are relics of our forefathers' nature worship. To them a storm in the night was Odin out hunting with his barking hell-hounds; thunder and lightning were Thor riding on his goats across the sky, flinging his hammer at the giants and causing the sparks to fly from the clouds.

There was a time when Swedes trembled before these mighty gods. But in the end, although it took three hundred years, the 'White Christ' overcame them. But in the depths of the folk-psyche notions of their power have survived right up to our own time.

The introduction of Christianity was a victory for humane values.

Even the bondsman was declared a human being. The White Christ demanded no living sacrifices. Once and for all, he had sacrificed himself for humankind, who thenceforth, in the bread and wine transubstantiated at the Mass, partook of the body he had given for them and the blood he had shed for their sakes. The old wooden gods had never eaten their fill of human flesh nor slaked their unquenchable thirst for human blood. More than anything else the temples of the Asa gods had been slaughterhouses. Now they were pulled down and on their sites were erected Christian churches where God could be worshipped without bloodshed.

The new religion also gave human life an inherent value from birth. So all children were now to be allowed to live. Previously, new-born babies had often been exposed in the forest to be devoured by wild beasts. Admittedly the custom had mostly been observed in time of famine. The food perhaps was giving out and here in a shack already overbrimming with children a new life had been born. Mostly such exposure had been the fate of girl babies, less valuable than male children, and of sickly and deformed infants who could only be a burden to their parents. The heathen, too, had poured water over their children; but this had not been a religious baptism, mostly a rite of physical purification. When a child was born, they carried it to the head of the household, who set it on his knee and decided whether it was to be allowed to live or should be put out into the forest. The father granted it the precious gift of life by sprinkling it with water.

All this was now forbidden. The custom is believed to have had a counterpart in the treatment of the old, the feeble and the infirm. Those whose lives were no longer of any use are supposed to have been killed by pushing them off 'ancestral cliffs' (*ättestup*) or by clubbing them to death with ancestral clubs (*ätteklubbor*). The prehistoric Swedes, as we have seen, were nothing if not rationalists; they had little interest in caring for the aged. But this particular charge against them, that they practised euthanasia, remains unproven. Modern research tends to reject ancestral cliffs and clubs as mere legend. Even so, we may surmise that the lot of the old who were past work was a heavy one. Social and practical considerations were paramount.

The Christians also thoroughly reformed the judicial system. Private revenge was now abolished. From time immemorial any Norseman who felt himself injured had taken justice into his own hands. If any member of his clan were slain, its other members had to be revenged by slaying the slayer. Such acts of manslaughter had always been regarded as self-evident, and were not punishable by law. A life for a life. It was an honourable act, the only way of wiping out an injury. Any clan that failed to exact vengeance for one of its members was put to shame. The Icelandic sagas give innumerable instances of such private justice. But now, after the triumph of Christianity, people had to be content with such justice as was done by the peasant council. Yet the custom of personal revenge has deep roots, and long ages were to pass before it wholly disappeared. Even in the 17th century the court rolls record cases of manslaughter for revenge.

Men began to be somewhat more considerate of each other's lives. This was Christianity's great accomplishment. Its humane achievement.

An English historian has asserted that Sweden was the last land in Europe to accept Christianity. But he was forgetting Finland, afterwards taken over and Christianized by the Swedes. Following the example of the Nordic Vikings, the peoples on the other side of the Baltic were ravaging Sweden's coasts. So the Swedes, in self-protection, had to convert them to the doctrines of the Prince of Peace.

But it was not done peaceably. The first crusade to Finland was led by King Eric, founder of the Erik clan. After his martyrdom he became Sweden's patron saint, Erik the Holy. The Danes for their part took care of the unbaptized peoples of the Baltic countries. It was during such a crusade in Esthonia they received their present flag as a gift from heaven. At a battle in 1219 the Danebrog came floating down to them out of the sky and under this red-and-white banner they gained a great victory over the barbarians.

The Swedish crusaders were equally successful. King Erik offered the Finns peace on condition they let themselves be baptized and adopted the Christian faith, but they turned down his offer. So the Swedes could only convince them with the edge of the sword that

Christianity was the one true faith. In this they succeeded. King Erik's crusading knights won a resounding victory over the recalcitrant Finns. After the struggle was over the king walked about the battlefield among the masses of the fallen heathen and was so deeply moved by the sight of their corpses that he wept. Legend reports his words on that occasion: 'I do much grieve that so many souls were lost this day who, had they been willing to accept Christianity, should have had eternal life.' This legendary tableau from the Christian missionary activities in Scandinavia, King Erik weeping over souls be believed he had himself sent to hell, is sublime. But it is legendary. 'The Swedes' crusade was carried on after the fashion of the age,' Odhner explains.

So the heathen also had their martyrs. And here of course we have the great contradiction at the heart of Christianity, a religion which in action denies the faith it confesses verbally: Jesus' message of peace on earth. His doctrine of the value of human life has been propagated by force. Apostles of the Prince of Peace advance over corpses. This was not how his first twelve disciples did their missionary work. The statues of St Paul which I have seen in Mediterranean lands, with the Old Testament under one arm and a long sword in the other, date from a later age and a time when the zeal to convert others had grown so strong and the faith so fanatical that Christians had completely forgotten Jesus' own doctrine of love and respect for the lives of others. It was their intolerance that caused the sanguinary wars of religion. How many lives have not been sacrificed to fanaticism!

By the 12th century all Swedes had been baptized. Not until four hundred years later did they realise that they had been baptized into the wrong church. Only when Luther's doctrines were preached in Sweden was the *true* Christian faith revealed to them. The Catholic Church, they were given to understand, did not provide the proper yardstick whereby a Christian could measure his life, nor did it show him the right path to salvation after death. The 16th-century Reformation revealed to the Swedish people that for four hundred years, throughout the Middle Ages, they had been living in the spiritual murk of catholicism. Now they were told that the Holy Catholic – i.e., universal – Church, with its supreme head in Rome, was not the right one for us Swedes. True Christianity was the Christianity preached by the Evangelical Lutheran Church which now, after four abysmal centuries, offered them the light of Protestantism. Whereupon the Swedes went through yet another conversion and accepted a third doctrine. Which survives to this day.

The struggle between heathendom and Christianity lasted for three hundred years. The armed struggle between Catholics and Protestants lasted for thirty, out of which the Swedes took part for eighteen. Several thousands of Swedish soldiers sacrificed their lives in the Thirty Years War, or else came home again as invalids to spend the rest of their days in the Vadstena hospital for invalided soldiers.

No doctrines cost so much human life as doctrines of salvation. Yet history teaches us that humanity cannot do without them.

A Family of Royal Criminals

Evil princes are the plague of countries; by them God punisheth his people.

Olaus Petri: *En Svensk Krönika*

. . . if the account does not wholly tally with all the crimes and all the misery typical of that age, it is because most has never been recorded. . . .

Hans Hildebrand: *Sveriges Historia*, The Middle Ages

P REHISTORY BECAME THE MIDDLE AGES. During the first mediaeval centuries Swedish society was transformed from the ground up. It was an age which left nothing unaffected. It could be the subject of an enormous volume. Here we only have room for the outlines.

Gradually the equality which – bondsmen apart – had existed between men in peasant society gave place to aristocratic, ecclesiastical and hierarchic institutions that set limits to their personal freedom. Social life continued to be regulated by the provincial laws, but the power of those organs whereby the Swedish peasant had freely governed himself – the *bondeting*, *häradsting* and *landsting* – were successively restricted. Most crucial decisions affecting the common man now came to be made at assemblies where the great lords spiritual and temporal held all the trump cards.

By the end of the 13th century the new social structure was complete. It was King Magnus Ladulås who put the roof on it. Out of the peasant class had arisen great men who, acquiring more and more land, formed a class of their own. Their new status was formally confirmed when King Magnus introduced the Order of Knighthood.

His Alsnö Decree, 1280, and the Skänninge Decree of 1284 put the finishing touches to a new temporal and spiritual nobility and laid the cornerstones of a society where king, nobility and church, dividing power between them, each struggled to increase their own share.

This new state was a class society, a pyramid. At its summit, on his throne, sat the king supported, immediately beneath him, by a new privileged class of the nobility and clergy who were exempt from all dues and taxes. Beneath them, still fewer in numbers and possessing but little power, came the town burghers. Lowest of all, but holding up the entire social structure, came the mass of the peasantry and the new class of 'servants' who had once been their bondsfolk. Together they made up the common people – *folket** – or ninety-five percent of the entire population. It was they who paid all dues and taxes; who did all the day-work on the farms, and upon whose shoulders rested the whole fabric of society.

With the institution of knighthood Sweden acquired a warrior class, totally exempt from taxation and enjoying other privileges in return for their armed service to the realm. It was by granting the nobility these special privileges that Magnus Ladulås attached it to the monarchy. They were to be its shield, a bulwark. Already, long ago, the monarchy had made its pact with the Church. As early as the year 1200 or thereabouts Sverker the Younger had laid the foundations of clerical privilege. By having himself crowned, Erik Knutsson had placed his kingdom under the Church's protection. He was the first Swedish king to be anointed with holy oil and who therefore ruled by the Grace of God. The Church had approved and confirmed his authority as proceeding from the will of God. All Church properties, in return, were exempted from tax and the Church itself was henceforth exempted from all dues. This alliance between Church and monarchy was to become a fixture, and in form at least, has survived up to our own time. Even today the king is the supreme protector of the Church of Sweden, and prayers are read for him in our churches.

It had been at the Skänninge Assembly of 1248 that the Roman

* The distinction, in Swedish, is between *frälse* (= exempt) and *ofrälse* (= unexempt). Translator.

Church had confirmed its power in Sweden. A papal legate had decreed that all bishops, priests, monks and clerics, having their one rightful lord and king in Rome, were exempt from any oath of fealty to the Swedish king. They should be obedient to the Pope alone. They were also to remain celibate. Sweden had been incorporated in an organization transcending all states: the Holy Universal Roman Catholic Church, a spiritual United States of Europe – the leading idea and great vision of the Middle Ages.

Social developments in 13th-century Sweden were marked by the expansion of the power of the magnates and by a long struggle between the most powerful clans. It was out of their ranks that the men who reached for the royal crown appeared. This struggle between two clans, the Sverker and the Erik, lasted throughout the 12th century and up to 1250. Before it was over, four kings were to suffer violent death. Then the Sverker dynasty died out and power remained with the Erik clan whose last king, Erik Eriksson, is known to history as The Lisping and The Lame. 'He did somewhat lisp; and to limp was also his way'. In Johannes Magnus' roll of Swedish kings he is numbered Erik XII. Being the legendary founder of the entirely mythical small town of Grönköping he has come to have an air of comedy about him.* But in historical tradition we find only positive evaluations of Erik Eriksson's reign. Olaus Petri writes of him: 'He was a pious and just man, and did justice upon one and all in the realm'. Could any king wish for a finer epitaph?

Perhaps because of his physical and speech handicaps, Erik the Lisper and the Lame seems to have had a predilection for peace, and for this reason is said to have been popular among the peasantry. In his *jarl*, Birger of Bjälbo, the last *riksjarl*, King Erik found an admirable servant and adviser: 'The government lay mostly in his hands, for the king himself was silly and little adept of speech.' So great was the king's confidence in his *jarl* that he gave him his own sister to wife.

Birger Jarl undertook a new crusade to Finland to suppress the Tavasts, a 'stiff-necked people', and to force them into the Christian

* Grönköping is an imaginary archetypal Swedish small town, whose doings are the perennial subject of *Grönköpings Veckoblad*, a satirical publication. Translator.

Church: 'unto all who were willing to be baptized he granted both life and goods: unto the others he gave no peace,' declares Olaus Petri. Victorious in Finland, Birger Jarl erected the fortress of Tavasthus, so that the local population 'should be so much the better held in thrall.'

While Birger Jarl was in Finland in 1250, King Erik the Lisper and the Lame died, and the Erik clan came to an end. A new royal dynasty was now to ascend the throne of Sweden. A great decision was at hand. Birger hurried back to Sweden, but arrived too late. In great haste, probably before the *jarl* should have time to return and intervene, the new king had already been elected. No doubt Birger had counted on becoming king himself. Instead, it was his son Valdemar who was elected. And with him began the Folkunga Dynasty.

The Folkungs were to rule the country for four generations and over a hundred years, from 1250 to the 1360's. I have followed their fascinating destinies through four generations. Anyone searching history for real human beings cannot fail to pause before them. Their century of power involved them in more dramatic events than any other Swedish dynasty. As a story of sheer gangsterdom, perhaps, the Folkungs' lives and behaviour would not offer much interest. As fiction they would beggar credulity, be too gross a caricature. The sheer impossibility of the thing would strip it of all verisimilitude. But since all this did in fact happen and cannot be denied, we have no option but to accept it as reality.

Murder and deeds of violence can occur exceptionally even in the best of families. But among the Folkungs they were an everyday affair. It is hardly too much to say the clan had a criminal heredity. Yes, the Folkungs were a family of criminals.

How the clan got its name is not known. In its royal chronicle the Law of Västergötland mentions the Folkungs as a group of inter-married magnates, who, at Gestilren in Västergötland, had taken the life of the younger King Sverker Karlsson. Folke Jarl is said to be one of the clan's ancestors, and Folke Filbyter, a mysterious figure popular in poetical-historical fiction, was another. Whether Folke Filbyter ever really existed is uncertain. In the 11th century his

D

grandson, Folke the Fat, was a powerful Östergötland peasant who is said to have been an ancestor of Birger Jarl of Bjälbo.

In the early Middle Ages the Folkungs had been one of the most powerful clans in the magnate class and their wealth during the 12th century had grown enormously. Of its earlier members Johannes Magnus writes: 'In those days the Folkungs were capable of all evil, straying with their armed flocks about the country, rather as robbers than as nobles.' They asserted themselves as a forceful and ruthless clan, predestined to wield supreme power in the realm. Afterwards, when they had come to the throne, they strengthened their own position in Sweden by allying themselves by marriage with the royal families of Denmark and Norway.

According to one historical tradition Birger Jarl's family took its name from the 'true' Folkungs; but it was an illegitimate branch of the clan which, in the person of his son, finally came to the throne. Birger himself had no drop of royal blood in his veins. In his second marriage, however, he was married to the Danish king's sister, by whom he had several sons. Thus, on his mother's side, King Valdemar was a royal half-blood.

In fact, if not in name, it was Birger who was the monarch. From 1250 until his death in 1266 he ruled absolutely, occupying much the same position as Mussolini was later to do vis-à-vis King Victor Emmanuel of Italy. Even after his son's majority Birger continued to govern, executing his rivals until his power was firmly established.

In 1251, a group of powerful men who regarded themselves as the legitimate Folkungs ('*Folkunga rot*') revolted against Birger. At the Battle of Herrevad Bridge in Västmanland, near the point where the Kolbäck River flows into Lake Mälaren, he crushed his opponents. It is said to have been the first time in Swedish history that a troop of horsemen took part in a pitched battle. According to the *Erik Chronicle*, our chief 13th-century source, the leaders of the revolt, Filip Knutsson, Knut Magnusson and Filip Pettersson, fell into Birger's clutches by an act of disgraceful treachery. They were to come and negotiate with him for their own capitulation against a promise of safe conduct; but as soon as they had crossed Herrevad Bridge he had all three seized and beheaded, and also took the lives of many of their supporters. Recent research has thrown doubt on the Chronicle's account, pointing out that several other sources say nothing whatever about this act of treachery. On the other hand Olaus Petri, usually a reliable source, supports the Chronicle. He praises Birger Jarl as a powerful prince who did the kingdom much good, but says that 'upon this point, wherein he so treacherously did take the lives of the Folkungs', he cannot praise him, 'inasmuch as one is also in duty bound to keep truth and faith with one's enemies. – For it is never praiseworthy with false oaths to betray any.'

One would very much like to acquit this great mediaeval legislator of breaking his word after granting a safe-conduct, as he had himself enacted a law against that very crime. It was also he who introduced our first laws protecting the inviolability of the home, of women, of the Church and, of meetings of the '*ting*', and who did away with ordeal by fire in the administration of justice.

Birger Jarl improved the realm's finances. He was largely responsible for the development of the city of Stockholm, and did much else familiar to students of Swedish history. Less well-known are his queer family relationships. Both King Valdemar and his father married into the Danish royal family. In 1250 the reigning King, Erik Plogpenning ('Plough-Penny'), was murdered by his bother Abel, who thereafter ascended the throne. It was a top-level murder. A couple of years later King Abel fell in battle against the Frisians. In 1260, King Valdemar of Sweden married Princess Sophia, a daughter of the murdered Danish king. And the following year Birger Jarl took the dowager queen, Mechtild – the murderer's widow – to wife. Queen Sofia of Sweden's mother-in-law, that is to say, was the very woman who had been married to Sofia's father's murderer. It is interesting to speculate just how cordial can have been the relationships between the Swedish royal family's two first ladies.

By having his son Valdemar crowned in Linköping Cathedral Birger Jarl had placed him under the protection of the Church. As long as Birger lived order was tolerably maintained in the kingdom. But soon after his death in 1266 conditions became chaotic. He had left behind him four sons. And now begins one of those fraternal life-and-death struggles for power which recur over and over again in Swedish history. Birger's second son, Magnus, had become Duke of the Svear, but aspired to the throne. The third son, Bengt, was content with the bishopric of Linköping. As for the fourth, Erik, who had received neither dukedom nor bishopric, he dubbed himself Duke Nothing Atall. The two discontented brothers, Magnus and Erik, joined forces and succeeded in driving their brother Valdemar from the throne.

Magnus became king, and Valdemar fled to Norway. Later he returned, and for a while with the help of Denmark, his wife's country, managed to seize part of the kingdom. Falling into his brother Magnus' clutches, however, he was first imprisoned and then freed. Finally, in 1288, as a prisoner-of-state, he was flung into the fortress of Nyköpingshus where he died in 1302. Having allegedly been born at the end of the 1230's, Valdemar must have been a little over sixty at the time of his death.

During his reign Valdemar Birgersson seems to have achieved nothing of note. Yet he must not be judged by the portrait painted for posterity by his victorious enemies. Valdemar appears to have been a man whom no one could have accused to cruelty or treachery. Chiefly he has gone down to history in connection with a sexual *faux pas*. He had a love affair with his sister-in-law, Princess Jutta of Denmark, who had fled from her nun's existence in St. Agnes Nunnery at Roskilde in Denmark – a calling for which God had clearly not created her – to her sister and brother-in-law at the Swedish court. The *Erik Chronicle* praises her for her beauty. With this runaway nun King Valdemar fell so deeply in love that, as the same chronicle discreetly puts it,' he came too nigh unto her' and the relationship bore fruit. 'He seduced her and begat upon her a child'. According to the Danish 16th-century historian Huitfeldt, Jutta also bore her brother-in-law a daughter, christened Sophia.

This was the great royal scandal of 13th-century Sweden. Such an affair today would sell our evening papers like hot cakes. In 1274 Valdemar, spared the pillory of the press, made a journey to Rome, supposedly a pilgrimage imposed upon him as a penance. Such was the Church's view of such matters in those days. A murderer might not even have to do penance. Marital infidelity with a nun was a much graver crime.

In his famous history, published in the latter part of the 19th century, Sven Lagerbring reproaches King Valdemar for 'allowing his indiscretion to become publicly known and so giving rise to widespread indignation'. 'Doubtless,' he writes, 'all could have transpired in perfect secrecy, and the public could have been kept either entirely in the dark or only dubiously informed of the matter.' As it was, Valdemar's adultery with his sister-in-law helped to bring about his fall.

For Jutta was not Valdemar's only lady-love. Several later liaisons, more or less well-documented, are also ascribed to him. History's scandal-mongers have much to say about him. Lagerbring writes that it was easier for Valdemar Birgersson to live without a crown than without a woman. And since in those days a royal crown was regarded as the highest joy life could afford, Valdemar must be considered a deviant among our mediaeval kings.

His human traits mark him out among other members of the Folkung family.

Like his father, Birger's son Magnus was a forceful monarch who, by the laws already described, wrought a permanent transformation of his realm. He asserted the power of the monarchy to the utmost. Dangerous rivals to his throne still existed in the great clans. A group of the Old Folkungs revolted. King Magnus suppressed the revolt and – following his father's precedent – had the leaders beheaded. Among them were two brothers, Johan and Birger Filipsson. Magnus caused them to be executed under a new decree, a Roman law of treason, or *lèse-majesté*, hitherto unknown in Sweden, but which was now applied for the first time. To secure his throne he had himself crowned in Uppsala Cathedral, thus confirming that he reigned by the Grace of God.

This blessing by the Church gave stability to Magnus' reign. Unlike that of his older brother, the reign was to have permanent effects. Besides confirming the privileges of Church and Nobility he reorganized his council. Known as the Council of State – *riksens råd* – it became a fixed institution. Magnus held several assemblies of the nobility. Supposedly representing the whole realm, they were mostly what their name declared them to be: feudal courts. Only the greatest in the land were summoned to them. Later, however, the commons were also allowed to be present.

Although an innovator in matters of state, King Magnus has chiefly gone down to history as the protector of the peasantry, whence his picturesque cognomen '*Ladulås*' – 'Barn-Lock'. By the Alsnö Decree he forbade the nobles their habit of extorting hospitality from the peasantry; he 'put a lock on their barns'. By unwritten law, a peasant had always been obliged to feed and put up any unbidden guests, travelling lords, bishops and their trains, as well as such troops and men-at-arms as might pass his way. All such travellers and their horses had had the right to demand, without recompense, night-quarters and hospitality at the peasant's table. What had been an old custom had degenerated into sheer banditry, a gross abuse.

All honour to King Magnus, then, for his ban. But how far, in practice, was his decree obeyed? New decrees soon had to be promulgated against the same abuses. As one reads of all these regulations against the extortion of hospitality from the Swedish peasant one cannot help reflecting how much easier it is to pass a law than to get people to obey it. The historian who says that King Magnus finally put an end to such excesses is simply not telling the truth.

Yet Olaus Petri calls Magnus a just king, worthy of all praise: 'Yea, few there be in the world that can be called Ladulås; everywhere hath crimes against barns been somewhat general.' Gustav Vasa objected strongly to Olaus Petri's way of putting the point in his chronicle. He had every reason to. The cap fitted all too well.

Doubts have later arisen whether King Magnus' contemporaries really called him Ladulås, a word which is actually believed to be a corruption of his second name, Ladislaus. And certainly it is remarkable that the *Erik Chronicle*, which otherwise praises and extols King Magnus in every context, should apparently be unaware of this honour. The name remains a puzzle.

Magnus Birgersson took strong measures to keep the royal crown in his own clan and family. He took to wife a countess, Hedvig of Holstein, and to make matters doubly sure crowned her too. As an action it was unique. Hedvig was the first Swedish queen to be honoured with a coronation. The historic event took place amid much pomp and feasting at Söderköping, in 1281 – historic also because it caused a fire which laid the town in ashes. In his history of the Middle Ages, H. Hildebrand writes: 'Someone must have acted carelessly at the feast, for the town burned down.' Further details are lacking, and indeed supererogatory. Hildebrand's remark is exquisitely laconic. Just how the fire started is not known; but as a royal occasion it must have been festive indeed. No queen has ever been honoured by a greater firework display, for which a whole town provided the fuel. Admittedly, the honour was involuntary – it was the homeless citizens of Söderköping who had to foot the bill. What help, one wonders, was given to those left homeless by the fire? The records are silent. Those citizens of Söderköping are among those whom history has forgotten: 'For most matters have never been recorded.' . . .

Sweden was an elective monarchy but the Folkungs did everything they could to keep the crown hereditary within their clan.

Magnus Ladulås had plenty of children to succeed him on the throne, three sons and two daughters, and in his own lifetime he had the foresight to arrange for his eldest son's election. That was in 1284, when the new king was only four years old and 'still not mature enough to take over the government of the country' as one historian puts it. Birger was called 'the younger king'. Until Magnus' death in 1290 Sweden had two, father and son. This, too, would appear to be unique in our annals.

When his father died, King Birger Magnusson had reached the age of ten. As his guardian his father had appointed the Lord High Constable, Torgils Knutsson, a man in whom he had the greatest confidence and who ruled the country during the last decade of the 13th century. His rule was capable and wise. Concerning the state of the kingdom at this time, the *Erik Chronicle* witnesses:

> So well was it with Sweden then
> that late it shall be thus again.

> Joy and dance and tournament,
> grain and pork were never spent;
> herring and fish came much ashore,
> the realm had neither wound nor sore.

This picture of the Swedish people dancing on a bed of roses, blithely unconcerned for their daily bread is, however, somewhat touched up. In the early 1290's the harvest failed. Besides famine the country was also ravaged by plague. Out in the countryside we have evidence of great want and misery. But neither for the weather nor for the plague baccillus can Torgils Knutsson be held responsible.

The Lord High Constable extended the Swedish empire in Finland and secured it by erecting the strong fortress of Viborg. By this campaign to the east he suppressed the heathen Karelians, who are said to have committed appalling cruelties, flaying people alive, so we are told, and extracting their entrails from their stomachs to eat them raw. But now the Swedes forced the Karelians to accept baptism and become 'Christians, at least officially', as one chronicler puts it. No doubt his reservation is justified.

It is at this point that Birger Magnusson's two brothers, Erik and Valdemar, who had been given the dukedom by his father, make their appearance in our history. Duke Erik is the hero and main personage of the *Erik Chronicle*. In the chronicle's doggerel he is described as manly and handsome, a nobleman possessed of the highest manly courage, fortunate in his friends, beyond all measure faithful and courtly, and adept at all sports that could be practised by a prince. In the chronicle, Duke Erik, that knight without fear and reproach, is the very embodiment of chivalry in the Swedish Middle Ages. His opponents saw him in a rather different light. To them he was an intriguer, false, faithless, ambitious, and obsessed by a lust for power. For anyone who studies the acts of Duke Erik's lifetime it is the latter portrait which most closely resembles its original.

Hardly had King Birger come of age than a struggle for the empire of Sweden began between him and his brother dukes. A complete account of their fraternal strife would fill a long chapter, and must be omitted. In brief what happened was as follows.

Duke Erik founded a kingdom of his own along the Göta River, in West Sweden. Valdemar meanwhile ruled over certain other regions, and at times the country seems to have been divided between three regents. Wishing to get rid of Torgils Knutsson and his great influence over his former ward, the dukes, surprisingly enough, enlisted the help of King Birger himself. On December 6, 1305, Torgils was treacherously attacked on his estate at Lena. Birger, Erik and Valdemar were all of the company that took him prisoner. Binding his hands and feet under his horse's belly, they took him 'through winter cold and short days' all the way from Lena to Stockholm Castle, where he was imprisoned. A couple of months later, on February 10, 1306, his head fell to the headsman's axe in the place of execution on the south side of the city. His body, like those of all decapitated criminals, was buried in unhallowed ground.

The Lord Constable seems to have had no trial; nor do we know of any sentence passed upon him. So what were his crimes? He was accused of treason against King Birger, but the nature of this treason is utterly obscure. Perhaps we can seek an explanation in the light of a later event – the 'Håtuna Games'. Torgils had seen through the dukes' treachery toward the king, and had become dangerous to them. Presumably, they had succeeded in convincing Birger that his wise and faithful old adviser was conspiring against him. How otherwise explain the king's participation in the crime?

A will, drawn up by Torgils Knutsson while in prison, has been preserved for posterity, though there are good grounds for doubting its authenticity. It is supposed to have been drawn up by the priest who confessed the prisoner before his execution. In this will Torgils begs 'his most gentle prince and lord Birger, by God's Grace King of the Götar' for forgiveness for the crime he had committed against him, and prays 'in all humility that he shall be the executor of this will'. Once again, nothing is said of the nature of the crime. It is also remarkable that the doomed man should have left the greater part of his property to churches and monasteries throughout the land: in his days of power he had been no friend of the church; on the contrary he stripped it of that part of its tithes which was supposed to go to the poor. The burial of his corpse in unhallowed ground, too, suggests that the church was hostile to him. The contents of the will suggest therefore that the prisoner's confession is a fabrication made at the orders of King Birger to justify his doom.

Duke Valdemar was married to Torgils Knutsson's daughter Kristina, but in connection with her father's murder he now put her aside.

The Grey Monks of Stockholm dug up Torgils Knutsson's corpse and moved it to their own monastery in the town, where a gravestone was erected to the executed man's memory. A facsimile of the stone has been preserved. It reads: 'He who rests here was condemned innocent'. And in the eyes of posterity, too, Torgils Knutsson has always been a martyr. Questionless, his removal was an act of political murder.

Nor was much time to pass before the next dramatic event in the dynamic Folkunga family. In September 1306, little more than six months after the liquidation of the Lord Constable, the time was ripe for a fresh act of treachery and brutality. Two of the three brothers who had done the deed at Lena attacked and imprisoned the third. With his Danish-born Queen Märta and his children Birger Magnusson was staying on his royal estate of Håtuna, there to celebrate, as a faithful Christian, the Archangel St. Michael's Day, which fell on September 29. Guest of the royal couple was one of the highest dignitaries of the church, the Bishop of Västerås, later Archbishop, Nils Kettilson. The festival was at hand and the royal family and the bishop very likely at mass, when some unexpected guests hammered at the door of the royal dwelling. Enter Birger's affectionate brothers Erik and Valdemar, accompanied by their guards. The guests, we are told, were well received by those who were celebrating the feast, but it was not long before they made plain the nature of their errand. King and queen, the bishop and a score of the royal couple's squires and servants were seized by the dukes' men-at-arms and taken to dungeons at Nyköping Castle. Only little Lord Magnus, Birger's eldest son, was saved. A servant who had his wits about him took him to safety to his father's brother-in-law, King Erik Menved of Denmark.

From time immemorial crimes committed during time of divine service, on Sundays or other ecclesiastical feast days, have been regarded in Sweden as peculiarly gross, and punished more severely than similar crimes committed on weekdays. The attack at Håtuna, committed at a church festival, could therefore be regarded as a crime of the first order. The name under which it has come down to posterity –_Håtunaleken_, the 'Håtuna Games' – has an almost poetic ring in our ears. A jousting, a gay tournament, perhaps, at the height of the Age of Chivalry in Sweden?

Be that as it may, the Håtuna Games had tragic consequences for many innocent persons. In the first place for the peasantry of Västergötland, little though they had to do with the royal family's internal quarrels. A border war broke out. King Erik Menved of Denmark came to the aid of his imprisoned brother-in-law and with his Danish men-of-war broke into Västergötland, ravaging the southern part of the province with fire and sword and penetrating as far north as to what is today the city of Ulricehamn. By and by an armistice was reached, but by then great areas of Västergötland's farmlands had already been laid waste. For the peasants of Väster-götland the Håtuna Games had become a game in deadly earnest.

Next year the Danes opened a new campaign. Dukes Erik and Valdemar fled before the enemy. On the battlefield they seem to have acted like anything but heroes.

The following years are full of confused, meaningless and indecis-ive campaigns. To describe them would only be monotonous. King Håkon of Norway, too, took part in these wars, and in 1309 Duke Erik ravaged Norway with fire and sword, plundering and killing; whereupon King Håkon replied by visiting Dalsland in the same way. At the same time a Danish army was ravaging Östergötland and Södermanland, until 'by reason of its difficulty in obtaining the necessities of life from the country it had plundered' it had to go home again to Denmark.

Not until all the barns in the countryside had been emptied did the men-at-arms depart. That the peasants should feed the troops as they passed through was self-evident. War had to be self-supporting. We can imagine what happened when the troops of men-at-arms came to a farm: they had to be entertained with the very best the house could provide, and board and lodging provided both for them and their horses. Any host who resisted was stabbed to death. A peasant could count himself happy if the warriors contented them-selves with 'fire-tax' instead of burning his home to the ground.

Unfortunately no peasant has left any detailed account of the hospitality he was forced to provide. The common man had no means of giving vent to his feelings. His mouth was closed; he could find no words for all he suffered in these endless campaigns across his countryside, campaigns which recur with dreadful regularity throughout the Middle Ages and far into later times. In the eyes of contemporary chroniclers they were so commonplace and natural that they did not even think it worth their while to describe them.

On the other hand we do have written evidence of the splendid courts and tournaments and the brilliant feasts at which Dukes Erik and Valdemar of Sweden did their best to emulate the chivalry of Europe. Such courts cost a great deal of money; an expense extorted from the peasantry by new dues and taxes, a special tax, the so-called *markgäld* – land-tax – being imposed for the purpose. Especially in the chronicle of Ericus Olai, our first historian, we find information as to the way in which the Dukes beggared the peasantry. In several provinces the peasants rose in revolt, risings which were obviously stifled in the cradle. It is only with all brevity that historians even mention these attempted rebellions at all. But the flame was time and time again to be relit down the centuries.

In 1310 a compact was reached between King Birger and Dukes Erik and Valdemar, dividing the kingdom between the three of them. This agreement Birger confirmed with a most solemn oath, and again became a reigning monarch. But his finances were in a bad state, and he was obliged to borrow money from his brother-in-law, Erik Menved of Denmark. Upon his demanding fresh taxes from the peasantry, the peasants of Gotland refused to pay them, and the situation became so serious that Birger had to send soldiery to the recalcitrant islanders to enforce his demands.

The annals from the first decades of the 14th century contain much information about the misery and oppression suffered by the common people as a result of all these campaigns, these taxes, these failed harvests and diseases. If, by way of relief, we should look for some cheerful lights in this dark picture, we should have to turn to some event in the Nordic royal families: a princely double wedding, for instance. Such a wedding took place at Oslo in 1312, when the Swedish Dukes Erik and Valdemar were simultaneously married to two Norwegian princesses.

Duke Erik's betrothal and marriage gives us a vivid picture of the royal marital customs of those days. At the age of eight Princess Ingeborg, daughter of King Håkon of Norway, had been betrothed to Duke Erik of Sweden. But immediately afterwards, the balance of war turning in Birger's favour and against his brother Erik, King Håkon had broken the betrothal contract, and instead promised his daughter to Birger's son, the nine-year-old Lord Magnus, heir to the Swedish throne. The new betrothal was confirmed at a stately ceremony held with the church's blessing in St Mary's Church in Oslo in the summer of 1309.

But once again the tide of war turned and, on Erik once more gaining the upper hand, he was allowed by Håkon to enter into a new betrothal; once again Princess Ingeborg was to become his bride. But now it was Duke Erik's turn to break the agreement. He chose another princess for himself, this time Sofia of Werle, the niece of King Eril Menved. Yet a third time, however, the chivalrous Erik changed his mind; with the Pope's permission he broke the contract of marriage with Princess Sofia, too, and made yet another with the Norwegian king to marry – Princess Ingeborg! Perhaps he had suddenly remembered that, as Håkon's eldest child, she was the heir apparent to the throne of Norway. Part of the contract stipulated that his brother Valdemar should be betrothed to one of Håkon's nieces, another princess who also bore the name Ingeborg.

On September 29, 1312, the anniversary of the Håtuna Games, the Swedish dukes' weddings took place in the Norwegian capital with all the brilliant pomp and circumstance a Scandinavian royal family could stage at the height of the Age of Chivalry. It was a royal double wedding, with two child-brides. The sum of the two princesses' ages was 26 years. Erik's wife was only 11, while Valdemar's had reached the mature age of 15. But marriage between minors was rather the rule than the exception in princely families of those days. The custom had its origins in parental foresight: the contracting parties wished in good time to secure for their children princes and princesses of such status that the marriage would augment their family's power and wealth. Nor was this type of parental love exclusive to royal houses – it was, and up to our own day still is – found in peasant families too.

Four years after the double wedding at Oslo the two young duchesses each bore her husband, certainly to his great joy, a son. In the struggle for the crown of Sweden, male heirs were indispensible. Duke Erik christened his child Magnus. This babe, under the name Magnus Eriksson, would later rule over both Sweden and Norway, together constituting the largest kingdom in the Europe of those days.

Five years passed without open conflict between King Birger and his brothers, now sharing Sweden between them. But that there were covert conspiracies and intrigues is certain. Posterity knows that Birger never forgot those 'games' at Håtuna. Duke Erik had furthermore deprived Birger's son Magnus of the King of Norway's daughter and so also of the Norwegian succession – an act which must have cut him to the quick. Birger brooded on revenge. No doubt he realised he could never be king of all Sweden until he had got rid of his brothers; and this he could only achieve by trickery and deceit and under a mask of pretended friendship.

By the end of 1317 the king's plans had ripened. In the fortress of Nyköpingshus the fraternal drama of the Folkungs reached its climax: the last act of our mediaeval Swedish Shakespearean tragedy.

It was during this epoch of our history that two convulsive happenings occurred, which made so deep an impression upon contemporaries that, surviving in popular imagination, they have been preserved by tradition and been passed down verbally from one generation to another: the murder of Engelbrekt, in 1436, and the Nyköping Banquet of 1317. To the latter the Håtuna Games were a prelude. As a mediaeval saying puts it:

> Nyköping Banquet
> and Håtuna Ale
> have turned many
> a cheek pale.

Popular accounts of these dire events display a wealth of fantasy. It is stuff for Shakespeare – what might not the creator of Hamlet and Richard III have made of Håtuna Games and Nyköping Banquet?

In the autumn of 1317 King Birger and his spouse Queen Märta were holding court at Nyköping Castle,* where they intended to

* Nyköpingshus. The termination *hus* means fortress or castle. Translator.

celebrate Christmas. Duke Valdemar visited his brother and sister-in-law and was made most heartily welcome. Queen Märta used the occasion to express her grief at so rarely seeing her brother-in-law Erik, who to her was most dear; and invited him to celebrate Christmas with the royal couple in Valdemar's company.

Warned of Birger's intentions, the dukes seem at first to have had their doubts whether to accept the invitation. Nevertheless, about a fortnight before Christmas, they arrived with their entourage at Nyköping Castle.

The banquet must have been held on the night between December 10 and 11, 1317. The following account of the drama is drawn partly from the *Erik Chronicle* and another Swedish annal, *Chronologia Anonymi*, and partly from two Danish chroniclers, but also from local historical works that repeat still living popular traditions. In honour of their great and worshipful guests King Birger and Queen Märta had arranged a stately banquet. The royal couple's chamberlain, a man of German extraction by name Johan von Brunkow, who was their adviser and is regarded as having played an important part in the drama, was also present. The day passed and so did the evening, and all was peace and harmony. A good deal was drunk:

> To mead and wine there was no end;
> and none 'tis said had ever seen
> so cheerful as was then the queen.

A Danish chronicle supplements the *Erik Chronicle* with these details of the feast:

> A little while they ate and drank
> then on the floor the queen would go;
> they danced within, they danced without . . .

Everything possible was done to lull Erik and Valdemar into a feeling of false security. Not even when King Birger had their entourage quartered in the town on pretext that there was no room for them in the castle did they become suspicious. Defenceless they fell into their brother's hands.

Weary and heavy with wine, the two dukes retired to bed in their own quarters in the castle. In the night while they lay sleeping 'naked and without clothes' in their beds, the King's men, led by

Johan von Brunkow, fell on them and seized them. Valdemar tried to resist, but Erik said: 'Useless it is to struggle here.' King Birger came 'walking down' and asked his brothers furiously whether they remembered the Håtuna Games.

Their hands bound, naked and barefoot, his guests were taken to a dungeon at the base of the inner keep of the castle and there had thick iron jougs placed round their necks, were manacled in iron fetters 'seven lispounds* weight', and their feet shackled. The floor of the dungeon between the prisoners was a pool of water. The Dukes were dealt 'cuts and blows'. A sharp splinter of wood from a heavy cudgel fastened in one of Erik's eyes as he was being flung into his prison.

Meanwhile, in their quarters out in the town, the dukes' guards were also made prisoner. One of their commanders, Arvid Gustafsson, a lawman of the Sparre clan, tried to resist and was cut down on the spot. Some of the king's men who refused to take part in the deed were also thrown into chains.

When the work was complete, King Birger shouted triumphantly to his Earl Marshal, Johan von Brunkow.

> Marshal mine, the Spirit be blessed;
> Now of all Sweden I'm possessed.

– a line worthy of one of Shakespeare's fated royal protagonists. Actually it was sated in tragic irony. At the moment when Birger uttered the words, believing he now ruled the whole realm, the kingdom finally slipped from his grasp.

All over the kingdom the dukes' supporters revolted against the king. Before he could occupy his brothers' fortresses and castles, their men-at-arms had assembled in Västergotland, Småland and Uppland. Once again the armies passed over the countryside.

Leaving its defence to a Livonian, Christian Scherbek, King Birger left Nyköping Castle, and set up his headquarters at Stegeborg. It was soon to be the only stronghold left to him in Sweden. His defeat was assured. He fled to Gotland, leaving his son, the young Lord Magnus, to defend Stegeborg to the bitter end.

What, meanwhile, was happening to the dukes imprisoned in

* 1 lispound = 18 lbs 12 ozs.

Nyköpingshus? From their brother Erik and Valdemar knew they could expect no mercy. They realised they would never get out of the castle tower with their lives – so much is obvious from the fact that, after five weeks in their dungeon, they made their will. The document, still extant, is dated January 18, 1318. In it they describe themselves as 'sound in mind and body', albeit in prison. They owned many estates throughout the country. Now they donate the greater part of their property to churches, monasteries, hospitals and houses of charity. Erik's and Valdemar's will shows great piety. They had made themselves ready to die; by these gifts to the Church they wished to make sure of heaven.

Before he left Nyköping Castle King Birger is said to have locked the keep where his brothers sat shackled to the wall and thrown the key into Nyköping River, which flows nearby. He intended to leave his brothers to an agonising death by starvation. According to one tradition, Erik lived for three more days, and Valdemar for eleven. Erik died eight days before his brother, 'having been miserably treated'.

Contemporary descriptions of the prisoners' sufferings are reminiscent of the *Divina Comedia*. When most fiercely tormented by hunger the brothers began eating each other. As the Danish chronicle puts it:

> Most pitiful it was to hear
> As each on other's shoulder gnawed,
> But greater yet doth now betide:
> Each brother ate of other's side.

In a ballad composed on the motif, we read:

> With pity those brothers smate the beholder
> As each ate of other's shoulder

And indeed the shoulder and arm of Erik's corpse bore marks of gnawing teeth, evidence that in his hunger Valdemar had tried to eat his brother's body. It was also Valdemar who, using the canine tooth of a wild boar, tried to dig his way out of the dungeon.

But how or exactly when the brothers met their death has never really been known. Here we only have theories to go on. They cannot be proved or disproved. What we do know for certain is that the brothers were still alive on January 18, the date of their will. But the question remains: how much longer did they live afterwards? In a detailed investigation, K. G. Blomberg, a local Nyköping historian, maintains that their death occurred about one month after January 18, some time in mid-February. But to the outside world their deaths were not known until August, when their supporters captured the castle.

The story about the keys to the keep, which King Birger is said to have flung into Nyköping River, seems apocryphal. After all, Birger had the fortress in his hand and his brothers were already in safe keeping. The action seems utterly senseless.

In a document of April 18, 1318, the imprisoned dukes are referred to as still alive; and in another, dated May 6, their duchesses call themselves their survivors. So we can only suppose the two men died between these dates. Yet according to H. Hildebrand the duchesses only call themselves their widows in a document dated August 1, 1318. And it was not until August that Nyköping Castle was captured by the dukes' soldiers, who discovered their bodies. Until they had been freed from their 'horrible filth' the prisoners were of dreadful aspect, and it aroused intense bitterness among their supporters. The bodies were placed on view outside the castle 'swathed in cloth of gold'. After which the dukes' remains were taken to Stockholm and there buried with all ceremony in St Nicholas' Church.

The epilogue to the Nyköping Banquet is thus well-known. But what actually happened to the Dukes during their eight months of imprisonment is obscure. We do not even know for certain how long they had been lying dead when the dungeon of the keep was opened. We can choose between three versions of their final fate. Either they were beaten to death; or died from the sickness that was raging among the garrison; or else died of hunger. Most historians have opted for hunger.

The Swedish princes' dreadful fate caused an outcry of contemporary indignation. Writings describing it were spread all over Northern Europe. To us the Dukes Erik and Valdemar seem to have been anything but children of light, but public judgment on their deeds while alive was mollified by the reports of their last sufferings. And it was in order to glorify Erik that our most celebrated mediaeval chronicle was written. By his ferocious treatment of his brothers Birger had given his enemies grist to their mill, and they certainly made the most of it. King Birger Magnusson became famous as the host at a banquet where the guests had starved to death.

His son, Lord Magnus, bravely defended Stegeborg, and when in the end that fortress had to capitulate gave himself up a prisoner against a safe conduct and promise of his life. He too was treated in the usual treacherous manner: after a period of imprisonment, on October 28, 1320, Lord Magnus, 'delightsome youngling that he was', laid his head under the axe. He was in his twentieth year.

Nothing is known of Birger's son. Unable to reach his father, the dukes' party exacted vengeance from the son, who, as heir apparent, stood in the way of another princeling, Duke Erik's son, also called Lord Magnus. Therefore he had to die. But he was buried in princely style with all honours, swathed in the most precious cloths and vestments.

Shortly thereafter King Birger Magnusson, who had been deposed, died in exile in Denmark, allegedly of grief at his son's fate. Thus 'the revenge', as Geijer, our 19th-century historian, puts it, 'was not less terrible than the crime'.

Lord Magnus' death made him the last victim of the struggle for the crown which had begun in 1251, when Birger Jarl had had three men of the so-called 'Folkunga Root' beheaded as pretenders to the throne, ridding them out of the way in order to place the crown on his own son's head. Then Magnus Ladulås, in his turn, had taken the lives of two rivals to the throne; after which there had been that banquet in Nyköping Castle which ended with the lives of two of his sons being taken by the third. Finally, this family feud had cost the life of his grandson. There had also been the political murder of Torgils Knutsson. Altogether nine murders, in which members of the Folkung family had been implicated in the course of seventy years. Eight had been committed to get that precious jewel, the crown of Sweden.

Visiting the scene of historic events one cannot but feel the influence of the past. At least I cannot. I call to mind what has happened in these places, and this affects my view of it. 'Here this and that happened!' It brings me closer to history than any document can do. Visiting Nyköping Castle and seeing its ancient keep, six hundred and fifty years after King Birger's historic banquet, I tried to envisage, against the background of all I had read of it, that past world. I breathed a lingering odour of those times. At Nyköping the Middle Ages still live on.

Nyköping Castle, on which the history of the Folkungs pivots, was built in the 1220's. In a number of other Swedish castles kings and dukes have sat imprisoned; but Nyköping Castle has held more royal prisoners than any other. It was here King Magnus Ladulås incarcerated his brother Valdemar. It was there King Birger was imprisoned by his brothers Erik and Valdemar, whom he in turn imprisoned here and left to die in the dungeon of the keep. As a prison for kings and princes Nyköping Castle is prëeminent in our annals.

The round tower where the dukes had died was demolished by their own supporters when they stormed the castle; but a large portion of the curtain wall still stands. Nicknamed the Hunger Tower, it is today the city of Nyköping's chief tourist attraction. At the bottom, several yards deep, where the two princes once sat chained to the wall, gleams a pool of water; and there is also a hole in the wall, said to have been gouged out by Duke Valdemar with his boar's tooth. All this seems to confirm popular tradition.

The story of the key, too, seems to be substantiated by something which happened about a hundred years ago. One day a boy was fishing in the river near the castle when he caught a big key on his hook. Today his find can be seen in the castle museum. As a key it is large and heavy, more than 8″ long. Its rust polished off, it gleams in its glass case – allegedly King Birger's key, after more than five hundred years in the water. This find from the river, too, agrees well with tradition; too well, perhaps, to be quite credible. But that the boy who found it should have known all about the Nyköping Banquet shows how its memory had survived among the local people.

Fascinating though the last act of the bloody drama of the Folkungs may be, to me it is no isolated royal drama. The Nyköping

Banquet had a profound effect on Swedish history, and for the Swedish people as a whole its consequences were exceedingly tragic. And this is why I have devoted so much space to it.

The banquet led to a new and lengthy civil war, gradually involving the whole of Scandinavia. While King Erik Menved of Denmark sent an army to help his brother-in-law King Birger, King Håkon of Norway, with Norwegian troops, supported the faction of his son-in-law Erik. Again Sweden became a theatre of war for foreign armies.

This is how Geijer sums up the final act of the Folkung drama: 'Since Sweden first came into being there can have hardly been any times unhappier than those of the fratricidal struggle which laid waste Magnus Ladulås' house'.

The nature of those disasters should be specified. Once again the troops of men-at-arms marched through the countryside; once again peasants were obliged to feed and quarter them; once again they were obliged to provide the materials of war. Once again destruction passed over the land, whose inhabitants were drawn into the struggle between Magnus Ladulås' sons, in a dispute which in no wise concerned them.

When all was said and done, it was the Swedish people who had to foot the heavy bill for the Nyköping Banquet.

'You Have Blood in Your Crown, King Magnus!'

~~~~~~

Strindberg: *The Saga of the Folkungs*

MAGNUS ERIKSSON, LAST OF THE FOLKUNGS, is the most interesting of our mediaeval Swedish kings. It is above all his destiny as a human being that we find so fascinating. He occupied the throne of Sweden longer than any other regent, from 1319 to 1365 – ' for six-and-forty years he had been king' – three years longer, that is, than Gustav V, who held it for 43 years (1907–1950). Even if at certain times Magnus only ruled part of the realm, he still holds the record.

During that reign – the first half of the 14th century – Sweden enjoyed a couple of decades of peaceful development and progress. The era is chiefly marked by thorough-going reforms in the administration of justice, most importantly the introduction of a code of laws for the whole country. In every way it was a time of flourishing spiritual culture. Clearly, the first decades of Magnus Eriksson's reign climaxed the Swedish Middle Ages.

It was then that the first Swedish constitution took shape; bondage was formally abolished; common laws were established for all provinces, so that a peasant no longer found himself judged in a neighbouring parish, situated in another province, by a law different from that which obtained in his own. Into the common code of laws was inserted a Royal Oath stipulating a king's duties to his people – Sweden's Magna Carta, admired to this very day for its language. The foundations were laid of a native literature: an anonymous and still unknown man wrote the *Erik Chronicle*, 'the first great work in our literature to treat of a Swedish theme' (Ingvar Andersson). This was also a time when a work that forms part of the world's religious literature was written down on parchment: St Bridget's *Revelationes.* Thanks to a translation of the *Euphemia Songs,* named after Duke Erik's mother-in-law Queen Euphemia of Norway, chivalrous poetry, too, became known in Sweden and had Swedish successors in song, folksong and legend.

In a primitive peasant country these were great cultural events to happen within so short a period of time.

But above all Magnus Eriksson's life was humanely interesting. At the age of only two he became king of two kingdoms, in extent the largest empire in all Europe. From his earliest years his lot had been a burdensome one, such as could have broken the strongest individual. After ruling for almost half a century he was closely confined for six years. And finally, driven out of his own country, he died as a king without a kingdom. Much slandered in his own lifetime, he was even more so after his death. Magnus was the typical loser, whose epitaph is written by his victorious enemies.

Magnus Eriksson's fate is worthy of the protagonist in some antique tragedy. It was his good qualities which brought him to his evil end. The fact is, he differed from the three preceding generations of his family in never treacherously taking the lives of his political opponents.

> Duke Erik's son, King Magnus they chose;
> So the story goes,
> No older was he
> than his years were three.

Thus – more or less – the *Rhymed Chronicle,* our earliest description of the election of a Swedish king.

Magnus had already inherited the crown of Norway from his maternal grandfather King Håkon, when, on July 8, 1319, in Mora Mead, outside Uppsala, he was proclaimed King of Sweden. In his chronicle, Ericus Olai, who had had access to sources no longer extant, states that both the commons and the privileged estates had assembled there to elect a king; so it can be assumed that the peasants too had been called to this council of the whole realm. Gottfried Carlsson, a historian writing six hundred years later, bases his account entirely on Ericus Olai's sources and maintains that the Assembly of 1319 in Mora Head can be called Sweden's first real parliament. Fredrik Lagerroth, on the basis of the extant source materials, agrees.

So Magnus, we can say, was a king elected by the whole people. The three-year-old babe, we are told, was present at his own election, seated on the so-called 'king's stone' in Mora Mead. He should have sworn his royal oath, but since the three-year-old had as yet hardly learnt to speak at all, he was exonerated from this first act of his reign by his chancellor, Matts Kettilmundsson, who, placing the babe on his shoulders, swore the oath on his behalf. Kettilmundsson had been Duke Erik's confidential adviser and was the most powerful man in the kingdom at that time.

For the first thirteen years of Magnus' reign the realm was ruled by a regency of some of the chief men in the kingdom, with Kettil-mundsson at their head. Historians are of the view that the regency did the country great services; but in saying this they overlook the circumstance that, during the regency, the finances fell into a parlous condition. When, in 1332, Magnus, then aged sixteen, was regarded as mature enough to take over the reins of government there was not a single mark left in the treasury. The king who ascended the throne was a king without cash.

What ensued was worthy of the beginning. Throughout his reign King Magnus was tormented by money troubles. In every work on him we come across the story of the warhorse which, having purchased for eighty silver marks, he did not have enough cash to pay for. Not having so much credit either, he had to find four men to stand surety for the debt. Probably the tale was invented by his enemies. That the ruler of the largest empire in Europe should not have possessed eighty marks credit seems undeniably comical.

This lack of money forced King Magnus to pawn both his two crowns, the Swedish and the Norwegian, to the Hanseatic city of Lübeck, at an extortionate rate of interest. When he could not repay within the allotted time another large loan which he had succeeded in raising from the papal treasury he was excommunicated by his creditor. Negligence in repaying debts due to the Church was quite enough to place one under its interdict.

Denmark, under the rule of the Counts of Holstein, was in a state of dissolution, and the provinces of Skåne wished to free themselves from the Danes. In 1332 Magnus seized his chance and incorporated the provinces in Sweden by purchase. For Skåne, Blekinge and parts of Halland he had to pay 34,000 marks solid silver, or 170,000 marks in money, a stupendous sum by the standards of those times. Initially it seems to have been a good stroke of business; but in the long run, when the cash had to be raised to pay for it, the whole affair plunged Magnus into the most frightful financial straits. For a while, however, he ruled not only over the whole of present-day Sweden, but also over Norway and Finland. Magnus Eriksson's empire stretched from Bergen in the west, to Viborg in the east; from the North Cape in the north, to the Öresund Strait in the south.

The first ten years of Magnus' reign were largely happy. The King took to wife the beautiful and lovable Countess Blanche (Blanka) of Namur. Her name is still preserved in a pretty little Swedish children's song (*Rida rida ranka . . .*). Contemporary writers say she was noted for great beauty. She is also said to have been loved by the common people. One chronicler remarks that she was also 'spiritually gifted', something he could not help noting in a member of the fair sex. The court kept by Magnus and his queen was more cultivated than any earlier Swedish royal court had been.

Magnus, however, had a good deal of trouble with his mother. The Duchess Ingeborg was a power-greedy woman who with the help of her Danish husband Knut Porse tried to gain influence over the government. Nor were the great men who had managed the realm's finances during the king's minority in any hurry to relinquish the reins of government. When Magnus tried to reassert the power of the monarchy, founded by his great-grandfather and consolidated by his grandfather, he ran into great difficulties.

Queen Blanche bore her husband two sons, Erik and Håkan. But the succession once secured, sexual relations with her husband seem to have come to an end; at least at certain times, when Magnus imposed complete continence upon himself. In this matter Fru* Birgitta Birgersdotter, a distant relative of the King and for a while mistress of his household, was only too keen to intervene. In his biography of this woman, afterwards to be known to the whole world as St Birgitta, or Bridget of Sweden, Johannes Jörgensen describes

* Fru = Mistress.

her energetic intervention in the royal couple's marital relationships. According to one source, Blanche accepted her husband's absence from the conjugal bed, and was content to comply with his wishes; according to another, their celibacy was also voluntary on her part. But this platonic – or, as the times called a marriage without sexual intercourse, 'Joseph' – marriage filled Birgitta Birgersdotter with indignation. While she regarded a marriage of abstinence between husband and wife as the highest of unions, such a relationship must have its roots in *Caritas Dei*. Here she found no evidence of any passionate love of God. On the contrary, in Bridget's view Blanche's motives for abstinence were purely selfish, a matter of mere convenience: she simply did not wish to give herself the trouble of bearing more children; and, as Bridget saw the matter, it was to 'bear fruit' that Blanche had come to Sweden. She was also shocked by the queen's behaviour at court. The fact was, Blanche had received a sinful French education. She devoted her time to vanities, bejewelled and painted herself, cultivated her own beauty and spoke frivolously. According to Bridget, she even went so far as to try to please the members of her entourage.

Eric Olai's chronicle accuses King Magnus of horrible and unnatural vices; and in her revelations St Bridget, too, declares that it was his marital continence which seduced him into homosexuality, most horrible and unnatural of all crimes. Since Magnus no longer shared Blanche's bed, he betook to himself instead a young man, whom he raised up above all others and whom he loved 'with all his heart', even more than he loved himself.

In St Bridget's *Revelationes* this youngling is called 'the devil's servant'. If the King does not rid himself of this monster, she says, he will be tormented by aches and pains from the crown of his head to the sole of his foot. True, St Bridget does not mention the monster by name; but an accusatory document composed by the magnates of the realm points out the handsome young knight, Duke Bengt Algotsson, as this *servus diaboli*. As the King's favourite and adviser, Algotsson certainly enjoyed his complete confidence; but we have no proof of any homosexual relationship. And then again, there were insinuations of a love affair between Queen Blanche and Sir Bengt. Again there is no proof.

Yet down the ages this king has had to bear the nickname Magnus Smek (Magnus Fondle), given him by his enemies among the aristocrats. When he was deposed, his 'lascivious mode of life, scandalous to all' was one of the chief heads of the indictment against him, but not a single concrete instance is adduced as to what this mode of life consisted in. The *Rhymed Chronicle*, too, says that he 'lived worse than a soulless Beast and sinned against right Nature'. But again this is an unproven statement. Whether Magnus Eriksson practised 'the most unnatural of vices' is a question that cannot be answered. Nor is his sexual behaviour, in itself, of any interest to posterity. Yet the historical fact remains; that this charge of homosexuality finally contributed to his fall. If Ericus Olai is to be believed, the first revolt against him was due to indignation at his mode of life. And no crime was more severely condemned by Holy Church than homosexuality. Compared with it, murder was a petty tort.

In one place in her writings Bridget says that three devils rule in this land: the first is the devil of drunkenness; the second, of lasciviousness. But the third demon, more horrible than either of the others, 'excites men to unnatural intercourse with men'. Yet, remarkably enough, it was not Magnus' 'lascivious life' that led to his excommunication. It was his delay in repaying his debts to the papal treasury. That the Church did not react to his alleged 'viciousness' may have been due to sheer lack of evidence. 'Let God judge', writes Olaus Petri concerning these indictments, 'against right nature'.

Of quite another order of interest to us are Magnus Eriksson's acts as regent; and from these it transpires that he wished to be a king for the whole people.* To this, two decrees especially bear witness. One is from 1335; the other from 1344. In them, 'peace' – *viz.* the reign of law, 'the king's peace' – is to be secured for the peasantry. In the first article it is stated that the 'hard customs' with which the peasantry have to put up are 'to us most displeasing'. And it is expressly declared that 'Sweden's commons shall have peace.' The decree was chiefly enacted against 'hospitality'; or in plain English, against its violent exaction.

The great nobles and ecclesiastics who were in the habit of travel-

* *all mogen* = all men = the commons.

ling through the country with huge trains of servants were, as we have seen, a scourge to the peasants. Now no one was to ride about with 'great flocks', demanding board and lodging in the farms for men and horses. The new decree permitted only thirty horses for bishops, twelve for knights and squires, and six horses for men of lesser degree; from which we conclude that these 'great flocks' must earlier have comprised an even greater number of horses. Further, the commons were henceforth to enjoy legal protection of life, limb and property. Severe punishments were decreed for all who resorted to violence. These harsher punishments, all things considered, were in high degree necessary. People who travelled along roads infested by robbers were particularly insecure, and when papal legates had to take their Peter's Pence out of the country especially rigorous measures had to be taken to protect such convoys from attack.

These enforcements of the reign of law, forbidding the exaction of hospitality under threat of violence, were repeated in the so-called Uppsala Decree of 1344. Under it, none should ride through the kingdom 'fully armed' unless by the king's permission. A bishop might ride as before, with thirty horses; but a royal official, unless accompanying the king, with no more than forty-five. To proceed against any disturbances of the peasants' 'peace', a twelve-man commission was to be appointed in each judicial district, and special regulations were issued concerning hospitality in the trading towns.

Clearly Magnus Ladulås' decree had not been obeyed, and stood in need of renewal. Despite the reiterated proclamation of such royal decrees, they obviously went unrespected. Why otherwise should these new injunctions always have been needed? That the peasantry, the common people of the realm, should '*hava frid*' – 'have peace' – is a formula we find many times over in our mediaeval royal decrees, until at length their very repetition comes to have an ironic ring about it. And we cannot help asking: When was the reign of law finally established? When did the Swedish peasant at long last come to enjoy 'peace'?

The late 1340's marked the beginning of a period of disasters for the king of Sweden-Norway-Finland. Eastwards there was war. The Russians allegedly having broken the peace, Magnus went crusading.

Though the Swedes had been struggling for two hundred years to rescue the reluctant Finns from heathendom, Christianity was still not firmly established in Karelia, along the Russian border.

St Bridget's revelations told her exactly how the war should be conducted, and she informed the king of her divinely inspired plan of campaign. She also informed him that if he did not follow it things would turn out badly for him. Birgitta Birgersdotter claimed, quite simply, to be God's inspired oracle. Magnus, however, according to Olaus Petri, regarded her revelations as 'idle female chatter' (*'höll för itt löst qvinnosnack'* – this historian adds: 'as indeed they appeared to be') and did not believe them. But in the event Bridget was proved right. Things went badly for the disobedient king. His campaign in Finland ended in a humiliating defeat that made Magnus the object of much scorn. Bridget denounced him in the strongest terms, and his enemies became still more powerful. Magnus was no commander in the field. It was a serious shortcoming in any mediaeval prince.

At the same time, in 1349, the realm was ravaged by the worst disaster ever to hit mediaeval Sweden: the Black Death or, as the Swedes called it, the Great Death – swept away one third of the population. (Our later expression, *Digerdöden*, The Thick Death, was not used by those who suffered from it. It first appears in Olaus Petri's *Chronicle*. That the greatest plague epidemic in the history of mankind should have spread to Sweden was also something for which Magnus, naturally, was given the blame. Bridget made it plain that the disease was God's judgment on the people for their king's sinful life. Already, before undertaking her pilgrimage to Rome, in 1349, she had prophesied and foreseen that the Scourge of the World would reach Magnus' kingdom. And had put down her prophesy in writing:

'Like a plough shall God's wrath pass over Sweden . . . for corpse shall lie upon corpse . . . Where formerly a thousand dwelled shall scantly a hundred be left alive; and the houses shall stand deserted'. These words of the prophetess are considered to have been fulfilled to the letter. Of the monks in Alvastra Monastery, for instance, Bridget had predicted that thirty-three would die, correctly naming each and every one of them – all in fact died from the plague. In her

Revelationes she had clearly described Death's Angel approaching the land. An undertone of satisfaction can be discerned in her words – afterwards she notes that the angel had in fact come and done his work, just as she had prophesied.

In the 1350's Magnus Eriksson's empire began to fall asunder. The preceding decade had seen a great increase in the power of the magnates, until in the end it outstripped the king's. After a revolt, to which he had been incited by his father's enemies among the nobility, Magnus' eldest son Erik ruled over a large part of Sweden, while Håkan, Magnus' second son, became King of Norway. Nor was it only Magnus' sons who proved faithless; he had a faithless brother-in-law, too. Duke Albrecht of Mecklenburg wanted to see his own son and namesake on the Swedish throne. More than anything else, Magnus Eriksson fell victim to the treachery of his own family.

In Denmark a powerful king, Valdemar Atterdag, arose and took back the Skanian provinces which Magnus at so great a price had purchased and even paid for. In the upshot, from the Swedish point of view, they had turned out to be a very bad piece of business. Valdemar's manoeuvres were partly cunning, partly violent. At times he was in secret alliance with Magnus' brother-in-law, Duke Albrecht, and later still further reduced the Swedish realm by invading and devastating the island of Gotland and plundering the Hanseatic city of Visby, the wealthiest trading town in all Sweden, and centre of her foreign trade.

Then Magnus' eldest son – Erik, part-ruler of the realm, died of plague – the allegation that he was poisoned by his mother, Queen Blanche, is wholly improbable – whereupon Magnus was reconciled to his second son, King Håkan of Norway, who thereafter became his main supporter. For a while Håkan, apparently with his mother's consent, was proclaimed King of Sweden.

It was a much shrunken kingdom for the possession of which the final struggle began in the mid-1360's. The lords of the council and others among the King's enemies offered the Swedish throne to his nephew, Duke Albrecht of Mecklenburg. Accompanied by many of his own countrymen, the Duke came to Sweden. After an army of Germans and traitrous Swedes had overcome King Magnus and his purely Swedish host in battle, he deposed his uncle. In 1365, Magnus

was incarcerated in Stockholm Castle, where he remained a prisoner
for six long years.

According to letters written by Magnus during his imprisonment,
he was infamously treated. He complains of being thrown into chains
and tormented by 'iron links'. The man responsible for his being
subjected to such rigorous confinement was his nephew Albrecht.
The new king is also accused by historians of treating his uncle un-
chivalrously and ungenerously. But rigorous incarceration, torture
and beatings-up recurred so regularly within princely dynasties, they
can only be called normal.

In 1371, for a ransom of 12,000 marks of solid silver, Magnus was
let out of his prison and betook himself to his son Håken in Norway.
There, in a kingdom which had once been his own, he was to spend
the last years of his life.

Dark years indeed. 'He was a man abandoned, and all ill was
spoken of him and his mode of life'. His death was true to style – as
dramatic as his life. On December 1, 1374, in a great storm in the
Bömmel Fjord, not far from Haugesund, he perished by shipwreck.
As his ship was about to sink he jumped overboard and swam ashore,
but no sooner had he reached land than he was overcome by cramp
and 'gave up the ghost'. All the rest of the ship's company had
found a watery grave. Only ex-King Magnus reached the shore and
was buried in hallowed ground. It was regarded as a miracle, and
'common men held him holy'.

Magnus Eriksson lived to be fifty-eight years of age, well beyond the
mediaeval average. His life had been packed with event. No other
Swedish king, one imagines, except possibly Gustav IV Adolf*
suffered such changes and disturbances in his path through life.

Magnus Eriksson really seems to have been persecuted by an un-
kind fate. It was his unfortunate lot to be a contemporary of the most
famous Swedish personality of all time, St Bridget of Vadstena. It
was she above all who played havoc with his history, behaving towards Magnus as the Old Testament prophets had behaved toward
the kings of the Jews: admonishing, accusing, threatening and,

---

* The eccentric son of Gustaf III, deposed in 1809, who fled abroad and ended
his days in a Swiss inn. *Translator.*

finally, condemning him. In her *Revelationes*, afterwards examined by a royal commission under the archbishop and approved as genuinely inspired by God, Magnus is condemned as a wretched creature, a gross sinner, a man of vice. And when, after her death, Birgitta Birgersdotter was declared a saint, she became an authority of the first order for European Christianity; so no one questioned her claim to have been specially chosen by God as His mouthpiece. Her allegations about King Magnus were regarded as uncontrovertible fact.

Magnus Eriksson's posthumous reputation was also much damaged by a denunciation under nine headings, *Libellus de Magno Erici rege*, written by his enemies in the council and the Swedish aristocracy. This final settlement of accounts with his reign reads like an extract from a list of criminals. The nine heads cover virtually every crime one imagines a human being could commit. As a document it is nothing but one long plaint; but in form it reads like an irrevocable judgment. Yet it was drawn up by the very men who had called in Duke Albrecht and his Germans, and who therefore can only be called traitors against their own country!

'Magnus let neither law nor justice be had in the realm' – thus reads the most grotesque among the heads of this indictment against the very king who first drew up a system of laws for the whole country and issued decree after decree to secure their enforcement, and thus established the reign of law throughout the land. It was as a legislator above all that Magnus had achieved great things, and here posterity has acknowledged him.

But for a long while Magnus Eriksson, because of Bridget's revelations and the accusations of his nobles, was regarded as having been a bad king through and through. In recent times this verdict has been revised to read 'Not bad, but weak . . .' Such is his new portrait. Redress could indeed go no further.

What can chiefly be held against Magnus is his enormous gullibility, a gullibility which Valdemar Atterdag and Albrecht of Mecklenburg both knew very well how to exploit. Both princes were sovereign in the arts of practical statesmanship, they ruthlessly broke their promises and agreements, lulled Magnus into a state of false security and then sprung a surprise attack on him. Magnus was no master of this efficacious type of diplomacy, so brilliantly implemented by his enemies.

On no occasion do we hear of Magnus breaking oaths, promises, or guarantees of safe conduct. Nor do we know of any circumstances in which he could be accused of a treacherous act of violence. Against the background of his forefathers' dark deeds we cannot help feeling sympathetic toward the last of the Folkungs. The struggle in which he foundered seems to have been altogether too unequal. Forces for which he was no match, Danes, Germans and Swedes, seem to have conspired against him. But no man who had Magnus' undoubted capacity for making powerful enemies can be called weak or insignificant.

In its judgment on Magnus Eriksson posterity should also see his reign against the epoch under King Albrecht's German rule which now followed. A period of profound humiliation for the Swedes, it was to last for 25 years. A quarter of a century of foreign government, reinforced by the power of native lords who at last had got a man on the throne who would serve their interests as Magnus had refused to, it became a period of new oppression for the common man. 'The foreigners with their hospitalities, their tallages and their levies, their tax upon tax, were the land's uttermost ruin, in such wise that peasants and townsfolk were utterly impoverished' (Olaus Petri). Admittedly, at an assembly of the lords of the realm in 1380, a new decree against enforced hospitality was proclaimed – the fifth such ban in succession, as far as I can see, during the High Middle Ages. No doubt it was a matter of pure routine. Nothing goes to show it was any better obeyed than its four predecessors.

From the sources it transpires that the common man wanted to have Magnus, the commons' king, back on the throne. While he was imprisoned in Stockholm Castle the peasantry of Uppland wrote a letter to their brethren in Östergötland and Västergötland. Calling King Albrecht and his father perjurors and traitors and acclaiming 'the good and honourable lord, King Magnus', they say they wish to free him from his prison. Many sources allow us to surmise that much was seriously amiss in the kingdom, and that only by King Magnus' return to power could the peasantry hope for a change. In Småland the peasants attempted a revolt. It was crushed.

E

These popular revolts to reinstate the deposed king are crucial to our final assessment of King Magnus' government. They showed that the common man preferred him on the throne to Albrecht. Even after only a few years, the latter's régime had become utterly intolerable. Historians have not sufficiently stressed these attempts by the commons to return the crown to Magnus.

In Norway, too, his second kingdom, the common people gave him the honourable name Magnus the Good; and an Icelandic annal states that after his death he was regarded as a saint. As far as we can see, the peasantry's view of him was quite different from that of the ruling class. 'He wished all men well', wrote one contemporary chronicler.

Had he had a more powerful nature, been more of a ruler and used the same methods against his opponents as his predecessor, it is possible he might have retained his throne. No doubt his negligence in refraining from shedding his enemies' blood contributed to his defeat. If so, his gentle disposition could qualify him as hero of some antique drama.

In Swedish literature we find one – Christian – explanation of his tragedy. 'Thou hast blood in thy crown, King Magnus!' cries the Madman, in Strindberg's play* about the last of the Folkungs. It is the key line of the whole play. The blood referred to is the blood of Sir Magnus – the young man who had had to go to the block because he had stood in the way of his namesake, Duke Erik's son. To Strindberg all the disasters of the last of the Folkung illustrate the commandment of a stern God: 'The sins of the fathers shall be visited upon their children, yea, even unto the third and fourth generation, who do hate me'.

Magnus was the last of the Folkung dynasty to reign over Sweden. He was the clan's fourth generation and its last; wherefore the Almighty, by the terms of his own Commandment, could crave of him punishment for the sins of his fathers. Divine vengeance was delayed to the last; but was the more dreadful when it finally struck. Magnus Eriksson had drawn down on himself the hereditary sins of three generations – and had to atone the cumulative guilt of all the blood they had spilt.

* *Folkungasagan* 1899. (The Saga of the Folkungs, J. Cape, London 1931.)

The Ship of Death

~~~~~~

ERGEN, FOUNDED ABOUT 1070, is Norway's oldest city except
for Tönsberg. Together with Visby, on the Baltic isle of Gotland, it was the most important port and trading city in all
Magnus Eriksson's realms. Like Visby, it was a centre of Hanseatic
trade with Scandinavia. In the Middle Ages the Hanseatic League
was the largest private enterprise in Northern Europe, a concern
of united shipping companies, asserting itself by the power of money
and capable of waging war as successfully as any empire or kingdom.
At the height of its power the concern comprised 160 cities in the
countries round the Baltic and the North Sea. The Hansa had a head
office in Bergen, which therefore stood in livelier contact with
Western Europe than any other Scandinavian port. We are in an age
when the land separated peoples, but water linked them. Bergen's
geographical position made it Scandinavia's chief port for trade with
Europe, the point of entry for all innovations from the West.

All this made the town the natural scene of an event more fateful
in its consequences to the Nordic peoples than any other in their
entire history.

One day in August, 1349, a ship came drifting into Bergen harbour
from the west. Expert eyes could discern at a distance that it was a
cog, the commonest type of Hansa merchant vessel at that time.

The men of Bergen piloted the helpless ship into port. Not a living
soul was aboard her. But many dead. The cog was manned by
corpses. Her crew had died to the last man. But the cargo of clothes
and woollens was in good condition, and as the ship had no master,
belonged to her salvagers. After unloading the cloths and woollens
the Bergen men took the cog and her lifeless crew out to sea and
scuttled her.

The same day, some of those who had unloaded her fell seriously ill. A few hours later they were dead. A Norwegian historian, Ernst Sars, has estimated that, in 1349, the diocese of Bergen had a population of about 100,000 people. Of these, two months after the cog's arrival, 40,000 had followed her crew to the grave.

It was the prelude to the greatest mass-death in Scandinavian history. Another fateful day for Scandinavia was April 9, 1940. But compared with that August day in 1349 when the unmanned vessel was sighted off Bergen, the Nazi invasion dwindles to insignificance. On board, the cog had the Black Death. Smitten by her terrible cargo, at least one-third of the entire populations of Norway and Sweden were to perish.

The Black Death was more important, humanly aud sociologically, than anything else that happened to Sweden during the Middle Ages. Although mentioned in all histories, it is often only cursorily described; and therefore, before I describe its effects and consequences for the population, something must also be said about its origins and European background.

It was no ordinary plague epidemic. It was a *pandemic* (Greek *pan* =all, *demos*=the people); the medical term denotes a sickness wiping out whole peoples and ravaging entire continents. This particular pandemic laid waste Europe and Asia and 'shook the Western world of those days to its foundations' (Lewis Mumford). The historians of the plague described it as the most terrific catastrophe ever to have afflicted humanity. Its name varies from land to land. 'The dark midnight hour of the Middle Ages' – our Swedish historian Grimberg* calls his picture of the Black Death, and orchestrates it with the Last Trump. Yet the plague does not appear under its Swedish name, '*Digerdöden*', until the 16th century, two centuries after the event. I have already indicated who probably coined the expression. In 14th-century Swedish sources it is called 'the great death', 'sudden death' (*braaddöhda*) and 'The Great Scourge'. But mostly it goes by Latin names: *Magna mortalitas, Grandis pestilentia* and *Febris pestilentialis*.

In Italy the pandemic was called *la mortalega grande*, in France *la peste noire*, in England the Black Death, in Germany *der schwarze*

* Grimberg: *Svenska folkets underbara öden.*

Tod, in the Netherlands *de groete doet*, in Iceland *Svartur daudi*, in Norway *Den store Manndauen*, in Finland *Iso Rutto* and in Denmark *Den sorte Død*. It got its English name, the Black Death, from the black spots which broke out on the patient's skin. In the chronicles the pandemic is also called '*Allhärjaren*' – the All-Devastater – and *Världshärjaren* – the World-Devastater, a popular translation of the medical term.

If the disease struck people with a peculiar horror it was because the victim almost always died. For anyone contracting to recover was regarded as a special act of God, a miracle. The Swedish word *braaddöhda* – the sudden death – indicates vividly how swift was its course. Death could follow on the spot, usually within a few hours, twenty-four perhaps, or, at the very utmost, three days and nights. Because it all occurred so horribly swiftly, the disease was also known as 'the furious sickness'.

It was believed to enter a person by the nose, and a violent attack of sneezing was regarded as the first symptom. Whence the old Swedish expression '*Gud hjälpe*' – much the same as the English 'Bless you'! – addressed to anyone who sneezes. He needs God's protection – because he has the Great Death in his nostrils. Anyone who caught the disease was eschewed by all around him. Parents abandoned their sick children, and the sick were even sometimes driven out into the forest and wastelands to perish.

Symptoms of the Great Death were manifold. Shiverings and heat, spasms of vomiting, headache and dizziness, bleary eyes, shortness of breath, a strangling sensation, a black tongue, an unslakeable thirst, a great weakness, a coughing up and excreting of blood, a stinking breath, bloodshot conjunctiva, bleeding skin. Great boils the size of a goose's egg – bubons – broke out under the armpits, in the angle of the jaw and in the crutch. The face of the diseased turned scarlet, his speech became incoherent and his gait staggering, as if in his cups. 'He was seized with a great terror and acted violently'. For, within three days he knew he would be dead.

The doctors were helpless. If they issued instructions to the population it was only to conceal their own ignorance. Petrarch writes plainly that the doctors knew no more than anyone else; *i.e.* nothing at all. The King of France called in the foremost and most learned expertise of the age, represented by the famous University of Paris, to investigate and explain the causes of *la peste noire*, which was so furiously ravaging the land, and thereafter proclaim to the people how best to avoid and combat it.

The faculty came to the conclusion that the pandemic had its origins in a struggle between the celestial bodies and the Indian Ocean. The sun's rays and the sky's warmth and fire were being so fiercely directed at this sea that much of its waters were being sucked up into the atmosphere. The steam thus formed was hiding the sun and, spreading through the various layers of the atmosphere to great areas of the earth, was swathing them in mist. Spread more especially by the ocean winds, these aerial currents contained lethal poisons which were spoiling the air. In them was inevitable death.

The medical faculty also issued instructions to the populace. They should eat very little, drink only a certain quantity. Burned and distilled drinks were efficacious, but water very dangerous. They should also sleep at certain times. Not only the water, but also the very air was declared poisonous; and to purify it, fire was recommended. Bonfires should be lit and kept burning in public places, streets and market places. Odiferous woods, camphor and other perfumes should form part of the fuel.

Latter-day medical science has other explanations of how the pandemic started. Its root-cause was a microbe, *Pasteurella pestis*, identified by the Japanese Kitasato and the Swiss Yersin during an outbreak of plague in Hong Kong in 1884. Rats, mice and guinea-pigs are particularly susceptible to this bacillus. Usually plague epidemics are preceded by the discovery of masses of dead rats, so it was long believed that it was the rats which spread the disease to humans. Today medical expertise knows that the rat itself is guiltless. Instead, a much smaller creature, the flea, must take the blame, more particularly those species of flea which, having settled on rats, transfer the microbe to human beings. After the rat is dead they leave its plague-smitten corpse, jump on to a human, and inject the deadly poison into the bloodstream. A fleabite is regarded as the least significant of wounds; but the stab of the plague-flea is lethal. Thus the widespread death of rats during the plague had quite a different implication from what was once believed.

We have our medical explanation of the Great Death, but its contemporaries found a supernatural cause in their own panic-stricken imaginations. In popular fancy the disease took the form of a Demon, or The Hunter, a giant of unthinkable size and height, whose feet trod the earth while his head was hid in the clouds. Striding across country after country in seven-league boots, he shot invisible arrows into human breasts. For the pious of the Middle Ages, living in a world circumscribed by their own ignorance and by the doctrines of the Church, this plague was no ordinary disease. It was *Death* itself. It was the Horseman of the Apocalypse (Revelation Chap. VI, v. 8,) who was riding over the earth on his pale horse and holding a fourth part of humanity in his grip. The Horseman was to slay men with sword, famine and pestilence. 'His name was Death'.

In the years before the disease broke out in Europe there had been many omens, rare signs and wonders. In 1334, a bloody rain had fallen at Locarno, in Switzerland and in two places in Hungary; in Swabia there had been a plenteous fall of red snow. In several places in Southern Germany the heavens had rained not only blood but also snakes and toads. These beasts were of unnatural size and the very sight of them had smitten people with horror. The Swedish physician Israel Hwasser (1790–1860) says such a fall of bloody rain is supposed to have fallen at Ringstaholm as early as 1316, thirty-three years before the Great Death appeared in Sweden. Fireballs and comets – or falling stars, as they were called – also appeared over several countries. On December 20, 1348, a great pillar of fire stood over the palace of the Pope at Avignon; remaining there for an hour it awakened the utmost terror and amazement in all who beheld it.

When the great catastrophe finally occurred, the popular mood in Europe was well prepared for it.

The Black Death – to give it its English name – is supposed to have come from India. Indian annals mention a great plague epidemic which ravaged the land for several decades after 1325. China, too, has been given as its place of origin.

But how did the pandemic reach Europe? It is thought to have followed the old caravan route from the Chinese Lake to the Black Sea and the Mediterranean, along which Persian merchants freighted silk and satin to Europe. Long forgotten, the Silk Route had been rediscovered at the beginning of the 14th century, just in time to spread the pandemic across whole continents.

By 1344 it had reached the city of Kaffa on the Crimean Peninsula. For nearly a century Kaffa had been in the possession of its Genoese conquerors, and its harbour was used by Italian merchants to store their wares. In 1344, the Tartars, then waging a victorious campaign, invested Kaffa. Bringing the infection with them, they gave it to the Genoese by hurling infected corpses over the walls of the besieged city with their catapults and ballistas. A primitive form of bacteriological warfare.

The Tartars did not take Kaffa; but when their besieging forces withdrew they left the city's inhabitants a frightful parting gift. And when the Genoese sailed for home, they had the Black Death on board.

La mortalega grande is known in Genoa, the first place it appeared at in our part of the world, from the spring of 1347. Thereafter, during the years 1347–1350, it spread swiftly over the whole of Europe.

There was one question to which no one could really know the answer: could disease be transferred from one human being to another? The concept of infection had still not been generally accepted, even by all doctors and men of learning and, above all, not by Churchmen. The Christian church declared the plague was a punishment sent by God to destroy sinful humanity. So it was impossible for humanity to check it. Therefore there could be no such thing as an infection, against which one could defend oneself. For who in that case, had infected the first victim?

But among the more enlightened and sensible a thought arose. They saw how the disease moved on from some ravaged area to others which were still healthy – just as people did. Therefore it could only be carried by travellers by land and sea, in their clothes and their commodities. Sheer self-preservation forced people to take measures to protect themselves. They barred the gates of their cities, they set a watch to turn away all strangers. When ships tried to put into their harbours they bombarded them with incendiary arrows. Plague-smitten houses were burned down. Stray animals – dogs, cats and pigs – were destroyed. And men and women who had contracted the disease were left alone to die, abandoned by all. Physicians provided themselves with face masks, animal masks of waxed cloth, and swathed themselves in long leather coats reaching down to their feet.

All to no avail. The All-Ravager, writes one chronicler, passed through locked doors, he paid no heed to moat or drawbridge, he marched remorselessly on over land and sea, crossing closed as well as open frontiers. Throughout the whole of Christendom, *Death* spread from village to village, from city to city, from kingdom to kingdom. And the Church seemed to be right. So vast a devastation could only be explained as having been sent by God. And no one could do anything against it.

Mankind's last days were believed to be at hand. The peoples expected the world to end.

Of European countries, with the possible exception of England, it was Italy that was hardest hit. Florence, 'the magnificent, more lovely than all the cities of Italy' was the greatest centre of the Black Death. The dead – though this surely must be a gross exaggeration – have been numbered at 100,000. Giovanni Boccaccio's description of the state of affairs there, in his introduction to his *Decamerone*, is well-known; so I shall not quote from it. Less well known, probably, are Petrarch's words to posterity. He knew what he was talking about. Laura, his beloved, had died of the plague on April 6, 1348. In *The Triumph of Death* he describes her sickness and last hours, and in his *Epistolae familiares* describes all the misery that followed in the wake of the pandemic. He writes of a father, by name Agniolo di Tura, who with his own hands buried five of his plague-smitten children in the same grave. But many of the corpses were so lightly buried that dogs dug them up again and ate them. There was no ceremony at the graveside. 'No bells, no tears. This is the end of the world.'

Concisely, simply, Petrarch has expressed his own feelings during the catastrophe: 'Woe am I. Woe on us' – and turning to generations yet unborn, cries: 'O, thou happy posterity! Thou that knowest not these weepings and wailings, perchance thou takest my words for a fabrication?'

But we have no reason whatever to doubt the poet's description of Florence in 1348. Following the advances of the Black Death through several European countries, I have found more memories of it in Florence than anywhere else. All the many thousands of victims are said to have been buried in one common grave outside the city. The city's art galleries too, contain many paintings and sculptures from those catastrophic years. But I made my most remarkable find in an old archive. A picture sculpted in wax. In all its realism its tangible vividness as an image of plague-stricken Italy, it is unsurpassed. A spacious market place is heaped with corpses, piled up like bundles of firewood. Here and there, between these heaps, odd corpses lie scattered about on the ground – corpses of women pressing dead babes to their breast. The rats have taken over these bodies. Swarming over bellies and breasts, the rodents dig their teeth into navels, eyes, noses, mouths.

An illustration for Boccaccio or Petrarch!

Petrarch has grippingly expressed the mood prevailing in his land: 'When ever was such a thing seen or heard of? Houses empty. Cities deserted and uncared for. Roads heaped with corpses. Everwhere a monstrous desolation. Ask the historians: they are silent. Ask the doctors: they stand dumbfounded. As for the philosophers: they furrow their brows and place a finger on their mouths, enjoining silence.'

Five hundred and fifty years were to pass before Petrarch's questions were to be answered – by the discovery of the plague baccillus.

It was not only the medical faculty in Paris that sought comprehensible, natural reasons for the world-wide catastrophe. So did other learned men. Astrologers found that, far out in space, the heavenly bodies were confronting one another in a new and unheard of constellation that was influencing the atmosphere and infesting it with poisonous elements. One explanation did not exclude another. In many lands the learned declared that the disease was being caused and spread by a thick, stinking and poisonous fog which during these years was sweeping over the earth. Contemporary science was largely agreed that the Great Death crept into a man with the air he breathed. Unsought analogies with our own age's pollution of the atmosphere by radioactivity after nuclear explosions suggest themselves.

But for the common people the explanations of the learned were not enough. Terror of death stripped human reason of its critical faculties. As to the cause of the plague, people believed the most monstrous rumours – and looked about them for some tangible object on which they could be revenged. A people who had immigrated into Europe were given the blame. The Jews. A pogrom broke out, unexceeded in extent or bestial cruelty until six centuries later – in the Age of Hitler.

Psychosis followed the plague. In his classic work on the plague, *Der Schwarze Tod*, 1924, the German historian Johannes Nohl has investigated in depth the persecution of the Jews during the Black Death. Two Nordic scientists, Hwasser, a Swede, and Ilmoni, a Finn, have also studied the subject. And 14th-century chroniclers in France, Germany and Switzerland, too, have much to tell us. The information in these documents is so fantastic that anyone who was not contemporary to Hitler would be inclined to dismiss them as sheer imagination.

Jews were accused of trying to extirpate the Christian peoples of Europe by poisoning their drinking water – an act in which they were supposed to be God's own tool. The quarrel between Pope and Emperor had thrown God into such indignation at the state of his Christendom that he had decided to extirpate it. Choosing the Jews for this task, he had provided them with a 'secret poison'. From their own wells and springs the people were to drink themselves to death. Different origins were ascribed to this poison. Some said it had come from the East. Others that the Jews themselves had manufactured it out of spiders, scorpions, snakes and other reptiles.

The action against the Jews began in 1348 in the south of France, where the pandemic was then raging. In several places in Provence the population were incited against the immigrants. At Norbonne and Carcassonne there were riots, the entire Jewish population of those cities falling victim to the mob. At Bourgogne, according to Nohl, 50,000 Jews were murdered 'in the cruellest fashion'.

The psychosis was to spread as swiftly as the plague itself. It claimed its greatest number of victims in Central Europe. Since time immemorial fire has been used as the most efficacious specific against evil. Now the Christians of Germany and Switzerland used it against the Jews, who perished in the flames. At Strasbourg, 6,000 were burned at the stake, and all Jews were forbidden to settle in the city for a century to come. The Bishop of Strasbourg, described as a 'wild fanatic', seems to have been the chief instigator of these human bonfires. In the market place at Mainz so great a fire was lit for the city's Jews that the bells of the nearby Quirinkirche melted in the heat and the church itself almost burned down.

In 1349, human bonfires were lit in a number of German cities: at Frankfurt, Nuremburg, Wismar, Rostock, Greifswald and Stralsund. Of the victims a contemporary record states that 'they turned black in the fire and smoke.' At Esslingen, in Swabia, the Jews gathered in their synagogue and themselves set fire to it 'out of despair'. At Erfurt 3,000 Jews cheated their executioners in similar fashion. At Speyer they were murdered by 'savage gangs' and their corpses, sewn into sacks or nailed up in wine barrels, were flung into the Rhine.

At Basel, in Switzerland, the Jews were put on the rack and 'by and by' forced to confess to having poisoned the city's drinking water. On an island in the bend of the Rhine near that city a wooden building was erected and a great number of Jews who were flung into it were burnt to death. The city chronicler who describes this event adds that the huge human bonfire was made necessary by the 'cannibal yells of the populace'. But although it may have been the furious crowds which committed these excesses, behind the scenes we can discern other forces at work, inciting them to these monstrous deeds.

All Jews were to be burnt 'to the glory of God and for the salvation of Christendom'. Their great courage when condemned to a fiery death made a tremendous impression on observers. One witness to a bonfire of Jews writes: 'Had I not seen it, I should never have believed it. With a smile on their lips they heard their doom; singing psalms and laughing jubilantly, they ran up on to the fire'.

Everywhere the common man believed it was the Jews who had poisoned his wells. In evidence it was alleged that, during the plague, the Jews had refrained from drinking well water. In many places in Germany and Switzerland wells and springs were walled up, and people drank rain and river water instead.

Though such pogroms were almost universal in the continental countries of Europe, none occurred in England, Poland or Lithuania. In these countries Jews were protected by the authorities. As early as the 13th century the Polish kings had given them the right to practice their own religion in peace. Of King Casimir the Great of Poland we are told that he had a Jewish mistress, by name Esther, and that it was for her sake he protected others of her race.

One small spur of these European pogroms is known in Sweden. The psychosis reached the Hanseatic city of Visby, which had many connections with the other Hanseatic cities of Northern Germany. An original source, still extant, describes what happened. In a letter sent by the mayor and council of Visby to the city of Rostock in 1350, it is stated that the city authorities had imprisoned and burned nine 'criminals or poisoners or traitors to all mankind'. One of them, described as an 'organist', had confessed to poisoning wells in Stockholm, Västerås, Arboga and other places on the Swedish mainland. Further, the man had compounded a 'powder' by means of which he had intended to extirpate the entire population of Gotland. He had spoken mysteriously of a 'Greek and Hebrew' conspiracy of many men in eminent positions, summing up its work in the words: 'All Christendom hath by the Jews and by us criminals been poisoned.' Two more of the 'criminals' were stated to be priests, who had poisoned the communion towels at mass in St Olof's church in Visby, causing the deaths of those who had used them. The letter says that altogether nine of the accused had been condemned and burnt at the stake.

We know of no Jewish immigration into Sweden in the 14th century, so these victims of the fire cannot have been Jews. Obviously, they must have been mentally disturbed individuals who had been infected by the continental psychosis and thought it their mission to help extirpate Christendom.

The supposed poisoning of wells was not the only pretext for these Black Death pogroms. An immemorial hatred of Christian peoples for the Jews which, latent for more than a thousand years, since the crucifixion of Christ, had risen to the surface. There was also an economic motive. Traditionally, the Jews were money-lenders. Canon law forbade Christians to take interest on loans. But this ban did not apply to Jews. Cities, communes, individuals, all were deeply in their debt. And now everyone seized this godsent chance to be quit of both debt and creditor.

The Pope at this time was Clement VI. He kept up a splendid court at Avignon, and he is said to have protected all Jews living in the south of France. He locked himself up in his chamber by a fire which was kept burning day and night as long as the plague lasted, and there composed a special prayer: *Oratio contra péstem*.

Many who have written the history of the plague level grave accusations against the authorities and the clergy for their attitude during the pogroms. There were instances of clerics who actually helped to pile up faggots on the bonfires; others, of their remaining wholly passive and simply letting the evil take its course. The more enlightened realised how insane it was to accuse the Jews of such crimes. But they left the ignorant masses to their aberration and, with few exceptions, did nothing to check the mobs' excesses.

In 1751, a work on the great 14th-century catastrophe was published in Stockholm: *Historisk Beskrifning om Then grufwelige Pesten Diger-Döden eller Then Stora och Swarta Döden*. It is the only major study of the subject written by a Swede. Its author was a clergyman, Henric Jacob Sivers. His titles were many: 'Royal Court Chaplain, Master of Arts, Dean of the Parishes in Northern Tjust, and Rector of Tryserum and Hannås'.

In his book, Sivers says the Jews were blamed for the Black Death and he gives a detailed account of the fiery vengeance taken on them by the Christians, adding:

'The Lord alone knows how the poor Hebrews can have been the cause of this plague.'

Two other consequences of the Black Death are of interest. They concern men's and women's reactions in the face of death. As instances of human behaviour they are perennially valid. One was the sexual orgies and excesses; the other, the trains of flagellants – in one case a mortal terror that expressed itself in a headlong embracing of life, in the other its equally headlong denial. Faced with sudden death, mankind divided itself up into the pleasure-seekers and the self-tormentors.

The first category tried to extract as much pleasure as possible from the senses while they still possessed them. Tomorrow, in an hour, life might be over. Most readily available were the pleasures of sex. Here, at least, the rich had no exclusive privilege. Sex cost nothing, and was just as accessible to the poor. Threatened by the All-Destroyer, conventions dissolved and inhibitions melted away. Ignoring both the Church's bans and the laws of society, men and women from all social levels and groups, but more especially the lower classes, sought each other out for sexual intercourse. From the Central European countries we even hear of special bi-sexual associations formed for the express purpose of freely elective sexual intercourse in a room apart. Group sex is a very ancient human phenomenon.

Johannes Nohl's history devotes a whole chapter to *Eroticism during the Plague* and describes in detail collective sexual intercourse within groups having hundreds of members. Particularly in the regions around the rivers Rhine and Moselle erotic deviation took peculiar forms. Dancing was a crucial element in these orgies. Sects were formed whose individual members were seized with *Tanzwut*, dance mania, leading to the most intimate advances between the sexes, and where it was the women who took the lead. Hundreds of women, attacked by *Tanzwut*, participated in public dances arranged in Cologne market place. Most are afterwards said to have found themselves pregnant.

Persons seized with *Tanzwut* were regarded by the Church as possessed by demons or evil spirits. The Devil, it was believed, had taken up his abode in their bosom and was subjecting them to horrible torments.

Such excesses were quite beyond both the spiritual and the temporal authorities. A time of terrible catastrophe, it seems to have abnormally stimulated people's sexual instincts. Perhaps the extreme fear of death is conducive to eroticism?

Wandering about in great flocks, people devoted themselves to group sex. At one point in his writings Radulfus de Rivo, a Dutchman, describes crowds of half-naked men and women who went from town to town in Holland, performing the most indecent dances. They evinced many symptoms of lunacy, flung themselves down wells, rolled in filth and dung like swine. The women who joined these processions, Radulfus de Rivo says, had lost all sense of shame.

All this went far beyond anything society could condone as

natural or normal. Against such excesses no measures had the least effect. Doctors warned people against sex in plague-time, even against permissible intercourse between married couples. There was the danger of infection. Also, by using up people's energy it reduced their powers of resistance.

Sex challenged the plague: *In peste Venus pestem provocat*. But lust also laid bodies open to the disease. The newly married, it seems, were more easily infected than others, and warning examples are given of several cases where the bridegroom had died on the third day after his wedding: 'Instead of white wedding candles, they were fain light black.'

But neither the spiritual nor the medical authorities could damp the common man's sexual desires. In spite of all warnings and admonitions, the marriage rate rose sharply: 'The plague worked like the cleverest bawd.' Twenty-four hours were as long as people were prepared to wait to get married. 'Widows, their faces still wet with the tears they had shed for their deceased husbands, took new men, who after a few days also died.' One woman at Nijmegen married three men within a period of only six weeks: the priests, realising how dire her need was, came to her assistance. Among the lower classes, especially, this rage for marriage assumed fantastic dimensions.

One historian of the plague sums up: 'Without caring for what is decent or indecent, people now lived only for their own lusts, and by day and by night, alone or in company, did whatever they desired.'

The other group, the scourgers, the self-tormenters, behaved in exactly contrary fashion. Scourging was an immemorial form of ecclesiastical punishment. Introduced with monasticism, it was recommended as a penance to those who dwelt within monastery walls. In the 13th century it had spread to private persons of piety who thereby wished to forestall God's punishments and judgment. By such self-punishment, inflicting on themselves with their own hand the sufferings merited by their sins, they hoped to expunge them. Great societies of such scourgers or flagellants were now formed, and going in procession through towns and villages practised their self-torments under the public gaze.

After the plague had broken out, flagellant trains, first mentioned in Italy as early as 1280, assumed the character of an epidemic. By appeasing God's wrath by such torments they hoped to prevent Him from annihilating mankind. They took upon themselves the burden of the world's sin. Their implements were short lengths of rope or leather straps with long dangling tails, to which had been attached heavy pieces of jagged lead. One old description says that a scourge consisted of 'three Whiplashes fastened together, in whose knots sat nails and thorns, wherewith they so mercilessly scourged themselves that the blood flowed'.

Apparently such flagellant trains were commonest of all in Germany. Persons of both sexes and all ages, men, women, old people and children joined in them. Day and night the flagellants were on the move. At nights they carried lighted candles in their hands, illumining their naked bleeding bodies. Clad only in a loincloth they went in procession through city streets, lashing 'their shoulders bloody'. As they scourged themselves they sang penitential songs, screaming and calling on God: 'The sound of the flagellants' dismal songs is heard by day and night, and fills town and country.' They crawled on their hands and knees around images of Christ, the Madonna and the saints, they crept around chapels, churches and temples. They literally humbled themselves to the dust before the Lord who was threatening to annihilate His own creation.

In all this, too, there was a sexual element. One chronicler states that 'the comeliest of virgins' joined these trains of flagellants, and adds: 'But women and maidens, so I have heard, return not seldom pregnant.' Obviously, the movement did not wholly succeed in mortifying the flesh.

The sight of these flocks of screaming, shouting, whimpering people, backs bare and bloodied, must have had a terrifying effect on all who lined the ways to watch them pass. Not only did such processions augment the general terror; they also helped to spread the plague.

The ecclesiastical authorities wanted no part of this flagellant movement. It had turned against the Church. So they condemned it emphatically. The Bishop of Lübeck, for instance, intervened against the processions and refused a flock of scourgers access to his town. Other German cities, too, closed their gates to this self-punishing fraternity. Flagellants trying to cross the border into Denmark were turned back by a royal ordinance, on account of what was termed their 'vicious mode of life'.

Nor have the historians of the plague found any traces, during the Black Death period, of flagellants in the Scandinavian countries. So if Ingmar Bergman's mediaeval film *The Seventh Seal* is supposed to take place in Scandinavia, the flagellant train in it lacks all historical basis.

Dance mania and scourgings, sexual excesses and self-torment to the point of lunacy – in all these ways man's fear of death put out the light of his reason. It was a vicious circle. Terror unleashed madness. And madness augmented the terror.

Truly, it was 'a time of great anxiety' (Ilmoni).

I have visited the scene of that historic event which, one August day in 1349, led to the Great Death in Scandinavia. In the Maritime Museum at Bergen can be seen *The Ship of the Great Death*, a model of the Hanseatic cog that brought the World-Devastator to our peninsula. Her dimensions were: length 78' 9″, beam 26', draught 9'. Her rigging: mainmast, foremast and mizzen. The vessel's beam is noteworthy in proportion to her length – she is a third as broad as she is long. The plague ship was certainly not a fast sailer. On the contrary she was a rather clumsy, almost barge-like vessel. If Columbus had sailed in cogs instead of caravels, the New World would probably have had to wait a further couple of weeks to be discovered. But 14th-century people were in no hurry. They had time on their hands. On their slow voyages they did not become hysterical with impatience, nor did they suffer from the mania for speed that afflicts their 20th-century descendents. As a cargo vessel the cog served her purpose admirably and a good many tons of cargo could be stowed away in her capacious hold. Nor did she need a large crew. A cog of this size had only some ten men on board. But ten corpses were enough – to reduce the population of Scandinavia by one-third.

Our knowledge of the plague ship's arrival in Bergen comes from an Icelandic annal, dated 1360. Scanty though it is, it is our only real source of information. Works on mediaeval Bergen can be searched in vain for any more detailed account of the terrible event. This lack of contemporary records is remarkable. For 40,000 people in the diocese of Bergen to die all at once was an unprecedented occurrence, and must have paralyzed the city and stunted its growth for a long time to come. Surely one would expect to find some trace of it in local history?

The explanation is doubtless simple enough. There was no one who survived to write it all down. Most of those who knew how to write belonged to a very limited circle of clerics. The Bishop of Bergen was himself one of the plague's first victims, and the greater part of the clergy of his diocese followed him to the grave. Priests, who had to administer the extreme unction to the sick and dying, were particularly exposed.

Otherwise Bergen, even today, retains so pungent an odour of its mediaeval centuries that a stranger might easily fancy himself in one of Germany's oldest cities. For a Scandinavian town, Bergen is oddly built. The German Quay, the Shipping House, the Mediaeval Brygge Museum and the Hanseatic Museum all bear eloquent witness to its past. Among Scandinavian cities only Visby is equally mediaeval. Here, if anywhere, one would have expected to find some memorials of the World-Destroyer.

It is also hard to explain why the men of Bergen were not more wary of the plague ship and her cargo. By 1349 the pandemic had been raging all over Europe for more than two and a half years. As early as August, 1348, it had reached England by the port of Melcombe Regis, now part of Weymouth in Dorset, and thence spread throughout the country. England, as I have said, was one of the most devastated countries in all Europe. British historians estimate the number of English deaths from the Black Death at upwards of two million. For England, too, this catastrophe was the most traumatic event of the Middle Ages. It changed the country's social structure and influenced developments for centuries to come. Which is why Trevelyan and other historians have devoted so much space to it.

But ships from Bergen sailed regularly for English ports, and one would have thought that news of so devastating a plague would soon have reached Norway. Surely people in Bergen would have been aware how dangerous it was to let a foreign vessel enter their port from the west? Suspect vessels were not allowed to tie up at the quays of other European ports, and it could even happen, as I have said, that ships trying to effect an entry were fired on and set ablaze with incendiary arrows. Yet the men of Bergen took charge of a ship whose crew were dead to the last man and unloaded her in the usual way. The mere aspect of all those corpses, one would have thought, should have deterred them. Why did they not immediately scuttle both ship and cargo?

Can the cog's cargo have been so valuable that for its sake they even accepted the risk of catching the plague? If so, it was not the first time that men have thrown away their lives for profit. The simple fact of the matter, however, is probably that the men of Bergen did not realise the highly infectious nature of the disease. Perhaps the ship's rats, too, infected with plague fleas, went ashore and helped to spread the pandemic.

Mediaeval communications were primitive, and the speed with which the disease spread through Scandinavia can only be described as remarkable. A mere two months after the Bergen outbreak it had already reached Sweden. In October, 1349, we hear of it in Halland, then temporarily under Swedish occupation. Probably it had arrived there by sea, having been brought by coasting vessels on the West Coast. Again, it was the water that united people; and the sea-route was more expeditious than that over the mountainous Norwegian frontier. In October, King Magnus Eriksson had received such dire tidings of the danger to his realm that he sounded the alarm. Obviously terror-stricken, he warned his subjects of the 'sudden death', which had 'ravaged the moster part of those folk that do dwell in the lands that lie to westward.'

King Magnus summoned his advisers to a council at Lödöse.* What was to be done to check the epidemic? The Council came to the conclusion that the plague was being visited on men by God for their sins. Therefore only one measure could avail against it. They must pray to God for mercy.

In a royal rescript issued at Lödöse the plague is called 'the great torment' which the Lord God 'hath universally cast into the world, with sudden death'. In his letter the king exhorts his subjects to fast

* Near present-day Gothenburg.

more particularly on Fridays. The whole people, men and women, the aged and the children, were to walk barefoot round their churches and bring offerings: 'Every Christian, man and woman, shall give one Swedish penny to the Honour of God and his blessed Mother Mary'. Thus and only thus would God be appeased and show mercy to the Swedes. Masses were also to be held in honour of the Virgin Mary, who was exhorted to pray for the Swedes to her 'blessed son'.

This royal letter contains every prescription issued by the Catholic Church against the plague in Christian countries.

So far, at the time when King Magnus issued his Lödöse warning, the disease had only appeared in Halland; but before the year was out it had invaded the neighbouring provinces of Småland and Västergötland. The year following, 1350, was to be the year of the Great Death in Sweden.

We do not know exactly what routes the pandemic took through the kingdom. But since King Magnus himself was in constant flight from it the best method of tracing its advances is to follow him on his journeys. Where the king was, the sickness was not; and where the sickness was, the king was not. Magnus Eriksson seems to have placed little trust in the prophylactics he had prescribed for his people.

Mortality was greatest in Southern and Central Sweden. Of the various provinces of the realm, Småland, Västergötland, Värmland and Uppland are thought to have suffered the worst losses. Among the clergy of Västergötland the death-rate was especially high.

Otherwise it was chiefly the poorest sort of folk who succumbed. In the uppermost level of society, among the nobility, few died – the well-to-do could always flee from infected to healthy districts. The indigent could not. In some parishes the so-called 'defenceless' (*försvarslösa*) perished almost to a man, thus solving one social problem at a blow. Since there were no more poor to 'defend', parishes were relieved of their obligation to support them. In several dioceses the cathedral chapters even suspended the poor-tithe as no longer necessary. There were no paupers left. In an extant source the Hälsingland provincial assembly speaks of 'the multitude of poor and pitiable persons who before the great plague had tilled our soil'.

By killing off such great numbers among the lowest classes of mediaeval society, the Black Death altered the balance between the social classes; and this was to have far-reaching consequences. For the survivors the material standard of living rose. There were fewer mouths to feed.

Another effect of the Black Death was greatly to increase ecclesiastical wealth. In wills preserved from around 1350 great men and nobles bequeathed either all or part of their property to the Church. Most of these donations date from the year of the Great Death when the Manslayer was doing his worst. From the manner in which these gifts are formulated it is clear they were being drawn up by people who expected to die at any moment and who by such bequests hoped to make sure of heaven. So great was the increase in the wealth of the Church thanks to the Manslayer 'whose name was death' that the Franciscans, a radical movement within Christendom, were of the view that the decadence of the papacy in the 14th century begun in consequence of it. Popes, cardinals, bishops and priests not only laid up treasures for themselves in heaven; they also acquired them on earth, as can be seen in the Vatican Museum, which houses such an accumulation of treasures, gold, silver, diamonds, precious stones and all sorts of valuable objects, as I for my part have never seen anywhere else.

In Sweden, as in other lands, people sought to escape the All-Destroyer by prayers, penances, fastings, and oblations. This is not to say they neglected to take practical measures, above all fire. Fires of purification were lit in streets and market places. Round one village in Halland, so we are told, a whole forest was set on fire to protect it by a ring of flames. Infected houses were fumigated with juniper smoke. One historian of the plague, W. Kock, has found other prophylactics used in Sweden. Strong spices and liquids were believed to have a preventive effect, particularly vinegar, with which they soused their food. Among drinks, water was especially to be eschewed as poisonous; perhaps the rumour of the Jews' poisoning of the wells had also reached Sweden. At all events they must have had news of the happenings at Visby. Extravenous medicines included the patient's own excrement, wiped on to his boils as a healing unguent.

One panacea was *teriak*. The name, derived from the Greek *theriakos* means a specific against animal poisons; on anyone bitten by a snake, by a mad dog or by wild beasts, its effect was infallible. As a medicine it had been used by Nero's imperial physician Andromachus, and it was still held in high esteem by doctors as late as the 18th century. Teriak was a powder compounded of no fewer than 71 constituents, among them opium and snake's flesh, dried and ground into a flour, which was then stirred into the powder. It was taken extravenously as a universal nostrum against the plague.

Fire and flame could annihilate microbes and thus limit the spread of the perilous disease; but whether the flesh of serpents and human excrement were equally effective may be doubted. The Church, too, could offer medicine in the shape of saints' relics. In their Churches, people could touch parts of the bodies of holy persons, preserved through the ages. The larger Swedish churches were veritable storehouses of fragments of skeletons, arms, legs, toes, nails, fingers and hair preserved in special shrines and reliquaries. According to an inventory of 1344, Uppsala Cathedral possessed at least 300 relics of saints, among them the head of John the Baptist, heads of the three Wise Men and the Innocents, and a tooth that had once been St Martin's. In the Middle Ages Lund Cathedral, too, could show for itself no fewer than 417 saints' relics, besides some of the Virgin Mary's milk, her hair and clothes. A biologist has identified one such bone, preserved as a holy relic, as the foot of a seal. Gumlösa Church, a small parish church in Skåne, preserved a piece of Christ's cross and the dish used by Jesus at the Last Supper.

The Catholic Church drove a thriving business in relics. In a circular to the churches in its diocese dated Sept. 1, 1277, the Cologne Cathedral chapter offered for sale a considerable quantity of bones from the bodies of female saints. Among them were fragments of the skeletons of Saint Basilia, Saint Emma and Saint Margaret.

But not everyone believed in the protective powers of Christian saints. Some Swedes turned to the old heathen gods and rituals. In time of plague and famine their forefathers had been wont to appease their gods with human sacrifices, even to the point of burying the victims alive. The most innocent, little children and pure virgins, had been put 'quick into the earth'; and now, as the Great Death swept over Sweden, tradition says that people again resorted to this way of worshipping and appeasing the divinity.

Such tales of sacrificed children and maidens are quite common, and one modern researcher, Hans-Egil Hauge, (*Studie i offer och magi*, 1965), has collated them. In his book Hauge describes twenty-six variants of what happened when someone was buried alive. Usually it was done in the borderlands between two villages or parishes, the idea being to 'bind' the disease and prevent it crossing the border.

In the Middle Ages the practise of burying people alive (*sätta kvick i jord*) had still not disappeared from Sweden, and there are sporadic instances of it being used as a punishment even up to the 17th century. King Kristoffer's national law of the 1440's prescribes it as the punishment for women taken in adultery.

And in fact, in Sweden, burying alive seems to have been a punishment specially reserved for female criminals.

In his great collection of myths and legends the Swedish poet and historian Afzelius (1785–1871) mentions cases of young maidens being buried alive at the time of the Black Death. A beautiful virgin from Kinnekulle sacrificed her own life to check the pestilence, of her own free will walking down into her grave. A peasant's daughter at Vartofta did the same, but on condition that a fence be raised round her grave and stand there for ever. But mostly it was small children who were sacrificed to the gods. From Western Värmland a local historian states that 'in their terror and panic' the people there 'reverted to their heathen faith', sacrificing two children, a boy and a girl, to induce the gods to relent. In this case the two children who were prevailed on to walk down into a ready-dug grave were two little paupers; 'whereupon the grave was hastily filled in.' As the first spadeful of soil fell on her, the little girl burst into tears and cried out: 'Don't throw earth on my bread and butter.'

We are also told of several cases of people buying up the children of indigent parents to bury them alive – a custom comparable to the exposure of newborn infants in the forest in famine years.

Whether human sacrifice occurred in Sweden as late into Christian times as the 14th century is a question on which, for lack of definite evidence, the experts differ. But so many and various are the popular traditions and legends of people being buried alive, they can hardly be altogether baseless. Chiefly they come from Västergötland and Småland, where heathendom lived on longer than it did in Svealand. There is also a Danish tradition of people being buried alive in the days of *Den sorte Død*.

Clearly, the lethally infectious disease met no obstacles. Infected places were not isolated. Quarantine – *quaranta* – was still unknown in Sweden; not until 1577 (another plague year) were any such regulations drawn up.

Over huge areas the entire population was wiped out. Not only parishes but also whole hundreds were left utterly desolate. Not a soul was left on farms where the animals strayed away and became wild beasts in the forest. In the mining district of eastern Värmland only four individuals survived. In Gunnarskog parish, also in Värmland, only two farms had anyone left alive. A single four-sided stone, placed outside the church door at Persnäs, on the island of Öland, was ample for all the surviving parishioners to stand on at once. At Hjorted, too, in the Småland district of Tjust, no more of the inhabitants remained than a little stone slab outside the church porch sufficed for all their names. In no time at all almost whole parishes had lost their population. Villages and farms, left uninhabited, were abandoned to their animals. For centuries people were continually coming across long-forgotten habitations, remains of human dwellings, fields gone wild, soil once arable but now overgrown with forest. The story of the huntsman whose arrow fastened in the moss-grown wall of a forgotten church in Ekshärad, in Värmland, is famous. Such tales are found in many places; in Västergotland, for instance, and in Norwegian legends.

One especially beautiful legend, found in various parts of Sweden, is about a young man and a young woman, each of whom had been left as the sole survivor on their own remote farm. One day, unable any longer to bear the solitude, both start walking through the countryside to see if anyone else has been left alive: meet, set up home together as man and wife and have children, found a new race, and are the original ancestors of all those now living in the parishes thereabouts.

This legend of a new Adam and Eve who recreated all life on earth anew after the Great Death is found in many European countries.

And, in fact, a great increase in women's fertility was noted all over Europe in the latter half of the 14th century. Several plague historians make mention of it. Nature herself seems to have made haste to repair the enormous losses of human life.

If the memory of the World-Ravager survives more vividly among Norwegians than among Swedes, this is probably because the Man-Slayer reaped an even greater harvest in Norway than he did in Sweden. A great many legends of The Black Death, to the number of about 200, have been published in Norwegian. Our Swedish legends of the great pestilence are few by comparison.

In a papal bull of March 1352 it is stated that the population of Magnus Eriksson's kingdom had been so reduced by the pestilence that his crusade to the east had been paralysed. But it was not only soldiers for crusades that were now in short supply; all over the countryside there was a shortage of agricultural labour. Much arable land had to be allowed to go to grass. As we have seen, it had above all been the lowest class of the population – the servants – who had been most cruelly ravaged. Now at long last people realised how indispensable the manual labourer is to life's continuance.

This catastrophic shortage of agricultural labour, the most trouble-some sociological result of the pandemic, made itself felt in all plague-smitten countries. English historians lay special stress on it. And in fact the Black Death seems to have been the chief cause of the agricultural crisis which, notoriously, set its stamp on late medieval Europe. In 1354, the great shortage of labourers and servants caused the King of Denmark to open his gaols and release a great number of criminals. These people, who would otherwise have been hanged or stayed behind bars for many years, were now put to forced labour. In Sweden, too, there were probably similar attempts to reintroduce bondage for the servant class: 'A tendency, known from several countries, to restrict the agricultural workers' freedom of movement can also be discerned in Sweden, though detailed studies are lacking', say the Swedish professor of history Ahnlund.

This expert on the period witnesses to the insuperable difficulties facing anyone who tries to retrieve the forgotten social classes for history. The field is unresearched. 'Detailed studies are lacking'.

In my childhood I remember hearing old people talk about the great '*dödin*' which, they said, had passed over the countryside 'in heathen times'. It was supposed to have left only one woman alive in the village, and all those that were then living there were supposed to be her descendents. Tradition had forgotten to provide her with a husband. No doubt a member of the male sex had survived in some neighbouring village.

The effects of the Black Death were felt for a couple of centuries to come. Witness, among other things, Peder Månsson's *Bondakonst*, a poem written down nearly two hundred years later:

> Now lieth in Sweden many an estate,
> though formerly much toiled upon, full desolate;
> As many a great stone wall sheweth,
> whereon the wild wood groweth.

Peder Månsson adds that the devastation was the result of 'black death'. In all their brevity his words vividly evoke the greatest event of the Middle Ages.

'As a plough shall God's wrath pass over Sweden', Saint Bridget had prophesied; all these thousands of people were to die because of the sinful life led by Magnus Eriksson. In the plague's very earliest stages, two of King Magnus' own half-brothers, Knut and Håkan, died of it. Later his son Erik was to die too. St Bridget's Avenging Angel visited both castle and cottage; he entered the dwellings of the rich as well as of the poor. 'Corpse lay upon corpse'. But hundreds of thousands of the victims are nameless. They belonged to the huge class of people who have found no place in history.

For lack of demographic records we can only arrive at approximate figures for the number of Swedes who died from the Black Death. Such estimates have been based on the Peter's Pence. This ecclesiastical tax, however, was levied on households not on individuals, and since we can only guess at the average size of the mediaeval Swedish household, the results are singularly uncertain.

Dr. Adolf Schück, an expert on Swedish social history in the Middle Ages, estimates the population of Sweden within its then limits, *before* the Black Death, at about 650,000 persons. But he has also reached about the same figure for the population at the end of the Middle Ages. In 1520, there seem to have been at least 615,000 and at most 700,000 Swedes. This would mean that the losses from the pandemic were so great that it took a hundred and seventy years to make them good. Another factor inhibiting population growth was the incessant late mediaeval wars and civil wars which, with brief intervals, lasted for more than a hundred years – from the Engelbrekt Rising of 1434 to the Dacke Rising of 1542. Not until the latter and more peaceful part of the reign of Gustav Vasa (1523–1560) did the Swedish population begin to grow. By 1560, according to Hecksher's *An Economic History of Sweden*, it had risen to about 750,000 souls. Even so, the population of that Sweden of four hundred years ago was smaller than that of Skåne today.

We have statements – among others, by Gustav Vasa himself – to the effect that during the Black Death his realm lost two-thirds of its population. Modern research has shown this statement to be exaggerated and fixes the number of dead at between 225,000 and 250,000, or slightly over one-third of the whole population. This estimate, in my view, comes closest to the truth. Yet the fact remains, the Black Death was the greatest catastrophe to afflict Sweden in historical times.

In Norway, proportionately to the population, the 'Manndauen' as we have seen, slew even more victims than it did in Sweden. According to one estimate acceptable to experts, about 175,000 of the total Norwegian population of 400,000 must have perished. How long the effects of the Manslayer's progress continued to be felt can be seen from the land statistics. Even as late as the year 1500, a century and a half later, six thousand Norwegian farms still remained desolate and what had once been their ploughed fields still remained uncultivated.

In the 14th century the Scandinavian countries were sparsely inhabited. Their total populations were extremely small. Magnus Eriksson's two kingdoms, together, measured some 300,000 sq. miles; but before the Black Death only about one million people were living in all this vast area, no more than one inhabitant per 0.38 sq., miles. The plague ship, that day it had drifted into Bergen, had brought death to more than one-third of this insignificant population. It is certainly justifiable to call it the most fateful day in the entire history of Scandinavia.

For mid-14th century Europe as a whole the total population has been estimated at about 100 millions. Plague historians are of the view that during the years 1347–52 the Black Death took about 25 million lives, reducing our continent's population by a quarter. (According to Lewis Mumford, by one-third.) So huge a reduction in the population necessarily affected developments in every aspect of social life. A universal tragedy, it intervened radically in both economic and spiritual life, and even to some extent led to a new view of life altogether. As I shall explain in my next chapter, a change also came about in mediaeval man's attitude to death.

Egon Friedel, a historian of culture, maintains that it was in the year of the Black Death that modern European man was born; and in 1832 J. F. Hecker, a historian of the plague, wrote that the catastrophe 'prepared the present state of Europe'.

We who are now alive, in 1970, will find parallels with our own age's catastrophes. But compared with that percentage of the European population which died in the Black Death the toll of life in the 20th century's two great wars has been small. On the other hand, the sort of nuclear warfare that now seems possible might well destroy as many lives as the plague did in the 14th century. Though they have six centuries between them, the World-Ravager and the Nuclear Bomb are fully comparable threats to mankind.

An American writer Millar Meiss has studied the plague's impact on Italian art (*Painting in Florence and Siena after the Black Death*, 1951). He writes: 'Never before or since has any calamity taken so great proportion of human life', while for the English historian Sir Arthur Bryant the Black Death, as a calamity, seems 'comparable to that which would today follow a nuclear war' (*The Story of England*). Antonin Artaud, a Frenchman, has seen another parallel. In *Le Théâtre et son Double* he has suggested the establishment of a special theatre, in which the plague would serve as an image of our epoch.

The idea seems strikingly apt. In the whole history of mankind I believe there has never been an era which for its feeling of impending disaster and its terror of annihilation shows such analogies with our own as the mid-14th century. In his fear of nuclear war, modern man should have no difficulty in recognizing himself in mediaeval man, especially in his feeling of impotence in the face of events. He, too, went in terror of the utter annihilation of his world.

Petrarch, describing the horrors of his plague-ravaged homeland, calls out to us across six centuries: 'O thou happy posterity!' Had he returned to life for a single day, on August 6, 1945, and seen what happened to Hiroshima – would he have called posterity happy? If it had come to Petrarch's ears that six million human beings were murdered in the 1940's just because they were Jews, and that in the 1930's an even greater number of Russian peasants were exterminated simply because they were peasants; and that on one night, in February 1945, 135,000 people lost their lives in the bombing of Dresden – would he still have envied posterity? Today, in 1972, it is possible to exterminate hundreds of thousands of people much more swiftly than was needed to annihilate the same number in Italy in 1347. In the efficient extermination of human beings our age is far superior to the Middle Ages. In this respect, at least, mankind has made the greatest thinkable progress in six hundred years.

Like 14th-century man, 20th-century man, too, lives in 'an age of great anxiety'. But the object of his fears is quite different. Mediaeval man went in terror of a supernatural almighty invisible power, beyond his control. He feared the wrath of God. Modern man goes in fear of what he can do to himself.

On Mediaeval People

‎〜〜〜〜〜〜〜〜〜〜〜〜〜〜〜〜

MEDIAEVAL SWEDES had but a short time to live. Magnus Eriksson lived to be fifty-eight, and Saint Bridget to be seventy. In reaching so great an age each was an exception. Average life-expectancy has been calculated as 25 years, rather more than one-third of ours today. War, pestilence and famine were three regularly recurrent scourges always threatening any human life. Most people were cut off in childhood. A high percentage of the new-born did not even survive their first year.

Mediaeval man, whose life-span was so pathetically short, is little known to posterity. We possess few biographies of that age's historical personages. Our material for depicting mediaeval lives is scanty. Mostly we are limited to a man's actions and outward circumstances. Of men's inner lives we catch only glimpses and the world of mediaeval people's thoughts and feelings is scarcely accessible to research. As for those documents still extant, which paint the characters of the main figures of that age, they are highly unreliable. To his friends the sitter is a figure of light, to his enemies an imp of darkness.

Within European Christendom, to which Sweden belonged, the peoples lived in a closed world, dominated by the spiritual power of the Church. God and the Devil, *Civitas Dei* and *Civitas Diaboli*, struggle incessantly for the souls of men. There were only two kingdoms, of God and of the Devil; and between them no reconciliation was possible. Man was caught between heaven and hell. When finally he quitted this earthly life he must infallibly spend another and infinite life, either in one place or the other. Either he was destined to eternal bliss or to eternal torment. This made death, in all its irrevocability, a horrible parting of the ways. This fated, inescapable either-or held sway over the life of mediaeval man. Only to those of us 20th-century people who reckon neither with heaven nor with hell is there a third alternative: total annihilation. A state where we shall never again experience suffering.

Mediaeval people do not seem to have reacted very strongly to their lot. On the whole they seem to have submitted to their world-order as something unshakable and to have adapted themselves to it as if it were to last for ever. There were some who thought their earthly existence might have been otherwise than it was; but no one questioned the existence of the Kingdom of God, or the Kingdom of the Devil. No one denied Heaven and Hell. And though earthly joys were certainly granted to a few, everyone else could console themselves with the knowledge that beyond death the heavenly kingdom in all its splendour stood waiting for all Christian men and women. At the heavenly gates they could, at last, expect equality.

The vast majority of people who lived in the Middle Ages passed away in silence, without ever having opened their hearts either to us or to their contemporaries. They were inarticulate. So we cannot even guess what they really thought of the conformist world they lived in. What mediaeval people felt at the back of their minds or in the bottom of their hearts is something we shall never know.

Only exceptional individuals have borne witness to themselves. Some were saints. Others were poets. The saints expose their spiritual life in their revelations. The poets reveal themselves in their works.

Among Swedes, the personality who has achieved the widest and most durable fame in the world was a woman. Not only is Saint Bridget the best-known individual to arise in mediaeval Sweden; her reputation has stood the test of the ages. Six hundred years will soon have passed since her death, but not a year goes by but some ten books are published about her in various languages. Sweden has produced other geniuses – Swedenborg, Linnaeus, Strindberg. But their fame dwindles beside that of St Bridget.

The girl who was to attain to a saint's halo and everlasting glory was born on the farm of Finsta, in Uppland, in 1303. At the moment of her birth a parish priest of the district saw the Virgin Mary sitting on a cloud in the sky with a book in her hand. Today Finsta is the name of a railway halt, a halt so small that passengers on the Roslagen line do not so much as notice it, and few trains even stop there. In fact the whole service has recently been suspended. Beside the station stands a memorial stone to our most famous personality.

Bridget was daughter of one of the wealthiest men in the kingdom, Birger Persson. According to his will, still extant, he owned at his death twenty-two large estates in various parts of the country. He was given a magnificent funeral, costing 275 marks, or more than £1,200 or $3,300 in modern money. Three sorts of wine, red, white French wine and Rhenish, were drunk at the funeral feast. Birger Persson's estate was divided between his three children, and on her father's death Birgitta Birgersdotter (Birgitta Daughter of Birger) became one of the richest women in Sweden.

She had received the best education the age could provide for a young noblewoman. She had learnt everything a woman of her estate should know. At the age of thirteen Birgitta married Ulv Gudmarsson of Ulvåsa, who was eighteen. They spent two years of marriage as brother and sister, and when they thereafter decided to have sexual relations they prayed to God before each intercourse 'that he might have forebearance with the sin they thereby committed, but that he might grant unto them such fruit of their bodies as should ever be ready to serve him', – this according to their daughter Katarina, who had heard it from her mother. At the age of sixteen Birgitta bore her first child. In being granted fruit of their bodies, at least, Ulv and Birgitta's prayers were heard abundantly. In twenty years she bore him eight children, four boys and four girls.

But physical intercourse between husband and wife was only permitted and legitimized by God if its end and goal was the procreation of children. Such pleasure as they might experience in intercourse was sinful, and God had to be asked to pardon it. Bridget does not seem to have sinned excessively in this respect. In one place in her writings – admittedly in the evening of her days – she says: 'The life of the flesh is bitter as venom.'

Bridget bore children to the greater glory of God, to serve him. She burned with love of God, who had once told her he would not willingly be unjust even to the Devil. In all matters she asked heaven's advice. For twenty years she was mistress of Ulvåsa,

F

thereafter serving for a while as mistress of King Magnus' household. Her acts as his adviser and judge have already been described. She called the king a disobedient and unnatural child, and held up to him a *Royal Mirror* containing, like the Laws of Moses, ten commandments, by which he ought to live. She instructed the king as to how he should fast. Each Friday, in emulation of Christ, he was to wash the feet of thirteen poor people and with his own hand give them food and money.

In 1349, Bridget left her fatherland for ever. She went to Rome and there, with brief intervals, lived for the rest of her life. In 1372, the year before her death, she made a pilgrimage to the Holy Sepulchre in Jerusalem. In Rome the investigations into her qualifications as a saint – the so-called canonization trial – went on, with occasional interruptions, from 1378 to 1391. Finally after thirteen years, the girl from Finsta was crowned a saint of the Catholic Church. She became Saint Bridget.

Historically, her destiny was unique. But what, apart from her status as God's chosen representative and mouthpiece, was this remarkable woman like, as a human being? Without a doubt she can be described as one who hungered and thirsted after power and glory. She was one of those people to whom power is everything. This is evident from her attempts to bend King Magnus to her will. Had not Christ himself once told her: 'Thou shalt attain to high respect, not only as my bride, but also as nun and mother at Vadstena'. All things considered, her greatest longing was for honour and worship. And she achieved her ambition. She has been more honoured, more respected, than any other Swede. After her death she has become the object of a cult within Catholic Christianity such as most of her saintly colleagues might well envy her.

The Swedish poet Heidenstam wrote a book about Bridget's pilgrimage and is said to have called her a veritable termagant. But only good can be said of her active and practical achievements in her own country. Birgitta Birgersdotter was no impractical dreamer, lacking in feeling for material reality. Her contemporaries bear witness to her immense ability and capacity for hard work. Never for a moment could she be idle. Always she must have something to do. She must have been a model mistress of her great Ulvåsa estate.

To give alms was a Christian duty, and Bridget gave generous alms to the poor and needy. She visited the sick and cared for them, working like any fearless slum sister today. She waged an energetic war on unchastity and immorality, strongly condemning priests who kept concubines or bought women's bodies for gold. She went about the Stockholm brothels trying to rescue whores from their degradation.

Once, during one of her visits to such a den of vice, something remarkable is said to have occurred. The Devil, as it happened, had chosen the same moment to visit the same brothel and had just got his claws into a woman, who was lying senseless on the floor. Bridget, we are told, took up the Devil's challenge and wrested his prey from his clutches. Panic-stricken, he jumped out of the window. The terror she inspired in the Prince of Darkness gives us some idea, perhaps, of her force of personality.

Bridget was also a great self-tormentor, always doing penance for her sins and fiercely mortifiying the flesh. Around her waist she tied her nun's girdle so tight that it cut great gashes in the flesh. Every Friday evening she would take a burning candle from a crucifix and drip the hot melting wax into her armpits. As soon as the sores began to heal she tore them open again with her fingernails, wishing to bear them perpetually in memory of Christ's wounds. Her hardest penance was fasting. She had always enjoyed good food, and the days and nights of fasting she regularly imposed on herself were a source of grievous suffering. No doubt the hallucinatory states she called her revelations were brought on by hunger induced by these self-imposed fasts.

Medicine acknowledges an intimate relationship between body and soul, between psychic and physical functions. Even while married, Bridget had chastened the flesh in various ways. Whenever her husband was away for a night she would stay awake weeping and praying, scourging her body until it bled. Such self-imposed torments cannot have failed to affect her psyche. Saint Bridget's spiritual reality, we may be sure, was influenced by her tormented and lacerated body.

In her lifetime Bridget experienced some seven hundred revelations. They exist in both Latin and Old Swedish versions, but only two are said to be written down with her own hand. When ecstasy came upon her she dictated her intuitions to a scribe, expressing in her revelations her views on the most varied and heterogeneous questions. And always it is at God's command; always it is a question of His Message of which she herself is only the mouthpiece. A latter-day reader is amazed at God's incessant preoccupation with current affairs in 14th-century Sweden and His intense commitment to the issues of the day. Not even the most trivial occurrences escape the Almighty's eye. He polemicizes on bagatelles. In her revelations, Bridget's enemies have their allotted place. The divine message also contains many purely practical injunctions and items of advice. Thus the plan of Vadstena Monastery, its furnishings and its functions, are drawn up for her down to the last detail by God. The Bridgettine Order had the All-Highest Himself for its architect.

Bridget's *Revelations* have been published in eight volumes, with appendices and commentary. But as to their source and origin, research is divided. In the 1340's, as I have said, they were declared genuine by a committee of experts chaired by the then Archbishop. But at several 15-century ecclesiastical councils sceptics arose, and the divinity or otherwise of her revelations has been a subject of argument in Christendom from that day to this. One Swedish novelist Selma Lagerlöf (1858–1940), who I suppose can only be regarded as a devout Evangelical Lutheran, did not believe in their divine inspiration. She thought they were susceptible to a material explanation. As a non-believer nothing less behoves me than to involve myself in a debate on the source of the *Revelations*. They astound and they captivate. But the enigma of their origin I shall leave respectfully aside.

As for her enemies, so far from killing them off, she made them immortal. In her writings they live for ever.

She belongs of right among the great personalities of Swedish history. The Bridgettine Order and its mother house on the shores of Lake Vättern made Vadstena the spiritual capital of Sweden's late mediaeval culture. Her monastery housed the largest library in Scandinavia. Within its walls innumerable manuscripts, the work of industrious monks, saw the light of day. As a social institution, as a place where the poor, the wretched and the sick were cared for, the monastery's value can hardly be exaggerated.

For a few years in my youth I lived at Vadstena, experiencing the place above all as St Bridget's town where the peaceful atmosphere of the cloister, an unworldly stillness, still lingered on. The saint's memory is remarkably alive. Catholics from all over the world still come to Vadstena on pilgrimages. Bridget died on July 23, 1373. In 1973 her sixth centenary is to be celebrated in the town she has made world-famous. It will be a great and solemn occasion, with participants from all Catholic lands.

Vadstena's prime tourist attraction is its reliquary, where Saint Bridget's bones are still preserved in her monastery church having been brought home from Rome on her own instructions to rest here. In the Middle Ages corpses were boiled down into skeletons for transport, and this was done to Bridget's body before it set out on its homeward journey. Later the saints' bones have obviously known their vicissitudes. During the Reformation, particularly towards the end of the 16th century when Catholicism again gained ground in Sweden, the cult of St Bridget's relics was felt to be inconvenient. Several historians repeat a traditional story, according to which in 1595, Duke Karl, the future King Karl IX, is said to have instructed Archbishop Abraham Angermannus to remove Bridget's bones from the monastery church and bury them in some secret spot. The historian Messenius (1580–1636) asserts that they were buried within the grounds of Vadstena Castle. If this story is true, then they must afterwards have been dug up again and returned to their former resting place.

In 1918, Carl M. Fürst, professor of anatomy at Lund, was commissioned to examine the contents of the Bridgettine reliquary, and the same year published his results in his *Birgitta-Utställningen*. The protocol of his examination takes up some ten ample pages, and describes the condition and probable origin of the relics. Professor Fürst found that the reliquary contained so many skeletal parts of the anatomy that they cannot possibly have all belonged to Bridget. 'The bones . . . may represent seventeen, possibly eighteen individuals!' Of the two skulls found there, the examiner regarded one as being that of Bridget's daughter, the Blessed Catherine. Fürst's most remarkable find in the reliquary was the upper bone of a man's arm, marked in mediaeval script *de Sto Sigfrido*, which he supposes must once have belonged to Saint Sigfrid, the apostle to Småland. Only saint's bones, of course, could have qualified for preservation in a reliquary.

Tradition and legend describe Bridget as small of limb and slight of stature. The professor of anatomy's examination confirms this tradition, at least as far as her stature is concerned. To judge from those bones he regards as authentic, she must have been quite short, between 5' ½" and 5' 1½" tall. Her daughter Catherine, on the other hand, is described by contemporaries as unusually tall; 'she was slim and straight as a lily, and she could reach bunches of grapes and other fruits that hung out over the walls of vineyards in the neighbourhood of Rome'. In his protocol, Fürst notes further that a thigh bone of an older woman, presumably St Bridget, shows marks of a double break which had healed but which had shortened it by 4cm (1½"), thus considerably reducing the leg's mobility, which in turn must have led to a severe limp.

It is not uncommon, of course, for older persons to break their thigh bones; but nowhere are we informed that in her old age the most famous of all Swedish women limped. At the age of sixty-nine Bridget was still active enough to go to the Holy Sepulchre at Jerusalem. Perhaps the solution of the problem lies in a miracle, whereby she escaped all hurt from her broken thigh.

Bones of St Bridget are preserved as relics and holy objects all over the world, and can be found in a number of Catholic churches. The girl from Finsta, the only Scandinavian woman ever to be canonized by the Roman church, is a mediaeval figure who still astounds and fascinates us after six centuries.

Originally poetry too, was regarded as divinely inspired. Its first practitioners were the gods themselves or their priests and interpreters, whose output consisted of incantations and prayers. Only these poets, originally, understood the secrets of runic letters. They enjoyed a monopoly of an art whose sources were magical.

Dead poets tell us about people in the past, and in antiquity the poetic art was highly regarded. In the Homeric Age the poet was a highly respected and venerated personage. 'Among all peoples on this earth, honour and worship are the poet's lot,' we read in the

Odyssey. Distinctions were awarded to poets at Homeric feasts, where the prizes were the fattest slices of roast pork and tastiest dishes, otherwise reserved only for kings. There was certainly sustenance in such grants. In the Viking North too – above all on Iceland – poets seem to have enjoyed superior status. They were much-valued members of the king's courts, and being on their staff did not suffer from material worries. They dined with the court. In the prehistoric North a skald's wages varied from precious ornaments and rings of gold and silver to whole oxen and swine, and at feasts in the king's hall the places of honour were often reserved for the practitioners of the poetic art.

The prehistoric and mediaeval skalds and tragedians were often as much at home in the military art as they were in the poetic, playing their part both on the sanguinary field of battle and in the literary lists, so their heroic epics and glorifications of warlike deeds were based on personal experience. Those 19th-century poets who sang of the supreme beauty of war and praised the happy lot of the warrior who fell in the foremost rank, on the other hand, had not themselves enjoyed the splendours and delights of such butchery. Indeed they were usually exempt from military service. In our own century, which has seen two world wars, the heroic poem, after a slow decline, has finally expired.

For absolute monarchs the court poet was an institution; he stood somewhat higher in rank than the court jester. Kings had great need of poets who would sing their deeds on the battlefield and at the same time praise their government as gentle, good and popular. Naturally they looked down on them – Gustav III (1772–1792) could not bring himself to dine at the same table as his court poet Leopold. But they were only too happy to be immortalized in their works.

The Middle Ages saw a decline in the status of poets. In earlier times, too, there had been a poetic proletariat whose members earned their daily bread as wandering troubadours and enjoyed scant respect. In the eyes of the common people there was hardly any difference between a poet and a tightrope walker. After the 13th century the poetic fraternity found themselves placed outside society altogether. For this we have the incontrovertible evidence of our provincial laws.

There the thralls of poetry were placed among players, a group that included all sorts of jesters, actors, jugglers, fiddlers, pipers and clowns. The poet in mediaeval society usually earned his living by his song. A person of no fixed abode, he wandered about the country's roads going from farm to farm to get food for the day and a roof over his head for the night. His place in the peasant's cottage was on top of the warm oven, where he shared his sleeping quarters with beggars and other homeless persons.

On the juridic status of poets the older Västergötland Law contains special paragraphs, headed *Lekarerätten* – the Player's Law. From it it transpires that the poet was virtually an outlaw. If any strike a player, says the Law of Västergötland (our oldest manuscript), it shall go unavenged and count for nothing. Anyone, that is, could abuse a common player without fear of prosecution. The player is described in this law as a man who went about with his fiddle, rebeck or drum. So most people in this social group must have been musicians, though of course they also sang songs and ditties of their own composition.

A player who had suffered dam or hurt could only obtain restitution in the following manner: he must take an untamed heifer, shave off all the hair on her tail and grease it, after which she is to be beaten with a sharp whip. Then the player is to try to grasp the heifer by her tail. If he succeeds, he may retain the heifer as his own and 'enjoy it as a dog enjoyeth grass'. If, on the other hand, he does not succeed, he shall 'have and put up with' the shame and hurt whereto he has been exposed. This farce, intended to ridicule the plaintiff, was played out inside a special compound, and was undoubtedly much relished by the spectators.

'Let player never ask more justice than a flayed female thrall,' declares the Law of Västergötland, a sentence which speaks volumes on his juridic status in those days. After the abolition of bondage there was an increase in the number of vagrants, people of no fixed abode who wandered about and refused to take regular work from the peasants. Strong laws, it was felt, were needed against this class of the populace, a source of much irritation to peasant society. 'Unquestionably this was why the player enjoyed no respect and was virtually an outlaw'. (Holmbäck – Wessén: *Svenska landskapslagar*).

From mediaeval days down to our own the player – or artist, as we now call him – has had to put up with his ignoble social status. One symptom of this is the fact that he is still not regarded as enjoying full legal rights to his own works, which society, by its denying him the right to intervene in those matters that most closely concern him, expropriates and exploits, a striking instance of how, after many centuries, the mediaeval view of things still survives in our modern society. History lives on in the present.

In the Middle Ages the knight was the chief and most admired of men. Mediaeval songs, ditties, chronicles in verse and prose, almost all poetry, are about the knight. Both poetry and art were dominated by the idea of chivalry, a notion which has its roots in Christianity. Chivalry was the Church's attempt to humanize the warrior, to transform him into a good and noble man who was treading in the footsteps of the Prince of Peace. His sword was to serve the Church. He was to be a Knight of Christ. The first knight was the Archangel Michael, the man-at-arms who in the Apocalypse overcomes the powers of evil personified by the Dragon. St Michael became the patron saint of knighthood. Always he was sculpted or painted in full armour, carrying an immense sword or long lance. He was a most military angel. The crusading knights fought for the Holy Sepulchre at Jerusalem, an angelic choir with the Archangel Michael as the commander-in-chief. Angels in armour, cultivating piety and every other virtue with sword and lance, they were to save the world from evil. And evil – that was the heathen, the infidel, who ruled in the holy city.

The Church showered her blessings lavishly on the order of chivalry. A prayer calling down God's blessing on the knight's weapons has been preserved from the age of the Roman Emperor Otto III. Included in the order of divine service, it no doubt formed part of every mass:

'We pray Thee, Lord, hear our prayers, and with the Majesty of Thy right hand bless this sword, with which Thy servant desireth to be buckled, that it may be a defender of churches, widows, orphans and of all who serve Thee, O God, against the fury of the heathen, and to the terror, dread and trembling of all who resist Thee.'

The knight had sworn a sacred oath to defend the true faith and likewise all weak and defenceless people. As an idea, the ideal of chivalry was a good and noble one. After the capture of Jerusalem the crusading knights put it into practice by killing innumerable defenceless infidel women and children.

The spirit of the Crusades, turning into religious fanaticism, expressed itself in the most horrible ways. Seized with Christian fervour and the most idealistic intent, the crusading knights marched to the Holy Land and there butchered hundreds of thousands of people. The climax of the whole insane enterprise, without counterpart in human history, was the levy of 30,000 French children who, in 1212, were sent out from their homeland to Jerusalem. On their voyage they fell in with pirates, who sold them all into slavery. Only six got home alive. The prelates of the Church had thought up the idea; it set a good example, they thought, to the adults. 'While we sleep they are joyfully on their way,' Pope Innocent III is supposed to have said, 'These children shame us all.' (Henry Treece: *The Crusades.* 1962).

The Pope uttered a great truth; though not perhaps in quite the sense he intended.

Inherent in the notion of chivalry was a measureless ecstatic worship of woman. As they struck at each other with their lances in their tournaments knights would wear their ladies' nightdresses; and then, wounded in the fray, hand them back all bloodied to their owners. Whereafter the women, proud and delighted that men should be shedding their blood for them, would wear them publicly over their normal apparel. Thousands of mediaeval epics, songs and ballads of chivalry spread a poetic shimmer over existence, singing of man's love for woman.

Unfortunately the motif of the chivalrous poem was utterly artificial. It was in no sense based on that natural healthy love which can afford men and women their highest happiness. In a chivalrous poem, woman had no physical existence. She was a supernatural being. In epic and doggerel she is eternally being praised, elevated to an idol, before whom the man humbly bows the knee. But in the real world, outside poetry, his attitude to her was entirely different.

In war, woman was often man's prey. As his partner in marriage and as a member of her own clan she was a mere chattel. A marriage was not decided by the young lovers themselves. It was decided by their families, both among the peasantry and among royalty and the nobility. In other respects, a woman's status varied with her estate and class.

Throughout the ages the Church, whether Catholic or Lutheran, has in high degree determined society's view of woman. The Old Testament saw her as Eve, who had brought sin into the world; and here, it would seem, we have the origin of the male's scorn for the female. The mediaeval church fathers represent her as sin itself: 'Woman is the Devil's gate, the thorn of iniquity, in other words a perilous thing', saith Hieronymus. St Paul had uttered views on her status in the congregation, and has possibly been misinterpreted. But those expressed by Aquinas formulated a practical maxim for men's and women's coexistence. There are, he writes, sundry necessary things, such as food and drink; and among these he also reckons women, whom he regards as 'necessary to the preservation of the race: woman was created to be man's helpmeet, but only in procreation . . . for in all his other works a man hath better help of a man than of a woman.'

Socially, the female sex was only regarded to the extent that man needed to exploit it. As for the chivalrous worship of Woman, it was mere verbiage.

Nowhere in world literature is there a more mendacious sort of poetry than the mediaeval epic of love and chivalry.

We Swedes hardly had any chivalrous poetry of our own, so we had to content ourselves with imitating and translating that of others. At least three famous novels of chivalry exist in Swedish translation. The *Euphemia Songs* got their name from the Norwegian Queen Euphemia, Erik Magnusson's mother-in-law, who is said to have personally instigated the translation of already existing poems on the occasion of her daughter Ingeborg's betrothal to Erik at Oslo, in 1312. In these songs the knight is represented as the incomparable hero of the age, in his gleaming armour galloping with raised lance at tournaments. He is bold, polite, magnanimous, noble-minded, without fear and without reproach; always faithful to his oath. He has promised to defend the weak and the defenceless and to sacrifice his life for them.

These poems were recited at the court of the Folkungs whose reigns coincided in point of time with the great age of chivalry in Sweden. We have already followed this royal clan's achievements and seen how well they abide by their knightly oaths and in what exemplary fashion they practised courtliness, high-mindedness and magnanimity, and how faithfully they kept their oaths.

If one thing is notable by its absence from Swedish history in the age of chivalry, it is chivalry.

As I have said, the *Erik Chronicle*, an epic in doggerel, is the most important Swedish work from this time. Its author pretends to be a historian. He assures us without blinking that what he is going to give us is the precise and incontrovertible truth. 'Here standeth writ that which hath happed', he says, in his introductory stanzas. The author of the *Erik Chronicle's* working principle for historical science was to be repeated, in word and deed, more than five centuries later, by Leopold von Ranke: *Wie es eigentlich gewesen.*

We may assume that the 19th-century historian applied this principle better than his 14th-century forerunner, and that his account is truer. Historians have long drawn deeply on the *Erik Chronicle*, that memorial to Duke Erik which only in recent times has been critically examined as historical source material. Its statements of fact have been found unreliable. Its virtues are mainly literary. In his preface the author gives an admirably concrete picture of the creation of the world. He acclaims the Creator, 'source of all virtue', who has made the world so well that each man in it lives in a state of bliss:

> This wide world hath he so well created,
> forest and lands, hills and vales,
> leaves and grass, water and sand,
> much joy and many a land,
> among them one yclept Sweden
>
> Good warriors find we there,
> chivalry and heroes good,
> that Didrik of Bern did help.
> How lords and princes there have lived,

that will ye find writ in this book.
How they have lived, what done, what acted.
here standeth writ, that which hath happed.

But what we know of these lords' and princes' real deeds agrees
but ill with the *Chronicle*'s glorification of them, and this contradiction pervades the whole work. Artistically it is best in its purely
descriptive passages. Here we meet pithy old Swedish in the hands
of a great artist who writes verse of laconic concreteness. In the
simplest manner in the world he gives us the atmosphere of the Age
of Chivalry; all its brilliance; its joustings; its banquets. Here and
there, even if only in swiftly passing verses, we find ourselves
close to mediaeval people. One famous section of the book is the
scene of the warriors' farewells to their wives as Birger Jarl embarks
for his crusade in Finland. Swedish crusaders are setting out to force
the Finns to accept baptism. The vessels which are to carry them
across the sea are lying ready at the shore. It is a vividly epic scene,
such as only mediaeval Swedish can do justice to:

> . . . *ther tha skuldo skilias vid thera hem*
> *ok vissto ej nar the kommo ater.*
> *Vridna hender ok starker grater*
> *vard tha af mange fruo seder.*
> *Tho gladdos the at Guds heder*
> *skulle meras as then färd.*
> *Mangt et gammalt fädernissvärd*
> *vart tha nider af naglom krängt,*
> *som ther hafde manga daga hängt.*
> *Them vart tha vänlika följt til strand,*
> *hälsados väl ok tokos i hand.*
> *Margin röder mun vart tha kusst,*
> *som aldrig kysstes sidan af hiärtans lust*
> *thy at the sagos summi aldrig mer.**

The description of their farewells rises to a moving climax: 'never
more!' The wife bids farewell to her man, who is going to the wars in

---

* There they must part from their homes, nor knew when they should return.
Many a wife then wrung her hands and wept bitterly, albeit they rejoiced that
Gods honour by this voyage should be augmented. Many an old ancestral sword
was then jerked off its nail, where it had hung for many a day. And they followed
them in friendship to the shore, took fond leave of them and shook their hands.
Many a red mouth there was kissed, which never more of heart's lust was kissed
again, for some never saw one another more.

lands the other side of the sea, never to return – a situation all too commonplace in Swedish life down the ages. How many soldiers' wives have not had to go through it? Gustavus Adolfus and Karl X Gustav, too, set out with great armies for the Baltic countries, Poland and Germany. And each time, as the armies grew, so did the numbers of women left behind. In 1700 Charles XII left Sweden with his army of conscripts. After twenty years only the wreckage returned. How many cottagers did not bid a lifelong farewell to their wives that time? Yet, crucial though they were to so many people, I have found no contemporary account of such occasions – and this is why I stress this passage in the *Erik Chronicle*.

The author only devotes a couple of lines to what the women felt about it. But it is enough. He cannot himself have witnessed that weeping and wringing of hands as they bade adieu to their husbands, for at that time he was still unborn. Yet Birger Jarl's crusade lay no further back in time than that people could still be heard talking about it. We also get the Christian's view of the crusade. Two lines, like a flash of lightning, illumine it. Though the women fear they may never see their men again, they console themselves with the thought that 'God's honour' will be increased by the lives sacrificed in the campaign – an eloquent index of the power wielded by the Church over people's minds in the Middle Ages.

The Swedes were victorious over the heathen Tavasts.

The *Erik Chronicle* relates:

> The heathen lost, the Christians won.
> All who wished them well
> and he who baptised would be,
> him they left both life and goods
> and peace without strife, therein to live.
> But him that had none lust thereto,
> him did they to death let go . . .

Few words; but enough to describe two centuries of Swedish missionary work in Finland.

The author of the *Erik Chronicle* has left no other trace of himself than his work. Even his name is unknown. In his book on 'the nameless poet', Ingvar Andersson, after studying his work for forty years, concludes that all attempts to reveal his identity 'can be no more than a game'. Much, he says, suggests that the chronicle was written some time in the 1320's, during Magnus Eriksson's minority. To judge by the poet's familiarity with life in the highest circles, he must himself have belonged to them. Probably he belonged to the entourage of Matts Kettilmundsson, the Earl Marshal and the most powerful man in the realm at that time.

Obviously the poet was a man who had received the highest education available in his time and place. He introduced the doggerel as a poetic genre into Sweden. He can be described as our first literary modernist. It is unlikely he was a churchman – his piety is altogether too conventional – but he seems to have been deeply read in law. There is a touch of Västergötland dialect about his mediaeval Swedish, so possibly that was where he came from.

Why did the author of the *Erik Chronicle* choose to hide himself behind anonymity? Very likely for political reasons. Duke Erik's faction, it is true, were in power at the probable date of writing, and the Duke's son sat on the throne. But in mediaeval Sweden régimes came and went so quickly that new men might come into power at any moment who disapproved of the poem's political gist. Then things might have turned out badly for its author. If it was his intention to hide his name from posterity, then he has certainly succeeded.

Half a century earlier than this nameless poet there had lived a Dominican monk, by name Petrus de Dacia. He has been called Sweden's first author. His autobiography is a classic of the mediaeval mysticism predominant in his own order. In its inwardness of feeling Petrus de Dacia's account of his passionate other-worldly love for a nun, Kristina of Stumbeln, makes moving reading. As a love lyric it is in quite another class from the lays of chivalry.

But on the whole the Swedish literature of that age can only be called meagre. The Swedes were not notable as wielders of the pen. The mediaeval knight was no man of letters; mostly he was trained to use his weapons. Few men, and they mostly clerics, mastered even the elements of reading and writing. Culture was the domain of the Church. In the monastery schools priests and monks were educated to read, write, speak Latin and do arithmetic. And among the nobility, the privileged and worldly class, even among the leading members of the government and within the council, there were many illiterates. A document dating from the 1470's and the government of Sten Sture the Older bears eloquent witness to this state of affairs. It refers to a state document which had been presented to the Lords of the Council for their signatures, and whose correctness had also been attested to by those councillors 'who could read'. Unfortunately, our source does not tell us how many of the Council of State 'could read' or whether they were in the majority or a minority; so we cannot assess the Council's level of education as a whole. But the fact remains: even in the Late Middle Ages some of the men who governed Sweden were illiterates.

What did mediaeval people read – when they did read? Only kings and a few magnates owned private libraries. An extant list of Magnus Eriksson's library reveals the many-sidedness of its owner's literary interests. Among his books were volumes on many subjects, not only Bibles and law books, but also poems and collections of poetry. Really large libraries, however, were only found in monasteries and cathedrals. The books there, although available to any who might wish to read them, might not be taken home, and were chained to shelves or lecterns against theft. As we have seen, the largest library in the land was at Vadstena Monastery, which is estimated to have comprised some 1500 volumes. Five hundred of its mediaeval manuscripts, rescued from Gustav Vasa's Reformation – which otherwise did irreparable damage to the monastery libraries' irreplaceable treasures – are now in Uppsala University Library. The libraries of Alvastra, Nydala and Sigtuna were all vandalized and destroyed.

Since mediaeval books could only be multiplied by transcribing them by hand on expensive parchment, they were costly to produce. In ancient Rome labour had been cheap; slaves did the transcribing, and brought down the price of books for the Romans. This was not so in the 10th century. Then the Countess of Anjou had to pay 200 sheep, 3 barrels of corn and several marten skins for a book of sermons; while, in the 14th century, the Prince of Orleans bought a two-volume prayer book for 200 gold francs, a huge sum of money in the currency of that time.

Discovered in the late Middle Ages, the art of printing books spread only slowly, and, until the new age had dawned, was of little importance. Gutenberg's invention was brought to Sweden by

printers who had immigrated from Lübeck, and Stockholm got its
first printing works in the 1480's. This did not lead to any revolution
in the country's cultural life. Even at the beginning of the 16th
century only some ten books had so far been printed in Sweden.

To the great mass of the common people a book was still a meaningless object. To understand written or printed *words* was still
utterly beyond them. It profited them nothing. For such illiterate
people the *image*, on the other hand, was so much the more meaningful. Instead of books, they enjoyed pictorial art. A major element in
their religion, it still survives in our old mediaeval churches. Men
bent the knee reverently before paintings and sculptures of the persons of the divinity, of the Virgin Mary and the saints. Some of these
brought answers to prayer. If only one's prayer was long and earnest
enough, one could be sure of being heard by God.

The popular imagination was nourished and sated with images,
symbols and allegories. Mediaeval man's cult of the image is an
enormous subject; it would fill several volumes of printed words.

The common people – peasants, servants, vagrants – probably made
up ninety-five per cent of the mediaeval population of Sweden.
Their tongues were tied. Neither to their contemporaries nor to posterity could they declare themselves; so we have scarcely any idea at
all how they experienced their daily lives, what they thought or felt.
Their outward circumstances were regulated by the provincial laws,
and will be discussed in connection with the texts of those laws – but
how, we wonder, did the individual view these rules of life? No
peasant or daily labourer kept a diary, or caused his thoughts to be
written down. So we lack all knowledge of how people reacted to their
circumstances.

For the man who tilled the soil, the world had strict geographical
limits. For a peasant or his servants to leave their farms or village
was rare indeed, and, their range of vision must have been extremely
constricted. But the farm was the family's abiding place and could
not be sold. At home, in one's own village, one was safe. But 'foreign
parts' were always dangerous and insecure.

The peasant was self-supporting. From his farm he obtained all
he needed, except for one indispensable commodity: salt. Salt was

always a great problem. Otherwise, the freeborn peasant, feeding his family, his wife, his children and his servants on his own land, was utterly independent of the outside world, and no doubt would have lived in perfect contentment, if only the outside world had left him in peace. Unfortunately the outside world needed him. It needed his grain, his meat, his pork, his butter, his wool, his flax and his leather. Upon him, the man who supported the whole social edifice on his shoulders, its one indispensable member, society imposed its heaviest demands. The tillers of the soil formed the base of the social pyramid; without them it would have collapsed. The peasant and his labourers had but one historic role: to work and be taxed.

The peasant did not move about. He stayed where he was born, living out his whole life from birth to death within the same walls of trimmed pine logs and under the same turf roof. This immobile state of affairs in peasant society persisted in Sweden right up to the mid-19th century and the beginning of the machine age. As a factor in our history, our peasant culture was a source of strength, fixed and inexhaustible. From it flowed 'great calm, patience and tolerance to bear grief, sickness, hunger and death'. This peasant immobility has survived, in places, even in our own time. My own mother, for instance, left this world after a long life spent in the same place where she had entered it. She was born in 1864, on a little peasant holding where she died in 1960, ninety-six years later. Her fate is not likely to be much emulated in the future.

Our peasant forefathers were plagued by the passage of fighting men; by lords who extorted 'hospitality'; by epidemics; by crop-failure; by years of famine. But they could never have survived these things had there not also been intermittent periods of peace, health and good harvests. Our ancestors' lot was a heavy one. But they endured it. And, even if not the same as ours, they had their great sources of happiness, their simple joys, natural and unaffected. Our ancestors were at one with Nature, spontaneously experiencing all that went on around them. Their senses were not enervated, nor were they dulled by that superfluity which brings death to pleasure.

To us life in peasant society, in all its monotony and eternal repetitiveness, seems to have been deadly dull. Yet it had an excitement, a sort of ever-changing quality, which we can only imagine with difficulty. The cycle of the seasons gave a definite rhythm to the peasant's year. Each season brought its own tasks: its feast days, its holidays. Workdays were many – so they enjoyed their days of rest the more heartily. Events which to us seem trivial were to our forefathers crucial. As for their mental world, it was largely magical. It endowed Nature with a soul. Water, springs, lakes, trees, stones – these were not just inanimate objects. In legends and tales, myths and fairy stories, by which the peasant enriched his daily life, they came to life. Magical happenings made meaningful the commonplace, lent it variety.

Every natural event, every seasonal change, was eagerly awaited by the farm people: the sprouting of the first grass, mowing, haymaking; the burgeoning leaf; the bird building her nest in a tree, laying her eggs at the appointed time and hatching her fledglings, the fish, too, spawning in lake or river at his appointed time – everything was forever repeating and coming back. All was at once fascinating and strange. Signs and marvels in Nature were welcomed as evidence of a world that could never be shaken out of its courses. The people of the soil lived in a world eternal and unchanging.

His life amid nature, in God's creation, opened the peasant's mind to the supernatural. To the very marrow of his being he was religious. Whatever his faith, whether heathen or Christian, he believed it with all his soul, with all his heart, with all his mind. He believed in miracles – and why not? Could not the whole of Creation, all that was happening round him every day, be regarded as one big miracle? His own hands scattered the seed-corn in the soil: they sprouted, became stalk and ear, and the ear became loaves of bread on his table. What was this, if not a miracle of God? In his religion he found security; and by promising him paradise it consoled him for death.

Mediaeval people ordered their lives according to the injunctions of the Church. They relied wholly on their spiritual pastors. Against such a background of a universal unshakeable piety the case of one peasant, burnt for not believing in the Sacrament, is striking indeed. We find it in the sources. And can read the judgment passed upon him.

It happened in 1311. A peasant by name Botolf, from Ostby in

Gottröra parish in Uppland, denied the presence of Christ in the Sacrament. When the priest offered him the host, he declared that it could not be the true body of Christ – if it had been, the priest would long ago have consumed him: 'For his part, although in other respects he was ready to serve the Church, he would have no part in eating of the body of Christ. He regarded it as evil to eat of another person's body. How much worse, then, to eat of God's?'

Botolf was examined by the archbishop, who commanded him to withdraw his denial. If he refused, he would be burnt at the stake as a heretic. Botolf refused. He said: 'The fire will soon burn out'. And on Shrove Tuesday, 1311, the Archbishop of Uppsala, Nils Kettilsson, condemned Botolf of Östby as a heretic, calling him 'this limb of Satan'. Whereupon he was handed over by the Church to the temporal authority, who carried out the sentence of death by having him burnt.

The examination of this martyr who died in the fire for his faith in 1311 is not wholly dissimilar to a much later case, from 1884. It was in that year that Strindberg was prosecuted for blasphemy for his book *Married*, in which he had made mock of Lettström's maize tablets, sold for 1 krona a pound, and Högstedt's Piccadon, 65 öre the can, alleged by the clergyman to be Jesus' very flesh and blood. Like Botolf, five hundred and seventy-three years earlier, Strindberg had denied the presence of Christ in the Sacrament. But Strindberg was acquitted.

In 1412, a peasant by name Hemming appeared in Bridget's monastic diocese of Vadstena. 'A simple-minded man', he preached certain heresies contradicting the faith of the Church and the rules of the Bridgettine Order. He alleged that he had been sent by the Virgin Mary to set to rights Bridget's erroneous views. Examined by the Bishop of Linköping, Hemming was thrown into prison, where he was left to starve until he withdrew his allegations. After which he was condemned to walk in procession with the clergy and common people round the cathedral of that city, the upper part of his body bare, and carrying a faggot of firewood on his back. The firewood was a reminder. If he relapsed into his heresy, he would be burnt at the stake.

But in the Sweden of their day heretics and sceptics like the peasants Botolf and Hemming were exceptions. Of the peasantry of the realm we can only say that to Church and clergy they were faithful, obedient and submissive.

Mediaeval people lived out their lives without book or newspaper; without electric light or even a parafin lamp; without telegraph or telephone; without films or plays; without radio or television; without railways, cars or buses. They lacked everything that we today regard as indispensable. In Sweden, furthermore, they lived in a sparsely populated country, from which for half a year the sun was largely absent and where solitude and darkness prevailed.

Man's joy is in man. For human communion people turned to the family, to the clan and village community. From solitude, darkness and cold the farm folk turned for warmth and light to the great open fireplace. It was here they spent the dark winter evenings. The hearth was the centre of the home. Both literally and metaphorically it was the source of light and warmth. From the nearby forest the peasant could get as much firewood as he wanted; when the fire began to die down, all he had to do was throw on more logs. The family and its servants gathered round the fireplace. It was our ancestor's book, their newspaper, their theatre and cinema, their radio and television, all in one.

Their gatherings were both useful and enjoyable. All sorts of activities went on; the hand's cunning – today vanished – was put to good uses by one and all. While father was making his wooden tools or a handle for his axe, mending his nets or whittling down heart of pine into tapers, mother sat at her spinning wheel and span linen thread from the year's flax. Meanwhile the household's daughters and servants would be carding wool, tramping the spinning wheel or swinging the reel. And closest to the fire, with their feet on the hearthslabs – for their old limbs are feeling the cold – sit grandmother and grandfather, both paternal and maternal. These old people may no longer have the use of their hands, but their tongues still perform a vital function. By telling tales they give pleasure and entertainment. They are the residuaries of something altogether irreplaceable: *memories*. Through them, and only through them, can the past of the race, its history, live on.

While the knife whittled, the spinning wheel hummed and the carders scraped and rasped, the oldest people on the farm would tell of the time that had been, before that which now was; of all that once had happened and would never happen again. They spoke of the strangest things; of trolls in the forest and giants in the hills; of water sprites in the streams; of elves under the barn floor; of all those magical things which happened in Nature – for him who had eyes to see. Through the old people's tales the younger could re-experience deeds performed by members of the family in time past. The old people also conjured up the dead who had walked, and the little circle of the living around the fire merged with ghosts and apparitions; they spoke of people who had died or had had spells cast upon them after seeing ghosts; and of those who after death had known no rest.

All the spirits of Nature joined that little circle of people round the fire, where legend and saga were kept alive as the logs crackled and flung their sparks out into the cottage. The fire itself was a living being, derived from the sun, mankind's primordial servant: provider of fire for heating, for light, for cooking, for signalling, for purification, for the camp fire. The old people repeated everything folk down the ages had heard and in their imagination transmuted into legends; stories which never came to an end, and which had been passed down verbally through countless generations. In the corner of the little cottage, scared and excited, sat the children, shivering with fright at the tales they so thoroughly enjoyed. What they are hearing just now will fix itself for ever in their memory. One day they too, will pass it on to their children; to new generations.

In each peasant home one corner was sacred. It spoke of another world than this. In that corner stood the image of God's mother, the Virgin Mary, the gentle and merciful maiden and mother, carved in wood by some local artist. A light burned before her, night and day. Morning and evening all who were of the household knelt before the Virgin and prayed to her in her wooden guise. And she passed their prayers on to her Son. It was through her intercession that their prayers would be heard and granted.

The following lovely vespers to Mary, dating from Catholic times, were recorded in 1864 in the parish of Moheda, in Värend:

Jungfru Maria, hon satt och sang.
Hon hade en bok uti sin hand.
Hon hade Jesum på sitt knä.
Gud bevare folk och fä!
Gud bevare qvinna och man!
Gud bevare eld och vann!
Gud låte icke döden för dörrarna stå
Gud låte icke synden in husen gå!
Denna lilla bön vilje vi sjunga
tre gånger, förr än vi gå till sänga,
så följa oss alla Guds änglar.
Två till hand och två till fot.
Två till varje ledamot.
Två mig söfva. Två mig väcka.
Två mig föra till Guds paradis
Och mina synder öfvertäcka.
Amen.

The Virgin Mary, she sat and sang.
She had a book in her hand.
And Jesus she held on her knee.
God preserve both men and beast!
God preserve both man and woman!
God preserve both fire and water!
God, let not death stand at our door!
God, let not sin walk in our house!
This little prayer we thrice would sing,
three times before we go to our beds,
that all God's angels with us may go.
Two for my hand and two for my foot.
Two for my every limb.
Two send me to sleep. Two me awake.
Two lead me to God's paradise
and cover up all my sins.
Amen.

The cottagers prayed this prayer, and slept soundly. They knew their place, their unchangeable destiny in the divine order of things. And none of the tribulations and hardships of this fleeting earthly life were of any importance – only what should happen to them in another. God's mother had their fate in her hand; and the candle-flame over there in the corner burned on at her foot through weekdays and holy days, shining on mankind's days and nights, through that great darkness which we call mediaeval.

Modern man finds his ancestors' circumstances intolerable. They had almost none of those things we so rejoice in. We could not have stood their life. But really all such parallels between past and present are invidious. Instead of the things they lacked, mediaeval people had others, which we have lost. We are in a position to compare our better lot with theirs, which was so much worse, and to pity them; but they could not compare their harder circumstances with ours, which are so much better, and envy us. No one can feel the lack of that which he has never known. Our ancestors' life was the only sort they knew; the only possible life. And since the degree of joy which people can feel in environments so different as those of the Middle Ages and the 20th century can in no wise be measured, all comparisons must remain null.

Nor can a people who are unable to write leave any written testimony to their lives. Those mediaeval poems which are called 'folk' art and 'folk' poetry have been attributed to the upper classes, to the educated. Concerning the so-called 'folksongs' from this time, Strindberg writes in his *Svenska Folket*:

'The song of the dove on the lily was not composed by some wretched peasant labourer behind his plough, nor was it composed in his spare time, for then he was asleep; but most certainly by some mediaeval cleric, a highly educated Catholic. *'Liten Karin'** is no peasant maid employed in the young king's house, but the Sicilian martyr Catherine, who long ago had died a martyr's death on the wheel. Nor is the song about Engelbrekt** written by some wood-chopper from Dalarna, but by a Bishop of Strängnäs.'

This account of the matter – in these particular instances – is correct. But there are many others where it is not. Research has revealed the existence during the Middle Ages of a genuine popular poetry, written down at some later date. There were folk-skalds, whose songs and ditties were widely sung. They did monotonous

---

* A Swedish mediaeval folk-song about Little Karin who rejected a king's improper approaches and was finally nailed up in a barrel.

** Swedish rebel and popular hero of the 15th century.

jobs, indoors or outdoors, and it was to make the working day pass more quickly and to flee from their own dreary reality that they made up their songs. Time hung especially heavy on the hands of the shepherd and of boys and girls set to watch the cattle; so they made up words and melodies, accompanying them on their primitive instruments, goat horns and horns of birch bark. Even the heavily burdened manual labourers took time off, played and sang, played and danced.

But a long time was to pass before the tillers of the soil in this land of peasants found a voice of their own in poetry, without the assistance of the upper classes. Even as late as the mid-19th century it was regarded as shocking for a peasant to appear in a novel except as a secondary figure. When Emilie Flygare-Carlén (1807–1892) was about to start work on her *The Rose of Thistle Isle* and told her publisher she had chosen a fisherman's family as her new novel's main characters, her publisher firmly advised her against so daring a plan. In literature 'lesser folk'* could only appear as secondary figures. But the authoress was not to be dissuaded. She became a pioneer.

Even the 20th century was well advanced before peasants, servants, outcroppers, and labourers came to be intimately described by authors of their own kith and by writers who had known such people personally and experienced their circumstances.

One thing we do know about our forefathers. On festive occasions, at feasts and on red letter days, they were immeasurably given to eating and drinking. This custom – or vice – persisted unchanged down the centuries, as any number of reliable witnesses from prehistoric times, from the Middle Ages and from later times all agree. The degree of excess varied with their material circumstances; but the desire to exploit such an opportunity to the full was exactly the same, at all levels of the population. Even in prehistoric times stern warnings had been issued against excess. Later they were to be repeated in various forms, all clearly to no avail.

'Worse fare for the road none chooseth than excess of ale,' saith the Havamal, that source of wise advice to heathen man, how he should daily comport himself. For Christianity excessive indulgence

* In Swedish the expression is '*sämre folk*' 'worse folk'.

in food and drink is a form of idolatry. It makes a man's belly his god. To the Catholic Church, gluttony was gross sin; even one of the Seven Deadly Sins. And Luther, too, listing sins in his catechism, puts gluttony drunkenness and (and not by mere chance, either) above fornication.

But for the peasantry and their servants there was little opportunity for such excesses. Chiefly it arose at the great annual holidays, above all at Christmas, at harvest time, weddings and funerals. Then the tubs of pork were emptied and the barrels of ale were drained, and the guests ate and, above all, drank more than they could stand. Their behaviour is explicable, even natural. After a hundred days of semi-starvation on short and hard rations came a feast-day; so rare an occasion had to be exploited to the utmost. Each man filled his belly to bursting-point and drank himself silly. But after its long mortification his body took a rest.

For the great mass of the people, days on short rations were many; days of superfluity few. But there were also the wealthy, who could daily gorge themselves, and get drunk if thereto inclined. Such orgies of food and drink certainly shortened the lives of the upper classes who dug themselves premature graves with their teeth. If malnutrition was all too common a cause of death among the poor, over-eating was its counterpart among the rich.

Extant menus tell us what was eaten in the Middle Ages at official banquets. On May 1, 1462, the Council in Stockholm gave a Walpurgis Eve dinner for some fifty eminent guests, whom the city delighted to honour. It was a representative gathering, and the main course was a whole roast ox. Large though this beast may have been, he was but a little fraction of the dinner as a whole. The Council also regaled its guests with roast mutton, roast deer, roast hare, hams, pies, tongues, sausages, boiled chicken, wildfowl, eel, salmon and pike – an array of dishes by no means unique in the Middle Ages. All this mass of food was washed down with 1,500 pints of beer, or an average of 30 pints or 45 of our modern bottles per head. The guests at such a feast must have left it in very high spirits.

Yet this mediaeval Walpurgis Eve feast in Stockholm seems simple, almost Spartan, besides a banquet given to visiting royalty ten years earlier, in 1452, by the French city of Lille. On that occasion the menu, still preserved, lists 192 dishes. The list of entremets, alone, bears witness to a gifted imagination. Besides cheese, which was *de rigueur*, there were pastries as tall as a two-storey house, and to round it all off, a vast iced *bombe* was placed on the table, out of which stepped a lovely nude girl. A dessert to climax a feast!

Naturally mediaeval Sweden could not offer so refined a cuisine. Compared to Renaissance France, Sweden was a barbarous land. To us our ancestors' festive gatherings may often seem crude affairs, lacking in all finesse. At the feasts and gatherings of the peasantry, quarrels were all too frequent, people lost their tempers, became violent and when all the tankards had been drained and the ale had gone to their heads, fists began to fly. At such a feast manslaughter was no rare occurrence.

Generally speaking, mead was the alcoholic drink in prehistoric times and ale, its heir, in the Middle Ages. In mead, honey was the prime ingredient – the Swedish word *mjöd* is the equivalent of 'honey' in other tongues. King Fjolner, who drowned in his tub of mead, was translated and became a god. By absorbing the king's soul the drink deified his spirit; for mead was a drink for the gods, endowing any who drained the horn with its magic power. Its alcohol content was much higher than that of modern beer. As far as we can judge, it must have been strongly intoxicating.

The ale, or, as we pronounce it in Swedish '*öl*', which supplanted mead, was probably weaker. As long as they could get hold of it, it was what the peasantry drank at table, and more of a necessity than a luxury. It was brewed from corn, dried in the open air or in an oven: 'black-malted corn its core', as the poet Karlfeldt says. An essential component of ale was the hop, cultivated by the peasants among the fruits and spices on their farms, but which also in places grew wild on cairns and stone walls.

After six hundred years in his grave there is one mediaeval Swede who has come back to us: Bocksten Man.

His tale begins as an exciting detective story, of the most classic sort. One day in June, 1936, a farmer at Bocksten, in the parish of Rolfstorp in Halland, was out harrowing his peatland when he made an exceptional find. Each year he had been taking up the topmost layer of white moss – sphagnum – for peat litter, with the result that in the course of time the surface had sunk by nearly three feet. As he was preparing his peat that day, something struck in his harrow, causing it to jam. The farmer assumed it must be a clump of heather; but on closer inspection discovered a human head. It had reddish brown hair and an almost black cranium, on which could still be distinguished the remains of skin and a beard. A human body, dressed in a garment of some antique material half rotted away, belonged to the detached head.

Naturally, the farmer thought he had come across a murder, the murderer having buried his victim in his peat-bog. He reported his find immediately to the chief constable of the district, who hastened to the spot with a doctor. But the chief constable and the doctor soon decided that this was no case for the police. A crime had unquestionably been committed; but a crime long since proscribed. The Statute of Limitation applies to murder, in Sweden, after 25 years, but six centuries had gone by since this murder had been committed.

Above all it was the way the corpse had been treated that put the crime so far back in time. Three stakes had been driven through the dead man's body. Two pointed slender birch trunks had gone straight through the loins, and a sturdy oaken stake, obviously fashioned from a plank, had been thrust through the heart. The dead man had been lying prone in his grave when the churning spikes of the farmer's harrow had brought the head to the light of day. What had come to light after all this time was a case of the immemorial custom of affixing a dead man so firmly into the earth that his spirit could not walk abroad. A modern murderer would have been content to bury his victim. It would never have occurred to him to stake down his corpse.

So the head of the local police passed the mystery on to historical science, in the person of Albert Sandklef, the director of Varberg Museum, for its solution. And it is thanks to him that Bocksten Man, risen from the dead, is to be seen in Varberg Museum, clad in every stitch of the 14th-century clothing he was wearing when he met his fate.

Who, in his own lifetime, was Bocksten Man?

Because of the specific quality of the peat where he was buried, both man and clothing had been remarkably preserved through the centuries. Not only the corpse itself, but every object found round about it have been thoroughly examined by experts in each field, until what we have today is a well-documented, reliable picture of one medieval human being, who is considered to have lived in the mid-14th century.

Probably he died from a blow with a weapon, which struck him on his left temple. He had splendid, well-preserved teeth, from which dental science deduces that he must have been about 35 years of age when he fell in with his murderer or murderers. In stature he was about six feet, almost to the inch, considerably taller, that is, than the average for his Swedish contemporaries. Like other peoples, the Swedes have grown taller with the passing of time. The dead man had been wearing a long coat or cape of a sort only worn by persons of social standing; peasants never wore such garments. 'It is the only complete mediaeval costume in the world' (Sandklef: *Bocksten Man*, 1943).

The rest of his attire consisted of hose (the garments worn on the legs), a frock, a cloak, a hood with a liripipe, and a belt, into which had been affixed two daggers; also puttee-like bandages round the calves. The dead man wore no underclothes: neither in the upper classes nor amongst the peasantry were underclothes worn until very much later – even as late as the 19th century peasant women in Dalarna went naked under their skirts. After comparing these garments with other finds of medieval clothing, experts on historical costume have concluded that his apparel dates from about 1360.

So much for Bocksten Man's dating and social status. The circumstances surrounding his death and the motives for the murder committed are less easy to determine.

The solution to the problem is believed to lie in an old folk legend from the place where the victim was found. Briefly, it runs as follows: In those days Halland was Swedish. But the Swedes were at war with the Danes, and officials were going about in the village recruiting the peasants and raising them against the enemy. But the peasants were unwilling to go to war, and killed the recruiting officer and buried him in a peat bog. Whereupon his spirit began to walk in the neighbourhood of his grave. Dogs, too, gathered and howled persistently all night long. So the peasants took up his corpse and pierced it with stakes. Whereupon the visitations ceased. All this, it is said, happened on a peat bog within the village confines.

Historically, it is quite correct that Halland, in the year 1360, was a theatre of war. Valdemar Atterdag was trying to recover the province for Denmark. In such a situation, it seems only natural that the Swedes should have tried to raise the peasantry against the Danish king's soldiers. But in the border provinces the peasantry were anything but nationalistically minded. It was not long since the men of Halland had themselves been Danes and their new-found affections for Sweden went no deeper, as yet, and to take up arms against their former compatriots went very much against the grain. It is by no means improbable that the peasants' opposition to their new masters may have led to the assassination of a Swedish lord who had come among them to drive them to the war.

The folk tale is at very least worthy of consideration as a putative explanation of the fate of Bocksten Man. Over and over again, old legends have been shown to be based on historically demonstrable events and been confirmed by archaeologists' diggings. In a study from 1921 Birger Nerman adduces numerous examples of popular traditions which have found archaeological confirmation. One notable instance is the discovery of a great new Norwegian gravefield at Meldalen in Søndertrøndelag. A plot of land in that valley has been famous for centuries as an abode of ghosts. For the locals, indeed, the spot was so fraught with terror that they dared not go past it at night. When, at last, diggings began there, a remarkable find was made: a prehistoric gravefield where more than a hundred people lay buried.

The stakes driven through the body of Bocksten Man speak to us of our forefathers' superstition and their fear of the power of the dead. From the remote past they had inherited a conviction that death is no complete divorce between soul and body. To die was called to *tryta* – literally, to 'run out', i.e., the thread of a man's life had run out – but they believed that the 'spirit' – the 'life itself', as they put it – continued to exist after the dead man had given up the ghost and his life-thread had come to an end. Therefore, a dead man could very well rise from his grave and wander about the earth as before. Of course, he could not appear in the same tangible, fleshly form as before, he was reduced to a shadow or wraith, transformed into an incorporeal ghost, a phantom.

Notions of the dead returning lived on long amongst the Swedish peasantry. My own grandmother was a firm believer in ghosts walking. Just before she died at the age of 80 she declared she had seen her husband, then dead for 35 years, standing out in the yard, clad in his winding sheet. He was 'calling her out.'

Life's end, the unfathomable mystery, never ceased to preoccupy our forefathers' imagination. They were deeply afraid of the dead, of ghosts. Dead spirits could harm the living, do them frightful damage. But there was one way to protect oneself from them: nail them down in their graves, fix them to the earth. And still to this very day we call a funeral – in Swedish – a *jordfästning* (i.e. *jord* = earth, *fästning* = fastening). But in those days the word was meant literally. The man or men who slew Bocksten Man believed the stakes they drove through his body would keep him in his grave. Nor was it mere chance that a peat bog was chosen for his burial place. As Sandklef points out in his book, he had many brothers in adversity. To lay the corpses of executed or murdered persons in peat bogs and stake them down is a custom known among Germanic peoples for 2,000 years. The fear of the living for the dead is immemorial.

But in this case even three stakes through the corpse were not enough to prevent a *nermanad* (i.e. *ner* = down, *mana* = admonish) human being from walking again. After 600 years in his peat grave a 14th-century Swede has come back, shown us the wounds left on him by his murderers and borne witness to his own death. Clad in the only mediaeval costume in the world, Bocksten Man stands in Varberg Museum. But his spirit no longer terrifies us.

Like our own age, the Middle Ages were an era of violence. Disputes, even within the country, were resolved by the sword, and disagreements among the mighty were decided on the block. This way of settling matters was not unknown among the peasantry: 'Mine axe shall decide the quarrel betwixt us'. He who could not obtain his just rights – or what he regarded as just – in any other way, resorted to violence as an irrefutable argument, while those in power for the most part thought no other proof necessary to substantiate their claims.

A human life was little worth. Here the Middle Ages held much the same view as our own. In a normal year 1,300 lives are sacrificed on our Swedish roads. But in another respect, in his attitude to and behaviour in face of death, mediaeval man, had a certain greatness. As far as possible twentieth-century man avoids the knowledge that he must die. But for mediaeval man death was always close at hand, an ever-present reality. Above all this was true in the later Middle Ages, after the Black Death.

In the *Erik Chronicle*, written before people had been through that shattering experience, death is only a personage hastily glimpsed in passing. The sheer joy of narration preponderates in this work, whose author is enchanted by all the brilliant colours of a knightly existence. To him it is all one long feast and spectacle. Death, accepted as self-evident, is almost always excluded from the actual course of events. Since it is inevitable, why waste words on it? 'Man dieth, though he willeth it not,' – and there's nothing can be done about that. The chronicler is a fatalist; and only a fatalist can enjoy the passing moment. Once or twice the poet of the *Erik Chronicle* dwells reluctantly for a moment or so on 'death's torment', and declares cryptically 'Death he is not sweet.'

But from the mid-14th century onward poetry and art take on a darker tone – and this is the Black Death's doing. After the five years of its dread passage, when Europe had been a charnel house, authors, painters and sculptors gave vent to people's obsessive fear of mortality in their poems, paintings and images. Inspired by the great sickness, they found innumerable ways of treating the Dance of Death motif. Dancing is usually a spontaneous expression of joy – but now it is the Skeleton with the Scythe who calls on men and women to dance with him.

Death assumed many forms: of an Angel, a Hunter, a Man with a Sickle, a Ploughman, as an Archer with his bow and arrow, as a Fisherman with his net, as a Bird-catcher with his snare. In St Bridget's *Revelations* Christ himself is the Ploughman who walks behind the plough. Wherever men turned, annihilation, concretely envisaged, seems to have faced them. Death, depicted in various realistic ways, appeared in the nobleman's castle, in the monk's cell, inside the burgher's city walls, in the peasant's cottage. And in these artists' work he becomes steadily less human, until in the end it is a Skeleton that leads the Death Dance.

The art of the late Middle Ages is largely an extravaganza, an orgy of deathly terror; of panic at our latter end.

Inscriptions on graves were wholly moralizing in intent. Always, man had to bear in mind the mortality of his own body: *memento mori*. Often epitaphs were drawn from the widespread legend of three live travellers who fell in with three dead men; the ensuing conversation reminds them of their own impending annihilation.

Here is one Swedish example. A succinct inscription on a grave dating from the 14th century in Sköllersta parish churchyard, in the province of Närke, gives us the whole sense of the legend:

> Thou who passest here
> halt by this stone.
> Behold, shed tears.
>
> I am what thou shalt be.
> What thou art, I have been.
> Pray for me!

For mediaeval people death was always present in the midst of life; and life went on after death.

What the Provincial Laws Relate

Land skola med lag byggas och ej med våldagärningar. Ty då går det landen väl, när lagen följes.

Land shall be built within the law, and not with violent deeds. For all fareth well with that land where the law is followed.
The Law of Västmanland

Much hath befallen, and full oft befalleth that which is evil.
The Law of Dalarna

POSTERITY'S CHIEF SOURCE of knowledge about our Swedish peasant culture is our mediaeval provincial laws. They originate in heathen antiquity. At first they had had only verbal existence. They were recited at the '*ting*', the provincial assembly of the free men, by its leader, the *lagman* (the 'lawman') who had learned them by heart and whose duty it was not only to 'tell' the law but also to administer justice and to put new laws into words ('*tälja, skilja och göra lag*') says the law. From this we have the concepts of '*lagsaga*' – lawman's jurisdiction – and '*domsaga*' – judge's assize. To a great extent these laws were rythmically constructed, like poems or lays, thereby the more easily to be fixed in memory. And even in their written form alliterations, end-rhyme and internal ryhme have been preserved. The lawmen who kept them in their heads must have been men with good memories.

The laws were written down from the 1220's, when work began on the older Västergötland Law, up to the 1340's, when the Laws of Dalarna, Hälsingland and Västmanland also assume written form. The Laws of Småland, Närke and Värmland are lost. Of the Småland

Law only the Ecclesiastical Statute has survived. That the older
Västergötland Law is immemorially ancient and dates from heathen
times is evident, for instance, in the way in which it formulates the
oath of testimony. He who gives evidence shall pray 'that the gods
may be gracious unto him.' Even if people in the 13th century no
longer generally believed in Odin, Thor and Frej, the oath followed
'the good customs of our fathers.'

These six-hundred-year-old texts are expressed in strong and
pithy language which in all its severity and simplicity still rings out
clearly. As language, it is direct and to the point; full of vivid
expressions and forceful basic words. No one can fail to admire such
Swedish. The flat exhausted language of our own day could well
renew itself at this fresh and healthy source. Present-day Swedish,
like most other European languages, is steadily being impoverished:
ancient native words, daily disappearing, are being replaced by
foreign ones. In the provincial laws' inexhaustible storehouse of
pithy expressions and vivid phrases we could find many a substitute
for all the vague and threadbare foreign interlopers that so spoil our
language today. In my own novels I have always taken up dialect
words and tried to use them in a fashion requiring no footnotes. Nor
do I ever use a foreign word without first having sought in vain for a
Swedish word of identical meaning. But usually the opposite habit is
beginning to set its stamp on our language. Only when no foreign
word can be found do we Swedes use one of our own.

Stylistically, the Laws of Uppland and Östergötland are pre-
eminent. Their paragraphs are often superbly phrased. The authors
of these and several other laws use an effective trick: they vividly
depict imaginary cases. The sentences begin with '*nu*' – 'now' – or,
as one might say: 'let us now suppose . . . ' and continue in the present
tense. The case they envisage comes alive before our eyes. *Now* a
man makes ready his wedding; *now* the peasants wish to build a
church; *now* a woman commits whoredom. And instantly we are in
the midst of a lively occurrence. We have an impression of its all
happening right *now*, in this very instant. Some of the men who
wrote down these laws were men of epic imagination.

These 'crafty' – in the mediaeval English sense of that word* –

* Crafty = strong powerful; *cf.* Swedish *kraftig.*

formulations recur in the subsequent *rikslagar* – laws for the whole land; and their echo is still heard in our present Statute Book. What norms and rules of law, then, were applied by our ancestors? Here we have our answer, in black and white. The provincial laws give us an insight into people's habits and customs, their views of right and wrong, their daily and holiday existence, their crucial values. They follow man as a social being from birth to death. This is not propaganda, worthless to the historian. These are no subjective documents, requiring strict examination before we can bring ourselves to accept them. These old provincial laws are something to be relied on. They have truth-value. And as sources, I think, are too little used.

Here a single chapter on what our provincial laws have to tell us about the way people then lived must suffice. I shall restrict myself to a few select and illustrative examples. My quotations are taken from Wessén-Holmbäck's admirable interpretation and explanation of the laws, which began to be published in 1933.

Our ancestor's legal norms are mainly based on immemorial Germanic right, and therefore, for the most part, can only seem strange to our modern view of law. At times they even shock us. A man's goods, for example, were more highly valued than his existence. To take away someone's possessions was a greater crime, and more severely punished, than to take away his life.

In his history of Swedish culture, Strindberg wrote that 'the spirit of these laws, generally speaking and judged from our point of view, was rather noble.' Personally, looking at them from our modern point of view, I cannot help finding their rules of law rather cruel and merciless, even if not without some lenient paragraphs. The laws were anyway presumably not interpreted after the strictest letter; and in the absence of a prosecutor there was not always a judge.

An unknown 18th-century author who made a thorough study of our provincial laws found in them eight negative traits, all highly typical of Swedes: wilfulness, ambition, sensitivity to affront, conceit, vengefulness, greed for property, violence, and envy of one's own fellow-countrymen. When the whitewash was scraped away during repairs to Riddarholm Church in Stockholm, a similar list of

Swedish defects, responsible for the country's troubles, was found. It, too, contained 'envy'. This notion of ourselves as an envious people, always begrudging our compatriots any success, is thus of very ancient date, and seems all too well founded.

But our old law texts also witness to the value set on honour and glory. A Swede, insulted, flies to avenge himself. The author of the insult pays with his life. In their dealings with each other our ancestors were excessively prone to violence, and sometimes of a sort which to us seems strange and odd. We find the regulations covering physical hurt caused by another person, for instance, surprising. 'Now putteth one out another's eye'; 'now cutteth one out another man's tongue'; 'now geldeth one another'. How often, one asks oneself, did people really put out each other's eyes, or cut out one another's tongues? How far, in reality, were our forefathers given to castrating each other? The crime precedes the law; but I should like to have some statistics on such odd crimes. 'Often befalleth that which is evil', declares the Law of Västmanland. All our provincial laws bear authoritative witness that this was so.

The old texts treat of all the crucial events of a human life from its inception to its end. They stipulate rules and customs valid from baptism to burial.

Concerning baptism, the Law of Dalarna says: 'Now is a child born in all good hap; it hath both nails and hair; draweth its breath in and bloweth it out. Such child shall have baptism.' A paragraph to be interpreted as follows: soundness of wind and limb shall be a condition of baptism, otherwise its parents may expose it in the forest. The Norwegian Burgher Council's Christian Law deprives misshapen children and the miscarried of all right to Christian baptism: 'Such shall be taken to an unholy place and there shall a heap of stones be cast upon it, where neither men nor beast passeth by; that place shall be sacred to the evil one.' But the Law of Gotland expressly forbids such treatment of infants: 'Every child that is born in our land shall be brought up, in no wise shall it be cast out.' Other Swedish provincial laws enjoin: 'A woman shall never baptise a child, if there is a man [available]. Let no child be baptised in aught but water.'

Children grew up, became ripe for marriage. Whereupon the law gave parents the right to choose a wife for their son, and a husband for their daughter. What could happen to a daughter who would not follow her parents' behest in entering the married state we read in the marriage statute of the Law of Södermanland. 'Father shall give away his daughter. If there be no father, then shall it be the brother. – If a maiden depart from her father's or mother's counsel, let her be cut off from her inheritance, both after her father and after her mother, unless they show her mercy while they yet live, and forgive her. Widow may decide upon her own marriage, with the counsel of her father and nearest relatives.'

It is nice to know that a girl could afterwards be forgiven for marrying the man of her choice.

On whoredom, the Law of Södermanland has detailed paragraphs: 'Now playeth a woman the whore, and entereth a bed whereunto other woman is wed. If she be taken therein by that woman who is wed to that bed, and her nose and eyes maimed or her clothes are seen to be torn, then shall no fine be payable; but for theft of that bed shall she pay a fine of three marks. Thereafter shall that woman be called a maimed whore.'

Concerning the same crime committed by a man, the Östergötland Law says: 'Now is a man slain in bed of whoredom, and bolster and sheets thereunto bear witness: he shall be fettered to the woman and both taken to the council. Witnesses shall appear against him: two men shall confirm him slain in bed of whoredom.' Touching a man who kills another in his wife's bed, the Västergötland Law has a similar paragraph: 'Take bolster and sheets and bring them before the council, let blood and wounds be seen, indict the dead man and confirm [the indictment] before two dozen commissioners and the chieftain of the hundred, and thereafter judge him [the slain man] unworthy of vengeance by the council.'

In certain cases of manslaughter the procedure seems peculiar to us: the man-slayer shall be fettered to his victim, and the living and the dead together be brought before the '*ting*' where the slain man shall witness to the crime before the council and the chieftain of the hundred. Such an assembly, with the accused bound to a corpse, must have been a horrible affair. |Hyena-minded spectators, no doubt, gazed their fill.

Punishments for sex crimes seem to have been made more severe in King Kristoffer's law of 1442, valid for the whole country, a law proclaimed as a result of 'the changing times and the distress of the kingdom'. Just then the Catholic Church in Sweden was at the height of its power, a circumstance which set its impress on legislation, particularly in what concerned whoredom and other sex-crimes. The law regards a wife as a man's most valuable possession. If another man takes her from him, the deed falls under the law against theft, in whose first paragraph we read: 'The best thing a peasant hath in his dwelling, it is his lawful wife. He who stealeth her from that peasant, he is the chiefest and worst of thieves. Wherefore he who lureth a peasant's wife from him and runneth away with her and is taken in the act, let him be led before the council and hanged above all other thieves. Should that peasant not grant his wife her life, then shall she, too, be brought before the council and be condemned to be buried alive.'

No woman condemned to death was ever hanged. Reasons of propriety – and of chivalry – required that no part of her body be exposed at her execution. Women were therefore either burnt, stoned or buried alive. 'Man shall be stoned, and woman burnt' – that was the rule. Persons guilty of arson should be condemned to the stake: 'He that hath set fire to a dwelling shall burn at the stake'.

Usually theft led to the gallows or a branch of a tree. Hanging was the most shameful punishment. Compared with it, beheading was almost honourable. Manslaughter, on the other hand, could be atoned for by surprisingly low fines, assessed according to the value assigned to the person slain; also to his nationality and which province he came from. The older Västergötland Law imposes quite diverse fines – or as we should say damages – for killing a man from Västergötland, from Småland, for a Dane or a German. If the victim is from Västergötland, the doer of the deed shall pay damages to his clan, but if he has slain any man, be he Swede or foreigner, not from Västergötland, he is exempt from such a fine. A foreigner was ill-seen in the land. Unless he had some powerful man of the country to defend him and be good lord unto him, he enjoyed virtually no legal protection at all. From these old laws it transpires that Swedish xenophobia, of which some traces still remain, is also of ancient date.

To judge from the detailed regulations punishing it, rape seems to have been far from unknown in mediaeval society. A rapist taken red-handed was, as a rule, to be beheaded. But the legislators are well aware how hard it is to prove rape. Mere accusation is not enough. The Law of Dalarna says: 'If a man rape a woman and the marks be seen upon her or him, such as he hath done to her or she to him; or if it be so near to a village or road that screams or cries for help can be heard, and all this be lawfully declared before witnesses, then shall a commission from the hundred try the truth thereof.' Several other laws, too, require judgment in such cases to be given according to what may be found to have been the truth of the matter. If a woman slays a rapist in the act, he shall not be avenged by the law or by her clan.

The statute of inheritance in the Law of Östergötland contains a rule concerning children begotten by rape: 'Now rapeth one a woman, and begetteth child upon her under struggles and screams; that child shall as well have its inheritance as those born of lawful spouse.' But, the Law adds, evidence shall be given under oath that the child was begotten 'under struggles and screams'.

In their basic view of justice the laws are strikingly alike, but one or another crime could be differently punished in Östergötland and Västergötland, in Uppland and Hälsingland. The punishment for incest, for example, was less severe in Dalarna than in Västergötland. If a son has intercourse with his mother, or a father with his daughter, the Dalarna Law imposes a fine of 9 marks* on each of the guilty parties. But in the Västergötland Law no fine is adequate punishment for such a crime: a man who lies with his daughter shall atone for it by a pilgrimage to Rome, there to seek forgiveness from the Pope. This law goes on: 'If father and son have the same woman, two brothers the same woman, mother and daughter the same man, or two sisters the same man, this work of abomination shall cost a fine of three marks to the bishop.'

After the Reformation, under the influence of the Lutheran Church, the punishment for incest was sharpened to beheading. In

---

* The late mediaeval Swedish currency was 1 mark = 8 öre, 1 öre = 3 örtugar, 1 örtugar = 8 penningar. A cow was valued at 1.5 marks, and a day's work at 2 penningar.

the Law of Dalarna, again, sodomy is a good deal more severely condemned than incest: 'Now committeth a man sodomy with some beast, with whatever beast it may be, and busseth with it as with a woman. If he be taken in the act, then shall that man be buried quick in the earth and that beast, wherewith he had sinned, with him.' As late as 1611 a case is recorded in the court rolls of Sunnerbo hundred, in Småland, of a peasant being buried 'quick in the earth' together with his mare, which he had used for intercourse.

Castration is everywhere regarded in our provincial laws as a terrible crime. The Law of Dalarna imposes heavy fines on anyone depriving a man of his ability to procreate: 'He who taketh an unmarried man, layeth him down upon the ground, cutteth out from him as from a boar and maketh him unable to beget children,' should be fined, for his unborn son, 40 marks: for his unborn daughter 80; and for the wounds inflicted on him by such castration, 40 marks. It is curious the victim should receive only half as great damages for the son he could no longer beget, as for an unborn daughter. The Law of Östergötland is even more severe: it fines the guilty party between 160 and 320 marks. And the Law of Uppland condemns him to a horrible physical punishment; he who gelds another shall lose both hands, and each of his accomplices one hand, if the victim is not prepared to accept such damages as he himself may determine.

In prehistoric times and the early Middle Ages, before the provincial laws were written down, polygamy was unquestionably permitted in Scandinavia (A. Holmbäck: *Ätten och arvet*, 1919). Where a man had many wives, his children, begotten with different mothers, enjoyed the same legal status as a matter of course. So the notion of illegitimacy can hardly have existed in heathen times. It can only have come in with Christianity and the Church.

After the Church had insisted on monogamy and had forbidden extra-marital relationships, the concept of *frillobarn* – concubine's child – was introduced into the laws. Extra-marital children do not seem to have been rare; wealthy peasants could have several. By the Law of Östergötland, such a child had no right to inherit, nor was its father obliged to support it. But a bastard could be legitimized by marriage bewteen its parents: 'If a man lie with a woman and beget a child upon her, it is a *frillobarn*. If he thereafter make her his lawful wife, then it is child of lawful wedded wife, inasmuch as he, on bettering the woman, hath bettered also the child.'

Christianity and monogamy improved woman's status, but it also meant that those children born of unmarried women lost their rights.

One paragraph in the Law of Östergötland, dark of interpretation, treats of him who, being innocent, had been beheaded, hanged or broken on the wheel. Whoever has executed the sentence shall namely be condemned to pay a fine for manslaughter, *i.e.*, be declared an outlaw and lose his property. Probably it is his accuser who is meant here – supposedly because he had also acted as executioner. If the innocent person had also been placed in the stocks 'so that his feet rotted away on him' a further fine of 40 marks was payable. The stocks were virtually an instrument of torture. Murderers were placed in them, but not persons guilty of manslaughter.

Almost all paragraphs in these laws, prescribing the manner in which accused persons shall be tried, also contain injunctions concerning the 'fiery-cross' – the *budkavle* – which, carried from one peasant to another, summoned the council. Anyone neglecting the call or leading it astray after it has been sent out at the king's command shall pay a fine of between 4 and 8 öre. Backwoodsmen who 'dwell in the forest', or persons living in islands far out in the seaboard, have no right to carry the fiery-cross.

The Law of Södermanland fixes the weapons to be borne when the populace are called to arms against an enemy. Every man eighteen years of age and capable of bearing arms shall be equipped with five weapons; sword or axe, iron hat, shield, mail coat or cuirass, and a bow with three dozen arrows.

As we have had reason to suspect, our ancestors were extremely touchy about their own honour, and suffered none to insult them. He who, for example, called another man a bondsman, or the son of a bondswoman, had to assuage the libel by payment of a fine.

Much of the provincial laws' text is devoted to their ecclesiastical statutes, regulating the common people's relations with their village priest and parish church.

The sanctity of the sabbath and of the Church's holy days is protected by law. The Law of Västergötland condemns men who by fighting on a holy day cause bruises to pay a fine of 3 marks to the bishop; and anyone committing manslaughter on a holy day has to pay a fine of 6 marks to that prelate. Anyone who in any way defiles the church's hallowed ground also has to answer for it. Anyone having sexual intercourse or ambushing another in a church or churchyard shall pay a fine of 6 marks and thereto shall provide a meal for the bishop when the latter re-sanctifies the church or churchyard after its defilement.

But the duties of the parish priest are also stipulated in detail. Above all, it is a question of his obligatory errands about the parish. Should he, at one and the same time, receive a call from a peasant who is lying on his deathbed and desires supreme unction, and another to baptise a new-born child, the Östergötland ecclesiastical statute says he shall first go and christen the child. In both cases it is a question of a human soul; but 'he cannot help them both', and the soul of the unchristened infant comes first. When a peasant has died, the priest shall come to him, bless his corpse, and watch over it for one night without recompense. If his wake over the dead man lasts several nights, he can demand one *örtug* for each such night.

For his services the priest shall enjoy a tenth part of all living creatures. All must pay this tithe to him, both poor and rich alike, as in duty bound. But of the peasant's corn the priest shall have a right to one-third; and he must reap it himself on the field. Otherwise the provincial laws can sometimes be contradictory as to the fashion in which the grain shall be distributed.

The ecclesiastical statute of the Law of Östergötland keeps a strict eye on parishioners' morals. 'Now seeth one another live wantonly, he shall tell it to the priest. Then shall the priest stand in the door on Sunday; likewise the next, and likewise the third, and speak thus: 'Such or such a thing hath befallen in my parish. Now do I pray him to seek me out and justify himself before God.' If the sinner thus reported fails to put in an appearance, the priest has the right to name him openly by name and impose a penance.

All this gave the parishioners wide license to play the informer; and they could accuse each other without offering any proof.

The ecclesiastical statute of the Law of Småland gives detailed instructions to peasants wishing to build a church. All who own land in the parish are obliged to lend a hand and contribute several days' work. Each household shall chop down timber for the church and transport those things which must be transported, according to the number of their draught beasts, and provide food for the building workers in proportion to the numbers of sheep and cattle on their farms. He who neglects to do his share of the work when a church is being built may be condemned out of hand, for breach of agreement. The statute also determines what objects shall stand in a church and how it shall be embellished and adorned. Vestments, chasuble, surplice, stole, head-cloth and towel must all be bought. Further, the church shall never be without candles. There shall be two altar candles, a candle over the font, and a bell that shall summon both him who comes into the world and him who is leaving it.

Sometimes the scribes of the law allow themselves to give vent to their sense of humour, even in the ecclesiastical statutes. This statute concludes with a worldly simile, somewhat at odds with the seriousness of its subject: 'There standeth the church, lit and locked, awaiting her suitor, like unto a peasant's daughter.'

Several of the provincial laws contain requisitions restricting the number of houses a peasant may have on his farm. He is not allowed to erect as many buildings as he may desire. 'Planning permission', that is, is nothing new to our own era. The laws also regulate the peasants' dealings in the *byalag*, and enjoin on them the manner in which they shall cultivate the land. A ditch shall be dug seven feet wide, and two foot of earth shall be taken to fill each ditch. When two peasants need a ditch between their fields, half shall be taken from either's strip of land. If man or beast fall into a ditch and die of it, then shall a fine for negligence be paid for each such person, and legal compensation also paid for the beast.

Before the land was redistributed, the peasants of a *byalag* could have their plots of ploughed land and meadow in up to as many as thirty different places. It was a most impractical arrangement, fraught with potential conflicts among the men of the village, who could not get at their fields without crossing those of others. In its regulations for the *byalag*, the Uppland Law lays down the fashion in which this shall be done: 'Now a peasant needs to drive his seed to his field; then may he on another's field reap and lay aside, bind in sheaves and lay aside the ears, whereafter he with impunity may drive across it. The same shall he do if he would make a path to his hayfield across another's land. In like fashion shall he mow and rake aside [the hay] on meadows, and [may] thereafter drive with impunity over [them]. If he doth not, then let him be fined as aforesaid.'

The same law tells us how the common labours of the *byalag* were to be undertaken: 'Now the peasants wish to harvest their fields; then a peasant's servant falleth sick or runneth away. Then shall each peasant in the fencing-team help him with one day's work, and then he hath had lawful aid.'

That is to say, the law laid down that the men of the village were in duty bound to help each other. Even in our own day they have fulfilled such duties, though no longer required to by law. This spirit of mutual assistance among the peasantry was characteristic of the *byalag*. It is a beautiful and humane tradition we have inherited from our old peasant society.

The Law of Uppland rounds off its statute on the *byalag* with a poem, also worthy of our consideration:

> Now hath this statute so been said and meant,
> that each with his own lot may be content.
> How each shall live in his own right,
> And they all build in common plight.

Scandinavia's Greatest Monarch

HE WAS THE DAUGHTER of a Danish king. She had a Swedish
education. She was united in marriage with a king of Norway.
By birth, upbringing and marriage she belonged to all three
Scandinavian countries. In the most real sense of the words she was
a citizen of the North. And became its supreme ruler. Her enemy,
King Albrecht, gave her the nickname Kung Bracklös – King Trouserless. The greatest Scandinavian monarch of all time was a woman.

Margareta, Queen of the Union, liked to call herself daughter of
Valdemar, King of the Danes. She is considered to have inherited
her father's best qualities: his strength of character, his inventiveness,
his enormous energy and power of endurance. True, Valdemar
Atterdag is also known for other less admirable traits. The inhabitants of Gotland had had a sharp taste of them. But the Danes had
honoured him with the cognomen Atterdag. When he ascended the
throne the Danish realm again saw daylight, after a long dark night.
King Valdemar himself is said to have constantly used the expression: '*det dagher*' – 'it's dawning', or as one might say, 'I see daylight'.

Of his daughter Margareta he said regretfully that she was an
error of nature. She should have been created a man, not a woman.
Presumably he would have withdrawn this remark had he been able
to follow her career.

Only exceptionally do our older Swedish histories speak well of
the queen who founded the Kalmar Union. But Olof von Dalin
(1708–1763) admits that Margareta possessed 'an acute male intelli-
gence', the highest compliment he could pay a woman.

A Danish historian has hit off her character to perfection: 'She
had a sure instinct for what was politically attainable.' Peter Ilsøe:

(*Nordens Historie*). In other words: She was perfect mistress of the art of diplomacy. One could also say that notwithstanding her sex, she was the very personification of the art of statesmanship.

The future regent of all Scandinavia was born in 1353. At the age of ten – for the usual dynastic reasons – she was given in marriage. The husband chosen for this child-wife was King Håkan of Norway. Not until six years after the wedding was the marriage consummated. Margareta spent the intervening time between her formal and her real wedding with her Swedish foster-mother, Mareta Ulfsdotter, a daughter of Saint Bridget. In her home the Danish princess was brought up in the Swedish style together with a foster-sister, Ingegärd. Both girls were brought up in severe discipline and fear of the Lord. It is stated that they often 'both tasted the same birch'.

Naturally, religious instruction was the crux of their education. Margareta's youthful soul, strongly influenced by Bridget's daughter, was receptive to Christ's doctrine, and as far as we can see she was a pious believer all her life. One sign of this is that she took Vadstena Monastery, the creation of her foster-grandmother Bridget, under her especial protection, supporting it with lavish gifts. She seems to have realised her faith in her actions, in practical life. This is worth stressing. Among the mighty there was apt to be a deep gulf fixed between doctrine and behaviour, between theory and practice. Though they paid lip service to the doctrine of Christian love, in practical matters of government they found it an inconvenient guide to action.

When Margareta was sixteen she was 'handed over' to her husband, King Håkan of Norway. She moved to his kingdom, made her home in Akerhus Castle, and about one year after the marriage was consummated, at the age of seventeen, bore her husband a son, who was christened Olof. Ever since the days of Saint Olof it had been the most revered name in Norway. But probably the young mother wanted to call her child after Scandinavia's greatest saint.

Margareta's Norwegian biographer (Halvdan Koht: *Dronning Margareta og Kalmar-Unionan*, 1955) assumes that she 'certainly came to be fond of her husband'. In point of fact no one really knows what her sentiments were for him. King Håkan was already thirty, in those days more than middle-aged, nearly twice as old as his spouse. He was incessantly travelling about his kingdom, so for long periods at a time the young Margareta was left alone at Akershus. Their wedded life seems to have been sporadic.

Being left for the most part to her own devices at Akershus, she early learnt to rely on herself. Already, she had a miniature realm to rule over and duties to be done; and these matured and developed her. The only witness we have to Margareta's concerns as mistress of a household is one of her letters, written in her own hand, the only one to be preserved for posterity. Written in 1369 and addressed to her husband, it is in Swedish, with only one or another Norvagism and begins:'You, my very dearest lord, I greet most heartily with God'. Margareta is writing to her husband to tell him that at Akershus she lacks the bare necessities of life. Both she herself and her servants are suffering acutely from want of food and drink. Their store will not suffice even for a day, and the sixteen-year-old mistress of the household fears lest her servant folk may leave her 'because of hunger'. It is a touching letter. She begs her husband to help her and wonders whether he may not be able to induce an Oslo merchant, mentioned by name, to advance her food on credit.

In 1380 King Håkan of Norway died. At the age of twenty-seven Margareta was a widow. But she pinned all her hopes on her son Olof, who had now become king both of Denmark and Norway. To him she devoted all her love and tenderness. He was, after all, her only child.

But seven years after her husband's death the widow was left childless. In 1387, her son, King Olof, too, died, aged only seventeen. With his death the ancient and very famous royal clan of Norway, whose blood was intermingled with the Swedish Folkungas, died out.

Margareta Valdemarsdotter was left alone. The tragedies she had been through would have broken a weaker nature. But her powers remained intact. Indeed she developed an extraordinary strength of character, and with it attained to the highest goals any man or woman could set for themselves. Seeking perhaps consolation for her personal sorrows, she became restlessly active. At all events, it was after the loss of her husband and son that she embarked on her historic career.

The age offered a tremendous political challenge. Confusion almost without parallel prevailed in the three Scandinavian countries. Throughout the 1380's one traumatic event followed another, and in all three kingdoms power was constantly changing hands. The young king's death had left no male heir to the Norwegian throne. Denmark, too, had neither king nor heir apparent. In Sweden a German king, Albrecht of Mecklenburg, who could not even speak the language of the country, was imposing an intolerable régime on the common people through his bailiffs. The embittered peasantry were trying to make a rising, but lacked leaders. The whole country was being torn apart by internecine strife, partly between the king and the magnates, partly among the magnates' own ranks. And all the while, in the background, the people were murmuring ominously.

At the head of the great men of the Swedish realm was the *Drots* (Lord High Steward) Bo Jonsson Grip, a man who owned more land than any other at any time in Swedish history. Altogether he ruled over 2,000 farms. His fiefs* are said to have comprehended nearly two-thirds of all of Sweden and Finland. Bo Jonsson was one of the group of traitorous lords who had called in a foreign king, but had afterwards fallen out with Albrecht and was now opposing him. His vast estates made him more powerful than the king himself. Patently he was above any law. In 1381 he stabbed to death the Södermanland nobleman Karl Nilsson, one of his colleagues in the Council of State, before the altar of the Grey Friars – now Riddarholm – Church in Stockholm; and the law had done nothing about it. Who, in the last instance, could have passed judgment on him? He himself, Bo Jonsson Grip, was Lord High Steward, the highest judicial authority in the land . . .

His first wife, Margareta, came from the wealthy Halland family of Porse. Upon her dying in childbirth at Kalmar, Bo Jonsson had done something unique. If he was to prevent her property from passing to her relatives and keep it for himself, it was necessary for him to prove that she had born him live offspring of his own begetting. So he ordered her body to be opened. The unborn child was extracted and found to be alive. They just had time to baptise the child before its life-spark went out; after which its father got the

* The Swedish fief, unlike the English, was not hereditary. *Translator.*

prior of Kalmar monastery to certify that it had been born alive. In this way he had made sure of his wife's great inheritance. The incident is characteristic. He was a man whose greed for land bordered on insanity.

Bo Johnsson was 'a highly gifted, strong-willed and ruthless climber' in the opinion of Sven Tunberg, who adds that his person-ality 'was not without idealistic traits'. To complete his portrait we can add that he was a warm friend of the Church and showered lavish gifts upon churches and monasteries.

Strong men would have been needed to bring order into the politi-cal chaos prevailing in Scandinavia in the 1380's. Instead, the con-temporary world saw it done by a woman. Within a mere couple of years Margareta, that remarkable statesman, had grasped the rudder of state in all three kingdoms.

There must reside some special voluptuousness in the exercise of power. Why otherwise should men so hotly desire it? Perhaps in the exercise of power Margareta found compensation for the happiness of which she had been deprived as wife and mother.

In Lund Cathedral, on August 10, 1387, she was elected regent of the Danish kingdom. On February 2 the following year she was elected at a general assembly in Oslo 'the puissant lady and rightful master of the whole realm.' In reality, it should be added, she had already seized power both in Norway and Denmark.

Never within the memory of man had a Scandinavian sceptre been wielded by a woman. As regent, therefore, Margareta was a unique phenomenon, and until the present Queen Margareta II was the only woman ever to have sat on the throne of Denmark. Arild Huitfeldt, who wrote the first history of her in 1602, as it were apologizes for her election to the Danish throne, pointing out that it was solely because she was of the ancient lineage royal and because the Danes had had time to accustom themselves to her even temperament and excellent government. A contemporary German chronicler, however, writes that, as the Danish nobles gradually discovered this woman's wisdom and strength of character, they became troubled and alarmed. Wis-dom and strength of mind, above all, were to typify the Queen of the Union. They were the two qualities by which she bent others' wills to her own. The Danish magnates were quite right to fear their queen. This woman was more man than they.

So Margareta was ruler of Denmark and Norway. Now it was Sweden's turn. In August, 1386, the country's real governor, Bo Johnsson Grip, died, and decisive events were at hand. Immediately, a bitter struggle broke out over the inheritance of Sweden's richest man between King Albrecht and the great men of the realm. As the aristocracy had sought outside help against Magnus Eriksson, so now they sought foreign aid against Albrecht. And their eyes turned to Margareta. Once again the great men were prepared to call in a foreign regent. In March, 1388, the executors of Bo Johnsson Grip's testament acclaimed Margareta as 'Sweden's all-powerful lady and rightful master.'

But Valdemar-King-of-the-Danes'-Daughter was about as unlike Duke Albrecht of Mecklenburg as anyone could be. If the Swedish aristocracy imagined they had found themselves a puppet regent, they were in for a disappointment. But to place her on the Swedish throne the Swedes first had to drive out their German king.

Resolutely Albrecht prepared to resist and, to strengthen his position, called in still more troops from Mecklenburg. The Swedes asked Queen Margareta for her help. It was more than willingly given. On February 24, 1389, the matter was decided by force of arms on the plain of Falan, near Falköping. Margareta, levying troops in all the Scandinavian countries, had assembled a sizeable army. It thoroughly defeated King Albrecht and his Germans. Both the king and the crown prince fell into Margareta's hands. Her triumph over her enemy, who had once called her King Trouserless and in every way mocked her for being a woman, was complete. Her proper place, he had said, was the embroidery frame; and he had sent her a whetstone to sharpen her needles on. The gift is still to be seen in Uppsala Castle. Scornfully Albrecht had also called Margareta 'the monks' milkmaid'. She was being accused, namely, of excessive intimacy with her confessor, the Abbot of Sora. Low rumour said he had fathered two children on her.

The battle of Falan Plain had warded off the serious German threat to Sweden and Norway for once and all, and this makes it one of the most important battles in the history of the Nordic peoples.

'God be praised for all eternity' exclaims one chronicler, 'for giving so unexpected a victory into the hands of a woman and shackling the feet of kings and placing manacles on their nobles.'

But the Germans still held Stockholm, and quite some time was to pass before they were wholly driven out of Sweden. Not until September, 1398, could the Queen of the Union make an entry into her Swedish capital or regard herself as regent of the whole country.

In the long run the Swedish nobility, too, had no reason to thank Margareta for her government. She undertook a 'reduction'. Crown lands on which the aristocracy had managed to lay their hands in King Albrecht's reign were forcibly returned to their proper owner, thus breaking the hegemony of the magnates and reducing the peasantry's discontent.

But the happiest outcome for the Swedes, as for the Danes and Norwegians, was peace between the three peoples. Now that all three had the same regent, war between them was impossible. Margareta Valdemarsdotter perceived clearly that they would have to stick together against the two great German powers, the Hansa League and the Holsteins.

It was this persistent German danger that gave her the idea of a permanent union between the three lands, a unified Scandinavia; an idea concretely formulated in a document presented at Kalmar in July 1397, and which came up for discussion on Margareta's saint's day, probably July 20 in the new calendar. The three peoples were to enter into an 'everlasting union'. 'All three realms should exist together in harmony and love, whatever befalleth one, wars and rumours of wars, or the onslaught of foreigners, that shall be for all three, and each kingdom shall help the others in all fealty' . . . 'and hereafter the Nordic realms shall have one king, and not several.' But it was only the monarch, their defence and their foreign policy they should have in common. In all other respects each land should be governed by its own people and according to its own laws.

For centuries Scandinavian historians have fought each other over the implications of the so-called Letter of Union. The document, as we have it, is incomplete, and seems chiefly to be a draft. The crux of the issue has been the question: was the Letter of Union ever ratified by the three kingdoms' plenipotentiaries? Its interpretation has been one of the great bones of contention in Nordic history. Its real implications are a problem that will now never be solved.

To posterity's objective eye this dispute among historians may well seem purely academic. What was decisive for the peoples of the North was the *consequences* of that meeting in Kalmar in July 1397. That its outcome was happy is something no historian disputes. A long period of peace between the Nordic peoples had begun.

With the commencement of Margareta's reign the longest period of peace ever enjoyed by Sweden in the Middle Ages commenced. It lasted right up to the Engelbrekt Revolt of 1434, or almost forty years. Nearly half a century of unbroken peace in Scandinavia – what must this not have meant to a peasantry ravaged and plagued by all those wars? No more men-at-arms marching hither and thither, no enforced hospitality, no more violent billeting of troops as they swept over the land, no popular levies against invading armies. It is true that in the reign of Margareta's successor war broke out again against the Hansa League and the Holsteins, but the war was mostly carried on outside the country's frontiers, and largely at sea, not on Swedish soil. The Swedish peasantry, of course, had to contribute to the cost of that war; and the levy was eventually to have great consequences.

Erik Lönnroth (*Sverige och Kalmarunionen 1397–1457*, 1934) has shown convincingly that the Kalmar Union was a defensive act, whose purpose was to ward off the German threat. And he has shown, too, that it saved the North from Germany hegemony. Unsought parallels with our own time suggest themselves. One likes to think that April 9, 1940 would not have been so disastrous a day for Scandinavia had Sweden, Norway and Denmark then – as they had 550 years earlier – constituted a single political and military unit.

Afterwards, in the 15th century, a regular orgy of hatred for the Danes emanated from the chancellery of King Karl Knutsson. It was said that the whole union plan had been nothing but an attempt by Margareta to place Sweden and Norway under Danish dominion. This anti-Union propaganda described her as a loving mother to her Danish subjects, but to the Swedes and Norwegians as a stony-hearted stepmother. For a long time these allegations – they were nothing more – won acceptance by Swedish historians. As

Gottfrid Carlsson has shown in the mediaeval section of his *Sveriges Historia*, they are utterly undocumented.

Yet we must bear in mind that at that time the population of Denmark was as great as the populations of Sweden and Norway put together. One Danish expert (Kr. Erslev: *Dronning Margarethe og Kalmarunionens Grundlaeggelse*, 1882) has estimated that, around the year 1400, Denmark had a population of about three quarters of a million, Sweden of half a million, and Norway a quarter of a million. It was therefore only natural if Denmark became the leading power in the Union. The Danes also had an older and more highly developed culture than either the Swedes or the Norwegians.

Between the three peoples over which she reigned Valdemar Atterdag's daughter strove for peaceful intercourse, a brotherly communion. She did everything she could to oppose the insular policies of a narrow-minded nationalism such as only spilled more blood and did the peoples mutual damage at each fresh conflict; a policy which for long ages had been the curse of the three peoples.

Her peace-making, no doubt, had something to do with her sex. True, her troops had defeated King Albrecht, who had to suffer much scorn for his defeat at the hands of a woman. But women and war did not go together. Margareta could not lead armies in the field. The heroic glory of the warrior must for ever be denied her. That once and for all, was a male privilege.

Had Margareta's idea of a union been realised, it would have proved to be the greatest event in the history of the Scandinavian kingdoms. Instead, the long peace was again succeeded by endless wars. For four hundred years to come the three peoples were to be always at war.

Traditionally, this is sometimes explained by saying that the time was not yet ripe for a unified Scandinavia. Geijer, the 19th-century historian, originated the view – afterwards adopted by many historians – that the prime obstacle to the union of the three countries lay in nationalistic feelings. But there is no evidence whatever of nationalistic prejudices among the peasantry of Sweden and Denmark. As yet, no hatred had grown up between the two peoples. What they longed for was peace, and only peace; as is proved by the many agreements to keep it, drawn up from the 15th to the 17th century by the peasantry on both sides of the border, in what is now Southern Sweden, the provinces of Skåne, Halland and Blekinge then being Danish. Nor is there the least indication that the peasants in other parts of Sweden and Denmark were less enamoured of peace than their brethren in Småland and Skåne. What could they have possibly have had against the peaceful communion of interests initiated by the Kalmar Union? Why should they conceivably have wished for anything else but its eternal preservation? Sweden was still not a national state, in the modern sense of the term. In reality, as we have seen, it was a federation of provinces. Geijer's romantic-nationalistic explanation of why the Union came to grief has recently been abandoned by Swedish historians.

Margareta's plan, as Queen of the Union, was rejected and her hopes for the future unity of Scandinavia dashed. And it was this that afterwards fixed her reputation in Swedish history. In Danish annals, of course, her position is unique.

In the 15th century her reputation among the Swedes was low, the anti-Union party missing no opportunity to blacken her memory. Among other things she was charged with having derided her Swedish subjects by issuing a coin called the Shame-penny, indecently stamped with the image of a woman's genitals. This coin, found in Västergötland, has since been found to have been minted as early as the 1340's, before Margareta was even born. But it is a vivid example of the sort of libel and rumour-mongering her memory was exposed to in Sweden.

Olaus Petri accused the Queen of the Union of having impoverished Sweden by taking its gold and silver to Denmark, thus trying to make the Swedes economically dependant upon the Danes. Olaus Petri was a highly qualified seeker after historical truth, but this indictment of Margareta has turned out to be baseless. Even at the time of her accession to the throne, Sweden's finances were already in a catastrophic state, its treasury having been emptied in King Albrecht's reign. A long time had to pass before order could be restored in the realm's finances. Fresh levies had to be imposed on the peasantry and in 1403 their obligation to work a certain number of days on the royal estates was established by law. Even under Margareta's government the peasantry had strong reasons for dissatisfaction. She herself admits it was justified, and concedes that excesses had been committed. 'We have well understood,' she declares in a proclamation to the diocese of Uppsala, in 1403, that the peasants have had great burden and much toil, more especially since we came to this realm; in part it hath been caused [by] the great warfare and burden, that hath lain upon the kingdom; in part [by] wantonness, greed and willfulness on our part and on that of our bailiffs and clerks; whereof somedeal could not have been bettered; and somedeal both we and they might peradventure have bettered, albeit this, alas, hath not come to pass'. Her rescript culminates in a prayer for the peasantry's forgiveness.

Its humility makes it a unique document to come from the hand of a monarch. I have failed to find any other in which a Swedish head of state openly makes confession to the people of 'wantonness, greed and willfulness', both on his own part and on that of his bailiffs and civil servants, and asks his subjects to forgive him for the harm inflicted on them by the authorities.

Yet this woman, absolute ruler of three countries which at that time together constituted the largest realm in Europe, was admired, respected and feared. Her finest laurels were not won on the battlefield. Recent Danish historical research into her reign suggests that Margareta despised war as a political instrument. For her, war was mostly a matter of luck; its outcome was always dependant on your officers' and soldiers' courage, their fidelity or whims, and on whether enormous sums of money could be raised to pay for it. Even then it was only necessary for plague to break out among the troops for a campaign to come to grief. The Queen of the Union's statesmanship bore throughout the stamp of one coldly consistent principle: to reach her goal by negotiation and strategic diplomacy.

All historians greatly admire Margareta's diplomatic ability. No one was her match at the negotiation table. Her grip on her opponent – and in her negotiations, of course, she always had to deal with the opposite sex – was sure and instinctive. One lone woman was their superior.

A Danish author (P. Lauring: *Unionskrigene*, 1962) says: 'Men's knees quaked when they stood before her, not because of any eroticism in the air, but at that ineluctible femininity of which certain women have such a command that they can use it for strategic and charmingly cynical ends. No man could resist her.'

To draw psychological portraits of historical personages, especially if they lived half a millennium ago, is a hopeless undertaking. But undeniably this woman, whom no one could controvert, invites us to such an attempt. She would make an attractive subject for a psychological study.

Queen Margareta died on board a ship in Flensburg, on October 28, 1412, probably from some pestilence.

The previous year she had made her will. In one respect it is a remarkable testament. In it she bequeathes great sums of money to people who had been the innocent victims of war during her reign and to those who in various ways had suffered from the misery which always follows in its wake. A fixed sum was to be paid to women and maidens who in the course of these campaigns had been 'violated and humiliated' by the military. Another sum was set aside to pay for masses for the souls of fallen soldiers, irrespective of whether they had fought for her or against her. Margareta even pities the man in the enemy ranks. To her, they too were human beings. The clause is a humanitarian act, elsewhere hardly to be found in a mediaeval monarch. Even in her last will and testament it is incontrovertibly obvious that to Margareta Valdemarsdotter war was a curse, and peace a great blessing.

The Queen of the Union was head of three kingdoms. She was one of the most powerful monarchs in the Europe of her day. Naturally, in many ways, she was a typical mediaeval ruler. A political characteristic of late-mediaeval Europe was a sharp increase in the power of princes. Of such power Margareta was a successful exponent. An absolute monarch, she wielded it with the greatest cleverness and, at times, even with rigour. To judge from contemporary accounts, her success was primarily due to her forceful personality. But what posterity finds most striking about her are her humane ideas, so unlike those of most late-mediaeval princes, who usually regarded war as the only means of achieving political ends.

The whole idea of a unified Scandinavia was hers from the outset. She was the first leading personality in the three countries to entertain and develop this great idea, fraught with a timeless, still unsolved problem. Latter-day Scandinavian politicians have long been trying – and are still trying – to turn it into a reality. No one can say whether they will ever succeed. In 1949, five hundred and fifty-two years after the Kalmar Meeting, they again took up Margareta's plan for a Nordic defensive federation. We can only assume that in her heaven the Queen of the Union gives her warmest blessing to all such attempts to achieve a single Nordic community.

Yet so far no Swede has written a biography of the Queen of the Union. Must another half millennium pass before the greatest of Scandinavian monarchs is granted her rightful place in Swedish history?